Judging IN Black & White

TEACHING TEXTS IN LAW AND POLITICS

David A. Schultz
General Editor

Vol. 31

PETER LANG
New York • Washington, D.C./Baltimore • Bern
Frankfurt am Main • Berlin • Brussels • Vienna • Oxford

Stacia L. Haynie

Judging IN Black & White

Decision Making in the South African Appellate Division, 1950–1990

PETER LANG
New York • Washington, D.C./Baltimore • Bern
Frankfurt am Main • Berlin • Brussels • Vienna • Oxford

Library of Congress Cataloging-in-Publication Data

Haynie, Stacia L.
Judging in black and white: decision making in the
South African Appellate Division, 1950–1990 / Stacia L. Haynie.
p. cm. — (Teaching texts in law and politics; v. 31)
Includes bibliographical references and index.
1. Judicial process—South Africa—History—20th century.
2. Judicial discretion—South Africa—History—20th century. 3. Political questions
and judicial power—South Africa—History—20th century. 4. Appellate courts—
South Africa—History—20th century. 5. Judicial discretion—
South Africa. I. Title. II. Series.
KTL1610 .H39   347.68'03—dc21   2002010659
ISBN 0-8204-6159-8
ISSN 1083-3447

Die Deutsche Bibliothek-CIP-Einheitsaufnahme

Haynie, Stacia L.
Judging in black and white: decision making in the
South African appellate division, 1950–1990 / Stacia L. Haynie.
–New York; Washington, D.C./Baltimore; Bern;
Frankfurt am Main; Berlin; Brussels; Vienna; Oxford: Lang.
(Teaching texts in law and politics; Vol. 31)
ISBN 0-8204-6159-8

Cover design by Dutton & Sherman Design

The paper in this book meets the guidelines for permanence and durability
of the Committee on Production Guidelines for Book Longevity
of the Council of Library Resources.

© 2003 Peter Lang Publishing, Inc., New York
275 Seventh Avenue, 28th Floor, New York, NY 10001
www.peterlangusa.com

All rights reserved.
Reprint or reproduction, even partially, in all forms such as microfilm,
xerography, microfiche, microcard, and offset strictly prohibited.

Printed in the United States of America

*For my parents,
Doyle and Leota Edwards,
my bulwark and my beacon*

*And always,
to Scott*

Contents

List of Tables　xi

List of Figures　xiii

Preface　xv

CHAPTER 1
Judging in Black and White　1
Courts, Judges and Judging　6
Developmental Approaches to Understanding Legal Systems　11
The Formal Law, Repressive Law and Judicial Discretion　15

CHAPTER 2
A Brief History of the South African Legal System　24
Arrival of the Dutch　25
Arrival of the British　26
The *Voortrekkers*　27
The Emerging Republics　27
Union　29
The Legal System　31
The Foundations of Apartheid　32
The National Party and the Constitutional Crisis　33
Implementing the Grand Scheme　36
Opposition　37
The Constitution Act of 1961　38
Increasing Tension—Soweto and Biko　39
The Beginning of the End—the Constitution Act of 1983　40
Courts and Repressive Regimes　42

CHAPTER 3
Winners and Losers in Cases Before the Appellate Division, 1950–1990 44
Facts, Law, Politics and Outcomes 50
A Deferential Division? 51
Analysis 56
Conclusion 60

CHAPTER 4
Individual Voting Behaviors of the Appellate Division Judges, 1950–1990 62
Analysis 72
Conclusion 85

CHAPTER 5
Longitudinal Analysis of the Outcomes Before the Appellate Division, 1950–1990 87
Assessing the Interventions 95
Discussion 101
Conclusion 102

CHAPTER 6
Judicial Decision Making in Repressive Legal Systems 104
Judging in Black and White 105
Winners, Losers and Discretion in South Africa 109
Alternative Explanations 111
Discretion, Outcomes and Politics 114
The Consequences and Possibilities for Courts in Repressive Systems 116
Conclusion 118

APPENDIX A
Logistic Regression Analysis of Outcomes Before the Appellate Division, 1950–1990 121

APPENDIX B
Codebook for the South African Data Set 123

APPENDIX C
Reliability Estimates for the South African Data Set 135

APPENDIX D
Measurement of Judicial Ideology 139

Notes 143

Bibliography 155

Index 161

Index of Statutes 167

Index of Cases 169

Tables

3.1	Decisions of the South African Appellate Division by Issue, 1950–1990	55
3.2	Net Advantage of Parties Before South Africa's Appellate Division, 1950–1990 (%)	56
3.3	Petitioner Success Rates Against Different Respondents Before South Africa's Appellate Division, 1950–1990 (%)	57
3.4	Net Advantage for Different Combinations of Parties (%)	57
3.5	Net Advantage for Party by Issue (%)	58
4.1	Concurring and Dissenting Opinions and Votes of the South African Appellate Division, 1950–1990	72
4.2	Percent of Votes Favoring the Underdog, All Cases, 1950–1990	78
4.3	Percent of Votes Favoring the Underdog by Issue, 1950–1990	81
4.4	Afrikaans-Speaking and English-Speaking Voting Patterns	83
4.5	Percent of Votes Favoring the Underdog by Issue: "The Emergency Team"	83
4.6	Percent of Votes Favoring the Underdog by Issue: Select Members, 1985–1990	84
5.1	Multiple Interrupted Times Series Results for Percentage of Cases Favoring the Government	100
A.1	Regression Coefficients for Pro-Government Decisions	122

Figures

4.1 Concurring and Dissenting Opinions, 1950–1990   73
5.1 Percentage of Afrikaans-Speaking Judges Serving on the Court, 1950–1990   96
5.2 Percentage of Cases Favoring the Government in All Decisions, 1950–1990   97
5.3 Percentage of Cases Favoring the Government in Civil Rights and Liberties, Criminal and Apartheid Cases, 1950–1990   98
5.4 Percentage of Cases Favoring the Government in Public Law Cases, 1950–1990   99

Preface

I had several objectives with this project. I wanted to create a comprehensive analysis focused on both the micro- and macro-level decision making of a court outside the boundaries of the United States. I sought to empirically and systematically evaluate the behavior of a judicial institution embedded in an authoritarian regime and to do so over a lengthy period of time. In doing so I wanted to answer three very specific questions. First, what constitutes a court? Second, what does a court do? Third, how do judges in a repressive regime behave? Apartheid South Africa proved an ideal setting to pursue the answers. My hope is that this text extends our understanding of judicial behavior and particularly judicial behavior in a non-democratic system.

This study of the South African Appellate Division emerged from a comparative courts project focused on a number of countries over a lengthy time frame. In seeking to develop a comparative high courts data base Reggie Sheehan of the University of Michigan, Donald Songer of the University of South Carolina and I evaluated our respective libraries as well as certain theoretically relevant requirements, and we selected four countries for an initial investigation. Reggie was assigned Australia; Don was to focus on Canada; and I was relegated to the Philippines, because of my previous research on its high court, and to South Africa. I was assigned South Africa because logistically Louisiana State University had an extensive collection on the South African legal system and theoretically because we wanted to include a non-democratic country. So Reggie would be off to the beauty of Australia. Don would enjoy the cool of Canada during hot summer months. I was headed to South Africa. I knew almost nothing of its judicial system or its controversial history in South African politics. With ignorance as no deterrence, I set off for Bloemfontein knowing no one on the continent. Looking back a decade later, it must have been nothing short of divine intervention that connected my interests in comparative judicial behavior with the South African legal system. South Africa represents a fascinating synthesis of a number of historically respected legal traditions along with the racist and paternalistic nature of apartheid. Most important, South Africa represents the capacity to persist, to change and to ultimately emerge stronger and better. I am so grateful I was rescued from those boring industrialized democracies.

As with any scholarly endeavor there are a number of individuals whose help and support were imperative. C. Neal Tate, as my advisor and mentor, directed my interest in comparative judicial behavior and has been instrumental in shaping my own understanding of courts, judges and judging. Both Reggie Sheehan and Donald Songer were fundamental in conceptualizing the book and the coding. My colleagues at Louisiana State University have supported my interest in comparative courts and have answered questions both substantive and inane. James Garand and Christopher Kenny were particularly helpful in answering methodological questions. Lori Hausegger read a complete draft of the manuscript and offered both a concrete critique and a helpful editorial hand. The state of Louisiana generously provided financial support through the Louisiana Educational Quality Support Fund (Grant (1996–98)-RD-A-06). The staff and administration of Louisiana State University have been supportive as well. A number of graduate students, Joseph Devore in particular, were instrumental in the project. A number of undergraduate students, Robin Rhodes in particular, were invaluable in the data entry and cleaning.

The United States National Science Foundation has supported the extension of this project into a multi-country comparative courts data set and provided travel support to South Africa in relationship to that project which benefitted the completion of this text as well (Grant #SES-9975237 and Grant #SES-0137055).

I am particularly indebted to the judges of both the Supreme Court of Appeal and the Constitutional Court. Without exception, the judges were helpful and tolerant of what I am sure at times seemed to be quite silly questions. Justice Richard Goldstone, currently at the Constitutional Court and previously on the Supreme Court of Appeal, was particularly helpful in providing introductions to a number of individuals and always was supportive and helpful in my own queries. Judge Louis Harms and Judge Pierre Olivier at the Supreme Court of Appeal were incredibly generous during my stays at the Court. Judge Harms continued his support answering innumerable e-mails on various minutiae despite his very hectic schedule. Chief Justice Corbett at the Supreme Court of Appeal was incredibly generous and provided me unbelievable support at the Court as well as tea at 10:00 A.M. and 2:00 P.M. His clerk, Ms. Lisa Botha, was also incredibly helpful providing crucial translations. Acting President Hefer was generous in facilitating access to oral arguments, archival material and the library facilities. The staff of both the Supreme Court of Appeal and the Constitutional Court were very helpful. In particular, Belissa Wilson at the Supreme Court of Appeal and Estelle Dehone at the

Constitutional Court were my designated baby sitters and provided me with computer access and various kindnesses. Hugh Corder, Dean of the Law School at the University of Cape Town, remains a constant source of insight. Amanda Gouws, Professor of Political Science at the University of Stellenbosch, was also instructive in shaping my thoughts. Gilbert Marcus was incredibly helpful with insights about the Appellate Division during the apartheid years. I reserve a special thanks for Judge Edwin Cameron who has served on the Constitutional Court and serves currently on the Supreme Court of Appeal. Judge Cameron read a full draft of the text and provided crucial feedback. He no doubt will recognize shamelessly plagiarized sections that flow from his suggestions in the final, revised version. However, the support and encouragement from these individuals are in no way indicative of their agreement with any of the assertions in this text.

I am thankful to David Schultz, Public Law Editor at Peter Lang for his belief in the importance of this book and in helping to shape its direction. I am grateful to Phyllis Korper and Lisa Dillon at Peter Lang who made the potential headache of publication a surprisingly pleasant experience. Special appreciation goes to the Peter Lang copy editor for providing comma therapy.

Finally and of course most importantly, I thank my family who has long supported my academic pursuits. My parents, Doyle and Leota Edwards, have gone beyond the call of duty moving in during my long absences to ensure that my husband was not left to single parenting. My children, Garrett and Taylor, are troopers in this endeavor. They endure my trips abroad and appear more concerned with the requisite souvenirs upon my return than my absences, as should be the case. And I thank my husband, Scott, who has tolerated the academic enterprise far better than I on many occasions. Not only would this book have been impossible without his support and confidence in me, my life would be far less fulfilling on innumerable levels without him. While South Africa's golf courses have not yet lured him away from the States, I remain hopeful.

This text would not have been possible without the help of each of these individuals and many more that will remain unnamed. While I consider this book a collaborative effort, I alone am responsible for this text and the inevitable errors that accompany it.

CHAPTER ONE

Judging in Black and White

In a small South African magistrate's court on March 20, 1958, Godfrey Pitje, an apprentice[1] to a local firm, was appearing before a magistrate in the defense of one Stefaans Niekerk. His employers were the partners of the black law firm in Johannesburg, Nelson Mandela and Oliver Tambo, both activists in the black oppositionist party, the African National Congress. While the latter would die just before the birth of a democratic South Africa, the former would go on to both forge and lead it. Like his employers, Mr. Pitje was black. Like his employers, the color of his skin determined where he could live, whom he could marry, what he could learn, what property he could own, what business he could enter or operate and where it could be located, whether he could vote and where he could sip a bit of water. All these limitations existed not simply because individuals elected to adhere to such racism but because the state had determined it to be so. Statute after statute had been enacted by the government to ensure that Mr. Pitje would never be treated equally with white South Africans.

On this particular day, Mr. Pitje faced yet another injustice. The presiding magistrate, on his own initiative, had added a table to the courtroom and designated it for "non-European practitioners." This was not a statutory mandate but an individual decision of the presiding magistrate. The magistrate utilized the discretion available to him, and of his own volition he dictated a new variation of the apartheid theme. Mr. Pitje protested his separation from the "European" table as had his principal attorney, Oliver Tambo, ten days before. Mr. Pitje requested an explanation from the judge for the new division of the races in a court of law.

 MR. PITJE: Is this an order of the court?

 THE MAGISTRATE: Yes, this is an order of court and unless you comply with
  it, I shall have no alternative but to fine you for contempt of court.

 MR. PITJE: I must protest . . .

THE MAGISTRATE: I have already warned you what the consequences will be unless you abide by the order of court.

MR. PITJE: But I demand an explanation.

THE MAGISTRATE: If you do not address me from the table I indicate, then I am not prepared to listen to any further argument.

MR. PITJE: I am not arguing or protesting. I . . .

THE MAGISTRATE: Are you or are you not prepared to occupy that table?

MR. PITJE: I must protest . . .

THE MAGISTRATE: In that case you are fined five pounds or five days for contempt of court.[2]

Mr. Pitje appealed his conviction to the highest court in the apartheid legal system, the Appellate Division. The appeal was an uphill battle indeed: Mr. Pitje was a black man in a white man's court, a black man in a white man's world. But the significance of his appeal should not be lost. Despite the authoritarian nature of the regime, South Africa's adherence to the rules of the law, as opposed to the rule of law, ensured that Mr. Pitje would be given his day in court to challenge the magistrate's order, even if at separate tables, and he would be evaluated by impeccably trained and scrupulously honest white South African judges.

These judges, however, have the same discretion in their application and interpretation of the rules as that available to the magistrate. In his appeal, Mr. Pitje noted that since there was no statutory requirement that the races be separated in a court of law, the Court would be required to adhere to the South African legal tradition that the rights of the individual must be granted the greatest protection unless otherwise dictated by Parliament. The Roman-Dutch law as well as its partner in the South African legal system, the British law, placed the greater significance on the equality and rights of the individual except in those circumstances where the law specifically denied those rights and equalities, as it did again and again in South African law. However, nowhere in the vast number of its statutes that separated the races in almost every aspect of public and private life in South Africa had Parliament required that in courts of law black and white attorneys be separated before the judge.

Despite the seeming advantage precedent provided Mr. Pitje, fate was not on his side. The majority opinion writer assigned to pen the judgment for his case was none other than Chief Justice Steyn. L. C. Steyn had been appointed to the Appellate Division in 1955 and elevated to Chief Justice in 1959 in flagrant violation of the norms of seniority.[3] But Chief Justice Steyn was "the Government's marked man" (Cameron 1982, 39), a staunch Afrikaner nationalist who raced to the head of the line of a number of English and other Afrikaner judges. Not surprisingly, his opinion supported the magistrate and ignored the underlying legal premise that without specific statutory requirement individual rights and equality should be protected. The Court determined that while Parliament may not have passed such a law, it clearly would have sanctioned such a practice. Chief Justice Steyn noted:

> A magistrate, like other judicial functionaries, is in control of his court-room and of the proceedings therein. Matters incidental to such proceedings, if they are not regulated by law, are largely within his discretion. The only ground on which the exercise of that discretion and the legal competence of the order might in this instance be called in question, would be unreasonableness arising from alleged inequality in the treatment of practitioners equally entitled to practise in the magistrate's court.[4]

Chief Justice Steyn saw nothing either unreasonable or inequitable in the behavior of the magistrate. Of course, Chief Justice Steyn was a white man in South Africa, and Chief Justice Steyn's concept of "unreasonable" and of "inequitable" behavior were completely different from that of Mr. Pitje's. For Chief Justice Steyn, the separation was inconsequential as he went on to indicate:

> ... it is clear that a practitioner would in every way be as well seated at the one table as the other, and that he could not possibly have been hampered in the slightest in the conduct of his case by having to use a particular table.[5]

Mr. Pitje, and Mr. Tambo before him, and the black attorneys who were to follow them into the courts of law, understood the order quite differently. For Mr. Pitje, the separation made it impossible for him to be "equally entitled to practise in the magistrate's court." For Mr. Pitje, the courtroom represented the last sanctuary for equal treatment before the law, particularly the vile and unjust laws of South Africa's apartheid. To be denied even the pretense of equal treatment within the courtroom meant that even judging would be in black and white. Mr. Pitje believed that "the special treatment meted out to me ... because I am an African"[6] made it impossible for his client to be fairly represented.[7] But such was life in apartheid South Africa. And eventually, black attorneys, including Mr. Pitje, who went on to become one of the senior black lawyers in South Africa, would be seated at separate tables in a number of South Africa's courts.[8] Eventually, all of the law, as with all of life, would be separated into black and white. Whether judges believed the laws to be fair or to be inequitable, they were one and all forced to judge in black and white.

Mr. Pitje's experience with racism did not begin in 1950s South Africa. Nor did separation of the races begin with the 1948 victory of the National Party and its apartheid platform. From the establishment of the Dutch settlement at the Cape of Good Hope in 1652, separation defined the lives of blacks and whites. The intersection of these two races, one white and one black, would result in an incredibly oppressive and racially divisive society. The divisions of black and white in South Africa go beyond race, however. Black and white, for this text, is synonymous with many differences: the racial divisions; the differences between the nondemocratic nature of the country yet its respect for rules and law; the professionalism of a judiciary that enforces iniquitous statutes; the formalism of positivist judging versus the reality of judicial policy making.

The central theme of this book is a simple one: judges are decision makers affected by both legal and extra-legal factors. I seek to answer three questions in this text. First, what constitutes a court? Second, what does a court do? Third, how do judges in a repressive regime behave? I hypothesize that judges in authoritarian regimes understand the limits on their independence and impartiality, and judges will defer to the regime in the major challenges that threaten the status quo. However, judges may use the remainder of their docket to challenge the regime in limited ways. I examine the behavior of an appellate court, the South African Appellate Division, that existed at the intersection of a developed legal structure and an oppressive legal system. The developed legal structure contained the requisite professional legal staff trained to respect the rule of law, equality and justice; the apartheid legal framework was based on rules of law, inequality and fundamental unfairness. I explore the decisions of the judges that emerged at that intersection exploring their function and role in South African politics.

Judges perform basic functions of social control and conflict resolution. Judges in authoritarian regimes with formalized legal structures contend with the overlapping natures of the repressive and the formal law. Judges who are ideologically aligned with the authoritarian nature of the regime face no moral or legal conflicts. Because their service ultimately legitimizes the authoritarian regime, judges who oppose authoritarian rule face difficult choices. How do judges rule when the reality of their judging differs so drastically from some of the philosophical bases of the rule of law? Specifically, what did the judges of apartheid South Africa do?

I am certainly not the first to attempt this, not even the first to evaluate the behavior of the South African judiciary generally or the Appellate Division specifically. This is, however, the first attempt to empirically examine the judicial activity of the Appellate Division in its entirety over the apartheid era. This text attempts to suggest broad trends in the interplay between the individuals who staff the bench and the social and political milieus which produce the disputes they must resolve. Ultimately, judges respond differently to the few high-profile cases they decide each year than to the whole of their docket. These few politically "sensitive" cases are those that are perceived by the regime to potentially threaten the status quo. Both structure and politics limit the independence and impartiality of courts in deciding these types of disputes, particularly in courts functioning under repressive regimes. However, the larger number of less controversial cases provides a better opportunity more generally to evaluate a court. High-profile cases, because of their significance, come to define a court, but focusing only on these few cases provides a distorted perception of any judicial institution and the judges who comprise it.

Three literatures are particularly critical to limiting the distortion and providing a clearer perception of courts and of judging. The first revolves around the role and function of courts. Courts are generally ascribed two functions: the resolution of conflicts and the imposition of social norms or values (Shapiro 1981). These two functions are evident even within less developed social systems. However, formal adjudicative structures with authorized arbiters imposing predetermined rules emerge as societies become more complex.

A second and related literature, the developmental approach to understanding courts and judging, suggests that increasing complexity combines with the need of the regime to resolve conflicts and impose social norms. Social and economic development drives the need to differentiate political structures and to establish institutions which are authorized to resolve the conflicts and enforce social norms. More repressive, coercive structures are replaced by formal law mechanisms that require some level of independence and impartiality to function appropriately. Ultimately, these formal structures lead to the potential for substantive justice or fairness in the imposition of the regime rules to protect against arbitrariness and abuse (Hund and Van der Merwe 1986).

The third literature emphasizes the discretion inherent in the judicial process. The inherent discretion in judicial decision making prevents mechanistic judging. Rules can never articulate the solution to every conflict that may arise. The law often is incapable of providing resolutions that are clearly right or wrong, black or white. This ambiguity provides judges the opportunity to respond imaginatively to the conflicts they resolve. Because judging requires *some* resolution, judges are responsible for elaborating the purpose, meaning and intention of the articulated rule. By doing so, judges engage in policy formulation and are thus involved in "making law." This capacity to make law can create tensions with the legislative and executive policy makers when the decisions differ from the preferences of these institutions.

These three literatures are important for our understanding of the behavior of judges generally. However, these literatures are particularly critical for understanding the decision making of judges in authoritarian regimes and in South Africa's apartheid regime specifically. Courts in authoritarian regimes are constrained by the repressive nature of the law. Courts do not develop linearly, as predicted by constitutional development theories, despite even the most professional of judiciaries. Moreover, the discretion inherent in judging is particularly problematic for authoritarian regimes which are unable to tolerate judicial decisions that carve out exceptions to the rules. The following pages articulate these three interrelated approaches to understanding courts and then apply these literatures to the South African legal system.

Courts, Judges and Judging

What constitutes a "court?"[9] By definition, courts—or more precisely, judges—embody the designated authority to decide the disputes brought before them. Shapiro (1981) argued that a continuum of "courtness," if you will, exists from very informal mediation processes, which require the consent of both individuals, to the more formal institutional arrangement encountered by Mr. Pitje in which consent is replaced by coercion.[10] Evaluating the particular context, facts and rules that define the dispute and determining some solution to the disagreement is the process of judging.

In many respects Godfrey Pitje's experience in a court of law differed little from that experienced by individuals across the globe, then or now. As social interactions become more complex and individuals are no longer able to resolve their disputes amicably, the regime establishes a formal adjudicative structure to resolve the disagreement. The regime enters the conflict, and the consensual nature of the dispute resolution process is replaced with specificity—the law. One party selects the judicial process as a means of settling the disagreement, and the other is forced by the regime to enter the resolution process and comply with the judge's decision. Thus, modern courts represent a forum of compelled adjudication in which a third party (the defendant) is forced to participate by the actions of the other two (the claimant and the courts) (Shapiro 1981, 1–17).

Modern courts, like the one Mr. Pitje faced, fulfill at least two basic functions for the regime: the control of social behavior and the resolution of conflict (Shapiro 1981, 1–28). Social control activities represent actions on behalf of the government to impose penalties or sanctions against individuals the courts deem in violation of regime rules, regulations or laws. The dispute arises not between two individuals but between the regime and one or more parties. The judge, theoretically, represents a neutral third party whose responsibility it is to impose the regime rules. Realistically, the judge is not a wholly independent party to the proceedings. In an obvious sense, the judiciary is an arm of the government, the "third" arm, and the judge is thus an arm of the regime in its regulation of society. Courts exist because of regime sanction, function because of regime support and decide disputes according to regime regulations or preferences. Courts choose between the arguments of the state and those accused of abridging the rule. For democratic societies, the population at large has at least the potential to influence the social norms that courts impose. For South Africa, the vast majority of the population, like Mr. Pitje, played no role in determining either the rules or the individuals who would impose them.

Mr. Pitje appeared in court on behalf of an individual accused of violating a social norm, and by refusing to sit at the "non-European" table, he also violated a social norm. Individuals, like Mr. Pitje's client, who are accused of acting against the "public interest," are required to face punishment following specified procedures. Individuals like Mr. Pitje, whose justifiable contempt for the rules dictated his own refusal to acquiesce to apartheid's social dictates, face punishment as well.

Courts are also responsible for resolving disputes between individuals or groups who are unable to resolve their conflict. The resolution of the conflict is theoretically dictated by the specific laws instituted by the regime. By bringing the conflict into the legal system, the regime hopes to avoid violent resolutions to individual disagreements or perpetual hostility between groups, individuals and businesses. The peaceful resolution of conflicts through courts of law is intended to bring civility and predictability to the political system. Moreover, the judge's resolution "is concerned not only with refereeing [the] two sets of interests, but with imposing a third set of interests on them both" (Shapiro 1981, 28).

The designation of an authority to resolve disputes and apply the sanctions necessitates the regime's delegating a certain amount of authority to the adjudicative body or, more precisely, the individual judge. Such delegation inevitably involves some risk that the judge may not rule in a manner that is acceptable or preferable to the regime.

Regimes can seek to control the ambit of judicial discretion in a number of ways. First, the regime creates the institution which is responsible for the resolution of the conflicts and the imposition of social control. The government can limit the types of disputes the court will have authority over and can limit the capacity of the courts to review the actions of the government. Second, the government can control the rules that structure the conflicts and dictate social behaviors. Governments can attempt great specificity in rules to limit discretion among judges, or governments can increase judicial discretion by developing intentionally vague rules, often the product of political compromise. Last, governments can attempt to control the individuals who staff the bench via recruitment, training and promotion (Shapiro 1981, 32–35). The South African legislative body and the executive of the apartheid government itself, which directly appointed all judges, utilized all three measures to limit the power of its courts.

Part of what comprises the judicial nature of a court of law are certain expectations concerning the behaviors of those who make the choices. For losing parties, like Mr. Pitje, to accept that they have lost and to accept the loss as a legitimate one, judges are expected to behave independently and impartially. Independent courts can and do rule against regime officials who could potentially retaliate. Independence may be exhibited by overturning statutes, or absent powers of judicial review, by interpreting regime rules in a manner contrary to the government's wishes (Tate and Haynie 1994; Verner 1984). Independence is evidenced by the fact that the court retains its authority to adversely affect regime interests. This is not to say that decisions which coincide with the ruling party's interests always lack independence, but that when decisions are contrary to the preferences of those in power, the decision of an independent court is tolerated, and the court retains its jurisdiction to rule similarly in future disputes.

Impartial courts rule objectively, without regard to the parties involved or the issues before them. Judges are expected to behave in an unbiased and neutral manner. Appellate Division Chief Justice Ogilvie Thompson asserted that:

> Independence, detachment and impartiality are the essence of judicial office. Justice, it is often rightly said, must not only be done; it must also be seen to be done. It is likewise highly desirable that the independence, detachment and impartiality of judges should be seen to be observed (1972, 32).

More recently, the South African Constitutional Court, established in 1994,[11] recognized the inability of judges to be completely independent or neutral. The Court noted in a *per curiam* opinion that:

> It has never been seriously suggested that judges do not have political preferences or views on law and society. Indeed, a judge who is so remote from the world that she or he has no such views would hardly be qualified to sit as a judge.[12]

However, in defining "neutrality" the Court went on to assert that what judges must do is "decide cases that come before them without fear or favour according to the facts and the law, and not according to their subjective personal views."[13] Further, "it must be assumed that they can disabuse their minds of any irrelevant personal beliefs or predispositions."[14]

Courts are expected to enforce impartially and independently the norms or behavioral expectations legitimately passed by the government. Thus the regime passes rules that dictate acceptable social behaviors, and appointed authorities are expected to enforce the rules through the established legal system, specifically the courts. The rules of authoritarian regimes are particularly problematic for judges who are the supposedly impartial arbiters. Are impartial and independent judges to ignore the normative character of the rules and simply apply the law, any law, to the specific factual circumstances? Are judges to neutrally impose the norms, even ones as inequitable as those imposed by the apartheid regime? Or are judges required to demonstrate their impartiality and their independence by refusing to enforce these rules or at least limiting their application?

In authoritarian regimes, and indeed some would argue in any regime, courts are not allowed the capacity to genuinely threaten the status quo. Because courts are staffed by judges who are products of the social context in which they serve, they are unlikely to be out of step with the will of the majority—in the South African context, the white majority—for long. Routine vacancies provide the regime with opportunities to staff the bench with like-minded individuals. The regime also has the capacity to rewrite the rules if the court differs dramatically in its interpretation from that preferred by the regime. Thus it is unlikely that any court will be out of step with the popular will for long periods of time (Dahl 1957; Dugard 1978; Kritzer 1979; Mishler and Sheehan 1993).[15]

But apartheid South Africa represented a unique twist. The social milieu which produced the apartheid reign also produced the judges who staffed the benches of South Africa's courts. Unlike their other political cohorts, judges were trained to appreciate the rule of law. Legal canons dictated that individual liberty be preserved against an onslaught unless clearly dictated by statute. Indeed Millner argued that Roman-Dutch law "shows a strong bias in favour of civil rights and has no room for inequalities grounded on racial differences" (1961, 284). Trengove further argued that South African courts accepted "at all times" that the South African common law embraced "certain inherent fundamental" civil rights and liberties (1988, 126–28). Thus, the political culture from which these judges emerged inevitably clashed with the legal training that accompanied the legal profession.

While political clashes between the popular majority and the bench are to be expected for short periods of time, the South African context provides a unique laboratory to explore the behavior of judges in a uniquely adverse context. If an individual accepts the appointment to the bench, will he or she attempt to translate into practice, where the opportunity arises, basic legal principles of equality and liberty? Are judges required by the dictates of fairness and basic respect for human rights to ensure that their decisions impose only social controls that are "just"? How do judges perform the function of social control within the parameters of independence and impartiality? Are they required by the dictates of impartiality to enforce the law without regard for its oppressive and inequitable character? Alternatively, do these judges embrace the will of the political majority in their decision making as the magistrate Mr. Pitje faced clearly did? If judges do defy the regime's authoritarian rule, what will be the government's response?

As it will become evident in the chapters to follow, the South African government did not allow courts the authority to establish broad precedents that could have limited the abuses of the racist nature of white South African rule. Indeed, the constitutional supremacy of Parliament gave the apartheid legislature the power to do as it wished. Courts were not given the power of judicial review, and the government was careful to place presumed supporters on the bench once the National Party gained control. Nonetheless, Mr. Pitje's case is an excellent example of the discretion available to judges that allows them to support or reject the government's thesis that black and white must be differentiated. Clearly the laws repeatedly separated individuals by race, but no statute dictated the magistrate's requirement of separate tables. The magistrate, however, interpreted the rules of the game to provide him with the authority to dictate just such a separation.

Part of his authority was derived from the fact that no statute can be sufficiently detailed to eliminate all potential conflict in its interpretation and application. As conflicts arise in social systems and the courts are accessed to resolve the dispute, judges are required to discern the meaning and substance of the words. Judgement involves some level of discretion to determine what a rule means and how it is applicable in the particular dispute at hand. The magistrate elected to use his discretion in a manner favoring the enforcement of apartheid values within the courtroom itself, and in this sense his decision lacked impartiality. In fact, the insistence on the separation of legal practitioners by race may well have been intended to connote the inequality of the individuals who appeared before his bench.

When the judge's decision is unacceptable to the losing party, as it clearly was for Mr. Pitje, modern judicial systems provide for appellate review to make the loss more tolerable. If the losing party perceives the decision to be unfair, either because the judge has misinterpreted the rules or applied them inappropriately or because the individual deems the judge to be biased, the fact that decisions can be reviewed by a higher authority increases the credibility of the system. There is at least the perception that errors can and will be corrected at higher levels.

Mr. Pitje, of course, did appeal his conviction. But appellate courts face the same regime controls—structure, rules and appointments—that are applicable to the lower courts, and regimes may be even more attentive to the behavior of appellate courts because appellate courts have the power to establish broad legal policy. While judges articulate that their choices represent merely an appropriate application of the law to the facts, once that application is rendered, it is considered precedent for future disputes. Thus once Chief Justice Steyn and his colleagues determined that the magistrate could require counsel to be seated at separate tables according to race, even though such distinction was not expressly mandated by statute, that became the policy; that became the law. Other magistrates and judges throughout the country were free to follow suit. Given that power, regimes are careful about the amount of independence and impartiality afforded to judges and to courts. Authoritarian regimes are expected to be particularly attentive.

South Africa represents an excellent case study to evaluate the interaction between the apartheid regime and the courts. While the judges represented a component of the legal system which legitimized the apartheid regime, the judges also sought to separate themselves from its abuses. The formal court structures, and more importantly the judges who comprised them, were essential to the government's ability to both resolve conflicts and to control social behaviors. Apartheid statutes enabled the government to regulate individual behaviors and conflicts but only through the maximum amount of coercion possible in the judicial process. Courts were an essential component for the administration of apartheid, both practically and theoretically. Practically, enforcement is essential if norms are to be established and adhered to by the majority of the population. By bringing punishment to bear, the sentences imposed by judges encouraged individuals to adhere to the apartheid rules. Theoretically, the courts gave legitimacy to the system by presenting a symbolically independent and impartial arbiter for those who found the rules unfair or unacceptable. The courts enhanced the perception that the government existed within a genuine rule of law. The courts also provided the necessary legal affirmation for the laws passed by the National Party government to be asserted as authoritative. A fierce debate emerged in the latter years of apartheid concerning the complicity of the judges in legitimizing apartheid.

Developmental Approaches to Understanding Legal Systems

The myth of the South African legal system, prior to the new constitution, was that it provided a foundation for the rule of law within a mixed-race society so that each race could individually and *separately* develop to its full potential. As in the Jim Crow era of the United States, the emphasis was overwhelmingly placed on the separate component of the equation. Theoretically, apartheid would provide the framework to resolve the conflicts and control behaviors in this racially polarized society. The reality of the South African legal system was one in which the law became a repressive tool to ensure white domination at the expense of the basic economic and political freedoms of the nonwhite population. The primary functions of social control and conflict resolution were embedded within the segregated system.

Industrialization, spurred by the discovery of gold and diamonds, required a legal structure that could produce some level of predictability and continuity in economic transactions. Laws were formalized, or more accurately adapted from the Roman-Dutch and British law, to resolve disputes. The underlying political instability of the apartheid system was masked in two ways. The first way in which apartheid masked political instability was through the use of traditional property rights to provide a sense of security for investors and other commercial enterprises. Thus if conflicts emerged, these would be resolved through legal rules generally accepted as legitimate though applied in a racially discriminatory matter. The second way in which apartheid masked political instability was through the assertion that the majority black population could be controlled. Elaborate rules dictating acceptable behaviors—for example, blacks could reside only in certain areas—were coercively enforced to ensure the separation of the races and the white supremacy norm. The apartheid edifice ensured white domination.

This approach to specification in the law is contrary to the developmental explanation. In general, legal systems are presumed to move from legal structures possessed of great discretion where control is maintained by brute force to a legal system with greater differentiation and institutionalized separation of powers respecting neutrally applicable laws (Hund and Van der Merwe 1986, 10–14). South Africa, and indeed many developing countries, represents an excellent example of why the developmental approach to understanding the functioning of courts is problematic. Judicial institutions do not progress neatly from one anticipated structure to a second in a clear pattern of predictable evolution. Like many systems, South Africa maintained aspects of the different "ideal" stages of development at the same time. The underlying repressive nature of less developed systems, whose existence is maintained through coercion and brute force, existed alongside those structures typically associated with more developed legal systems: professionally trained judges, generally free of corruption, who apply statutes in a nonpartisan manner.

In their classic work on the development of legal structures, Nonet and Selznick (1978) argued that the first stage of legal development is *repressive law*. Repressive law has two features: "close integration of law and politics in the form of direct subordination of legal institutions to the source of power" and "rampant official discretion" (Hund and Van der Merwe 1986, 10–12). Repressive law ensures that the weak remain weak and that the strong remain strong, producing a system of "dual law" in which the punitive nature of the penal system is reserved for the underprivileged, and the private law facilitates the maintenance of power for the privileged who remain "relatively insulated from political intrusion" (Hund and Van der Merwe 1986, 11). Every political order is repressive in some sense and has the potential for even greater repression (Nonet and Selznick 1978, 29–52).

Certainly the apartheid statutes were prototypically repressive. Parliamentary sovereignty ensured the subordination of the courts. Moreover, the capacity of Parliament to sanction any action through statute merely codified the discretion available to it. The law was a means of domination for the ruling class, ensuring the subordination, economically and politically, of the black majority. The coercive nature of the apartheid system inevitably led to conflict between the ruling elites and the subservient masses. This conflict, in turn, led the ruling elites to pass even more repressive laws to stop any threat to the status quo. Thus, the typical functions of conflict resolution and social control were introduced as the formal law mechanisms of the repressive legal structure. For the majority of South Africans, the law was viewed as a means of coercion rather than a legitimate use of authority to ensure predictable and equitable treatment of individuals and to peacefully resolve conflicts.

Hund and Van der Merwe (1986) argued that two forces in society will pressure the adoption of a more differentiated rule structure. The first of these is trade and commerce. As trade and commerce become more important within the society, the need for stability and predictability among those involved in these economic transactions increases. Repressive law is incapable of providing the security demanded by these commercial interests. Demands emerge for rules to structure economic interactions that will exist above and beyond the political infrastructure.

The second force that leads to greater differentiation is the need for continuity in the governance of the society. With no formalized mechanism for succession, every transition from one regime to the next represents the potential for chaos threatening business interests. Legal rules are established to ensure peaceful transitions of power, which, in turn, secure the continuity of governance, avoiding the instability surrounding regime changes under the repressive law.

These two forces, the rise of commercial interests and the need for continuity, represent the impetus necessary to bring about the second stage of development. This second stage of development according to Hund and Van der Merwe is the *formal law*,[16] which is characterized by the separation of law and politics secured by an independent judiciary; the legal system is bound by a "model of rules"; and judges remain faithful to the rules regardless of the consequences (1986, 12). Emphasis is placed on fair and consistent treatment rather than substantive justice (Nonet and Selznick 1978, 54).

These aspects of the legal structure allow for the development of the rule of law in which the judiciary acquires sufficient institutional legitimacy and authority to restrain "the exercise of power politics" (Hund and Van der Merwe 1986, 12). Institutional legitimacy, however, must be garnered by the judges through the reasoning they proffer in their decisions. These decisions must be based on an independent and impartial evaluation of the law or the rules. This evaluation is guided by "neutral principles" that transcend the particular facts of any given case.[17] The principles are developed from historical traditions and from the strict interpretation of the law which should remain objective and be independent of individual preferences or ideologies. Politics determines the rules, not the subsequent interpretation or application of them. Law and politics are separate entities. To meld the two undermines the authority and legitimacy of the courts and their rulings (Hund and Van der Merwe 1986, 12–14).

However, frustration with increasing conservatism and self-restraint in judicial decision making leads to pressure for the last stage of development, *responsive law*. Responsive law is concerned not with mere mechanical application of the rules, regardless of the end result, but with substantive fairness, with justice. Whereas the formal law focuses on procedural fairness and neutral application of the rules with fair and equitable treatment of parties, responsive law seeks fair and equitable outcomes (Hund and Van der Merwe 1986, 12–14).

The authors argued that South African legal ideology melded the first two stages of the law.[18] The denial of basic rights to the majority of the South African population represented a very repressive component of the rule structure in South Africa. Alongside this, a formal rule framework existed to provide predictability in commercial interactions.[19] But even these economic sectors, with legal rules to protect white property rights and economic transactions, were infused with segregation. Blacks were excluded from economic competition within certain sectors of the economy and excluded from property ownership over the vast majority of the land. Thus for whites, the rules were structured to provide the protection anticipated in a formal legal structure, but for blacks, the rules ensured economic subjugation associated with the repressive law.

The overlapping nature of the two ideal types, rather than the progression from one to the other, demonstrates the problematic nature of developmental approaches to understanding legal change and its relationship to judging. Indeed, the South African case is a particularly problematic one because there was no progression from the repressive nature of, for example, the Dutch trading company to more democratic formal law. The formal law of the Roman-Dutch legal system, and then subsequently the British common law, was transplanted to the colonies. Moreover, the indigenous tribal law remained largely intact except where the African population interacted with the newly arrived Europeans. While the inevitably repressive nature of colonization remained a force within the socio-political environment of South Africa, the National Party's system of apartheid moved the legal system to a much more repressive legal regime. Thus instead of progressing from repressive to formal, the legal structure was overlaid with a formal legal system which then became progressively more repressive.[20]

A second problem with the developmental approach, recognized by Hund and Van der Merwe, is that repressive law and formal law do not represent stages of development as much as ideal types, and development is not the systematic progression from one ideal type to the other. Aspects of these ideal types can coexist, and the simultaneous existence of the two types posed a particular problem for the judges of South Africa. While espousing a positivist legal ideology derived from the formal component of the law, these judges nonetheless applied, and thus legitimated, the repressive component of the apartheid political structure. Judges were thus incapable of separating politics and the law because of their inability to divorce their decisions from the fundamental unfairness of the rules they were to interpret and apply.

Thus the formal law articulated the repressive legal rules that were to resolve the conflicts and control society. Cases brought before the judges were to be decided within a formal law perspective that differentiated disputes and disputants by race.

The Formal Law, Repressive Law and Judicial Discretion

The separation of law and politics is, of course, the apogee of ideal judging. This mechanical perception of judicial decision making provides great protection for judges. Their decisions are the product of the laws and the facts and are completely independent of any discretion or personal bias. However, as noted above, judging is inherently a function imbued with discretion. Laws are never sufficiently detailed to resolve all potential conflicts. As the unsuccessful efforts with specificity in code law proved, laws will never be able to cover all possible conflicts, nor is it politically feasible to avoid ambiguity in legislation. If a mechanically derived "correct answer" were so clearly obvious from the statutes or the constitution, the need for courts and judging would be superfluous. If conflicts concerning the laws are to be resolved, some entity must be given the discretion to assess the law and end the dispute.

Courts are allotted the functions of social control and conflict resolution and required to determine who wins and who loses in such disputes. The fundamental assertion of the formal law is that judging, at least proper judging, leads to a singularly correct interpretation or application of the rules. But judging is never so black and white. The manner by which judges reach their decisions is infused with the unavoidable individuality that is the core of the judicial process. If judging were a simple technique of divining objective principles, then every judge should reach the same evaluation of the facts and the law. Indeed, appellate courts would be of no value because every judge would reach the same conclusion given the same facts, the same law and the same objective principles.

Of course, this is a fundamentally flawed perspective of judging. While adhering staunchly to the formal law mode of decision making, each judge understands the facts *individually,* and each judge understands the law *individually,* and each judge adduces the appropriate application of the law *individually*. As Cardozo noted, "There is in each of us a stream of tendency, whether you choose to call it philosophy or not, which gives coherence and direction to thought and action. Judges cannot escape that current any more than other mortals" (1921, 12). Cardozo does not imply that judges are free to replace the rules of the regime for those they prefer. The capacity of the judge to shape the law is limited, and judges are clearly bound by logic, history and custom. However, Cardozo noted that the "ideal of objective vision" is never attained because judges "may try to see things as objectively as we please. None the less, we can never see [them] with any eyes except our own" (1921, 13).

The formal law myth is valuable to judges in any political system but particularly to those who function in systems with the repressive legal component of the law so strongly intact. Judges distance themselves from the brutality of the law by reiterating their mechanistic interaction with the rules. They neither embrace nor reprove the law; they merely provide the inevitable conclusions to be derived from it.

Many scholars echo this theme of the juxtaposition of the repressive and formal elements of the South African legal system broadly and of the Appellate Division specifically. One of the first to study the relationship between judging and the unjust laws of South Africa was Millner in 1961. He argued that the "incurable positivism" of the judges led to an inability to declare unjust laws "non-laws." By using a formal law perspective to uphold repressive laws, he argued that the "judge, dedicated to uphold the principle of justice, becomes its executioner" (1961, 280).

"Positivism" became the label associated with the South African formal law perspective. This perspective was the product of the dominant English legal philosophy of both John Austin and Jeremy Bentham transported to South Africa during the British annexation of the Cape during the 1800s (Dugard 1971, 184). The rise of positivism is attributed to the "decline of natural-law doctrine" and "the pervasiveness of English legal influence" (Dugard 1971, 184). Dugard (1971) asserted that the South African approach to the legal process—legal positivism—is based on two core principles: the "command" theory of law and the separation of law and morality. The command theory of law requires the judicial branch to determine the will of Parliament in the interpretation of statutes without analysis of the motivation for the rules. The separation of law and morality requires judges to reject policy considerations in the adoption of positive legal rules. These aspects of positivism allow judges to apply and legitimate the harshest of statutes with no personal or institutional blame for the inevitably unjust outcomes (Dugard 1971, 184–189; 1987, 496–498).

Evidence of this is apparent in Judge Didcott's judgement in the decision of *In re Dube* (1979).[21] The case involved an appeal from the Commissioner of the Department of Plural Relations and Development declaring Mr. Dube an "idle person" and ordering him from Durban to a "farm colony" for two years.[22] In evaluating the commissioner's decision, Judge Didcott noted:

> When the commissioner has finished with you, the papers in your case go on review to a Judge of the Supreme Court. He is expected, if everything is in order, to certify that what happened to you appears to him to have been "in accordance with justice."
>
> The trouble is that it was not. It may have been in accordance with the legislation and, because what appears in legislation is the law, in accordance with that too. But it can hardly be said to have been "in accordance with justice." Parliament has the power to pass the statutes it likes, and there is nothing the Courts can do about that. The result is law. But that is not always the same as justice. The only way that Parliament can ever make legislation just is by making just legislation.[23]

Former Chief Justice Ogilvie Thompson similarly suggested that:

... a judge is ... required to be wholly divorced from politics. ... Unlike the system that obtains in the United States, where, in certain spheres, the Supreme Court in effect legislates by pronouncing its own constructions of the general precepts of the Constitution, in our country a judge must interpret the enactments of Parliament and the provincial councils and administer the law, not as he perhaps would like it to be, or as he might consider it ought to be, but as set out in the relevant statutory provisions so interpreted (1972, 32,33).

This particular jurisprudential approach, Dugard suggested, is merely an "inarticulate premise" which provided a justification for conservative outcomes that coincided with the white judiciary's adherence to political and social norms regardless of their own racial prejudices. Thus Dugard claimed that "[w]hether they support[ed] the government or not, most [had] one basic premiss in common—loyalty to the *status quo*"(Dugard 1971, 190).[24]

Corder's analysis of the early years of the Appellate Division, 1910–1950, suggested that the Court in the early 1900s was an essential precursor to the more conservative, Afrikaner-dominated, apartheid-era Appellate Division. Corder suggested that the support of the repressive nature of segregation prior to the National Party's victory in 1948 was less a function of the Court's adoption of the formal law perspective than a product of the inevitable influence of the political and social environment in which the Court existed. Its support of the repressive law made the Court an "integral" part of the structure that created and maintained injustice, and "from which they made little effort to extricate themselves" (1984, 240).

In her evaluation of the South African judicial system, Van Blerk argued that in a system with parliamentary supremacy, judges are by definition limited in their discretion. The primary function of the courts is to "apply the law—any law" which Parliament elects to pass (Van Blerk 1988, 155). To criticize the judge who merely carries out the law is to criticize the inevitable duty of those who staff the bench. Van Blerk argued that such criticisms can be detrimental to the judiciary. Criticisms should be aimed at the legislators, if criticisms are warranted, but critics of the judges cast blame for actions which are the inescapable outcomes of legal rulings dictated by statute. Van Blerk did not distinguish between repressive law or formal law but suggested that judges are independent of the laws, whatever their nature, that they enforce.

Dyzenhaus argued that for those who adhere to the theory of the formal law, "law has no inherent moral worth" (1991, 2). Judges are required to apply or interpret the law as written. The legitimacy of the law is dependent upon the legitimacy afforded to the lawmakers, not judges, since judges are inherently incapable of "making" law. Judging is a separate and distinct phenomenon from politics (1991, 2).

Dyzenhaus evaluated the "hard" decisions that faced the South African judges in the "wicked legal system" of South Africa. According to Dyzenhaus, positivists would argue that the formal law does not provide a legitimacy for the decisions of judges who are applying the repressive statutes of the regime but that, in every decision, judges have a range of possible outcomes from which to select. Since judges should be guided by morality, judges would select the outcome that best frustrates the repressive laws. Judges must exercise moral judgement, and judges in wicked legal systems will decide according to their moral attitudes. Dyzenhaus evaluated judicial decision making in South Africa, and he determined that the typically liberal ideals associated with progressive law were either strongly perverted or never existed at all. Judges were trained to respect the legal order producing a "morality" that equated this allegiance to enforcing the repressive laws with "the rule of law."

Forsyth's (1985) exceptional study of the Appellate Division from 1950 through 1980 found that South African judges embraced the notion of the formal law, and within that positivist context, judges were reasonably consistently pro-government. Forsyth suggested this "pro-executive" mentality was not simply a product of completely neutral judicial entities that adhere to the intent and letter of the law to produce the one correct answer. Nor did he suggest that the decisions were the simple by-product of consciously racist, conservative judges. Instead, Forsyth suggested that these decisions were "related to the more conservative background of the judges, the political tensions in South Africa, and similar matters. Judicial adherence to a mechanical approach to interpretation of statutes [was] at best a symptom, not the cause, of the judiciary's pro-executive stance" (1985, 230).

Forsyth asserted that these judges not only embraced a formal approach to the law, but did so in a manner that consistently ignored the "pro-democratic" or more liberal, egalitarian options. Forsyth argued that cases arose before the Appellate Division when, from his perspective, the Roman-Dutch law clearly favored the individual as opposed to the government. Forsyth suggested that, particularly in the violations of the Group Areas Act[25] and many of the security cases, the Appellate Division seemingly abandoned the "right" decision in order to reach a conclusion that favored the government. These conservative choices, he suggested, were not the only alternatives available but were certainly the ones that appealed to individuals raised in a moral climate that feared black rule and the perceived catastrophic consequences sure to follow it.

Davis (1987a) argued that judges choose a theory of legal reasoning which then guides them to a particular outcome in legal disputes. Davis evaluated the "pro-executive" and "pro-democratic" options detailed by Forsyth (1985) and suggested that the latter is concerned with the "very idea and fabric of a legal system" (1987a, 96). Judges who seek to interpret this "fabric" will follow the pro-democratic approach requiring judges to self-consciously search for the moral meaning in legal materials, rather than "the interpretation of the prevailing mental state of the legislator" (1987a, 96). Davis recognized the complexity of the decision making process by which judges will select their theoretical approach to decision making—a process influenced by personality, background, social class and education. Nonetheless, Davis believed that individuals like Forsyth and Dyzenhaus were incorrect in their assertions that the similarities in background and social class inevitably lead judges to favor the status quo. Davis argued that both of the authors attempted to divide the sociological from the normative explanation of judicial behavior. This fault, he argued, ignored the importance of the nature of the law, particularly the influence of social structure on language and thus "is doomed to irrelevance" (1987a, 105).

Wacks (1984) argued that the judges of apartheid South Africa were indeed faced with the unacceptable task of legitimating repressive law. While Wacks adopted a positivist or formal law approach to judicial decision making, he rejected the notion that judges have sufficient substantive discretion to alter the rules or create some tradition of responsive law. Proper judging, he argued, *should* separate politics from interpretation. When the judge is interpreting racist statutes, he or she should never allow individual preferences for more egalitarian legal rules to alter the legally appropriate choice. When the law was unclear or ambiguous, Wacks asserted that the judge should follow Dworkin's (1978) exhortation in these "hard cases" to "decide on the theory of law and justice which best coheres with the 'institutional history' of his community"(Wacks 1984, 271). Former Chief Justice Corbett echoed this approach in his 1986 address, noting that when judges are required to create policies because the laws do not address the issue at hand, the judge must:

> ... draw upon his knowledge and experience gained as an educated, responsible and enlightened member of society, upon the contact with and insight into his fellow humans which his professional career has given him; and he would draw upon his continuing perceptions of the attitudes of the community around him (1987, 68).[26]

Of course for apartheid-era South Africa, the judge's community was a nondemocratic, racist and oppressive one. These judges, if true to the formal legal approach, have no choice but to reach a right legal answer that is always morally wrong. For Wacks, resignation is the only solution for judges who are faced with the overlapping repressive and formal laws.

The most noted critic of the South African legal system, Dugard, refused to accept resignation as the only solution for judges in repressive legal systems. Dugard suggested that the myth of the mechanistic formal law was used by South African judges to avoid the personal responsibility of decisions that ignore basic human rights. Dugard suggested that the positivism of John Austin and Jeremy Bentham became entrenched in the legal philosophy of South African jurisprudence. Judges embraced the concept of a single choice mandated by proper statutory construction, a fallacious concept according to Dugard, but one that "exonerates judges and lawyers from any responsibility for the implementation of evil laws" (Dugard 1988, 61).

For Dugard, judging inevitably involves discretion. If statutes were unambiguous, disputes concerning various statutory applications would not arise in the first place. This ambiguity provides the essence of judging for Dugard: choice. Judges choose one resolution or interpretation over others that are possible. Embracing the positivism of the formal law removes accountability from judges for the policies they articulate. Dugard suggested that, given the inevitable discretion and ambiguity of judging in repressive legal systems or in any system for that matter, those decisions that support individual liberty should be embraced (1978, 366–388).

Ironically, in the case of Jabulani Sydney Dube discussed above, Judge Didcott, though asserting a positivist or formal law approach, followed Dugard's advice exactly. The statute allowed that individuals incapable of work fell outside its jurisdiction. Judge Didcott determined that Mr. Dube was not capable of work because of frequent epileptic seizures. The commissioner, who had been aware of this information, had required Mr. Dube to locate "special work of a sheltered kind" that would accommodate his malady, which he had not been able to do. Lacking the requisite employment, the commissioner deemed Mr. Dube "idle." Judge Didcott ruled that Dube's physical disability rendered him incapable of work and prevented his removal. Despite the formal law verbiage that followed Judge Didcott's ruling, his *decision* limited the repressive nature of the law. Judge Didcott went on to note that "on this occasion at least, it is possible to apply the Act and to do justice simultaneously."[27] Dugard would argue that it was possible on other occasions ignored by the South African bench. Judge Didcott's decision in *Dube* exemplified the type of judging that Dugard thought the judiciary should embrace.

For Dugard, the answer for the apartheid-era judges was not resignation, but a return to the roots of the Roman-Dutch law which provided for freedom from, among other things, arbitrary arrest, detention without trial, cruel and unusual punishment and freedom for counsel, for speech, for press, for expression, for assembly and for movement (Dugard 1971, 197). These should be the principles guiding judicial discretion, not the traditions, norms and values of the "white" community within which the judge presides (Dugard 1984, 289). Otherwise, in systems like apartheid South Africa, justice is perceived very differently depending on the pigment of your skin.

The critics of the South African legal system during the apartheid regime were thus divided into two camps. Those led by Wacks believed that the judges who embraced the formal or positivist approach to judging had no choice but to enforce and thus legitimize the repressive components of the law. Even by deciding cases involving family or contract law, these judges were coopted into the system and inevitably integrated into the political machinery that was apartheid South Africa. These critics did not believe that judges were imbued with discretion, at least not of any measurable or meaningful amount. The dictates of the repressive law within a system of parliamentary supremacy left no choice to the judges who opposed the repressive nature of apartheid but to resign.

The second contingent of critics, helmed by Dugard, contended that resignation would be a futile endeavor. Not only would conscientious judges most surely be replaced by less oppositionist ones,[28] but these resignations would embody the positivist, formal law understanding of judging which, argued Dugard, was wrong. Judges indeed have discretion available. The vague and ambiguous nature of "facts" and "rules" provided judges with opportunities to choose interpretations that embraced the more liberal, egalitarian English and Roman-Dutch law of South Africa.

Both of these approaches are empirically inaccurate. Dugard was correct in his assertion that choice is always available to the judge. Discretion is inevitably inherent in judicial decision making. If the law were as clear and dictatorial as the positivist approach would suggest, societies could quickly dispense with courts all together. The law, of course, is not so black and white.

Wacks, however, was correct in noting the limitations on that discretion, but he suggested that the law dictates the outcomes, I suggest that politics does so, at least in the high-profile cases that come to define these legal systems and the judges who comprise them. The outcome is black and white for politically charged cases. In systems like South Africa with no constitutional protections of rights or liberties and with Parliament supreme, courts ultimately will fail, regardless of their opposition to the government, when the will of the regime is well defined and unified. Thus the court, whether reluctantly or loyally, will support the regime in significant challenges brought by the opposition to test or reverse major government actions. While the courts may be able to confront the regime on isolated occasions, the majority of the legal battles that seek statutory interpretations that could significantly limit the will of the regime will fail.

The politically attuned "liberal-minded" judge may prefer to oppose the oppressive rules or, in fact, may prefer to oppose the regime in general to limit any legitimacy afforded it by the courts. But realizing the ultimate supremacy of Parliament, the politically expedient judge will support the regime in the high-profile challenges. To battle and lose repeatedly will sacrifice precious institutional resources. However, the remainder of the docket, the less sensitive, less visible cases, will provide opportunities for the politically expedient judge, or court, to follow the advice of Dugard and rule in a manner favorable to the individual.[29]

It may be that the support for the regime is not relegated to those cases in which judges realize they inevitably will be overturned. Decisions supporting the government may be the result of political expedience, but they may also be the result of judges who are ideologically aligned with the will of the apartheid state. The ideologically aligned judge will consistently support the state in the majority of the docket, regardless of the political importance of the case. The judge will demonstrate the pro-executive stance consistently in his or her decision making.

The third alternative, is that the judge is not influenced either by what is politically expedient or by his or her own personal ideology but merely by the facts and the law. This of course is the formal law approach to the judicial process, one which I, like Dugard and others, reject. While the facts and the law restrict the options, for appellate courts in particular, resolution is not dictated clearly by the facts and the law, or appeals would be superfluous or at a minimum, consistently predictable.

Judges are required to resolve the conflicts that come before them. Judges are required to enforce and determine the appropriate social norms. Formal law emerges to establish the parameters within which judges are to perform these functions. The existence and continuation of the repressive law complicate the mechanistic myth of judging. Understanding this intersection is essential to understanding judicial decisions in authoritarian regimes.

Judging, as stated before, is not a decision-making process in which outcomes are clearly black and white. Facts, at least for those cases that reach the highest appeal courts, are rarely obvious or clearly agreed upon. Moreover, laws are saturated with language that is elusive and equivocal, the product of the political necessity of compromise. Judges are required to take the uncertainty that is the reality of the law and create from it an appearance of a singular, inevitable interpretation. The judge proclaims the law within the judgement, asserting that this choice was compelled by the assessment of the facts and the law. This process of judging, like any human enterprise, is inevitably filled with the bias and prejudice that accompanies the judge to that specific social, political and historical moment in which the decision is made. *Judging is not black and white—judging is a process by which the grey is given the appearance of black and white.*

When courts in repressive regimes are faced with decisions that clearly represent a threat to the status quo, courts are not likely to challenge the regime often. The independence of the court will be reduced even further, and the impartiality of the court will lean toward the executive in most, but not all, of the cases. The discretion available to judges will allow them to reach conclusions which minimize the threat to the regime. Should the court use its discretion to reach conclusions that follow legal tradition and canon favoring the individual at the expense of the government, it can be easily negated through a statute. Courts that seek to limit repeated reversals will limit direct challenges. That is not to say that the court will always favor the government in high-profile cases, but the lack of enforcement powers as well as parliamentary sovereignty will logically force the court to limit these challenges. However, the bulk of the docket does not represent important challenges to the status quo and can provide the court with opportunities to demonstrate its independence and impartiality, or at a minimum, can be used to better assess the court's ideological position. Empirical evaluation of the decision making of the South African Appellate Division can provide evidence of judges who are consistently ideological in their decisions or who exhibit politically expedient behaviors.

Judges, as political actors, realize the utility of the mechanistic myth, but they also realize the limit of its utility. Regardless of their adherence to a formal law approach to judging, the adjudicative function cannot be fully separated from the larger moral questions embedded in these systems. This text evaluates the response of judges to this dilemma.

In the chapters that follow, I evaluate the decision-making behavior of the institution at the apex of the South African legal structure during the 41-year period, 1950–1990,[30] which basically corresponds to the rise and fall of the National Party's apartheid regime. Chapter 2 outlines the history of the South African legal system broadly and the Appellate Division specifically. Chapter 3 explores the winners and losers before the Court across various issue areas. Chapter 4 explores the individual decision making of the judges. Chapter 5 does so for the Court over time, and Chapter 6 provides a conclusion with thoughts for the future. I assess both legal and extra-legal factors, attempting to uncover statistically significant patterns that provide clues to understanding, if only partially, the behaviors of the individuals known as judges who, through their decisions, determined the fates of millions of South Africans like Mr. Pitje.

CHAPTER TWO

A Brief History of the South African Legal System

Mr. Pitje encountered a legal system that emerged from a unique set of forces that converged some three hundred years before he walked into the Transvaal magistrate's court. As Nonet and Selznick (1978) suggested, there was no neat trajectory from a simple social structure to the modern court system that determined the fate of Mr. Pitje. Without colonial intervention, no doubt a very different legal structure rooted in tribal custom and folkway would have led to a different destiny for Mr. Pitje. With the clash of colonial and indigenous social structures and the desire by all for political and economic control, the necessity to resolve conflicts and to control social interactions soon compelled the creation of a formal judicial system. Melding these disparate forces while balancing political interests created a legal structure that eventually relegated Mr. Pitje to a separate table in the small courtroom in the South African legal system.

Hahlo and Kahn's classic treatise noted three layers in the South African legal system: Roman, Dutch and English (1968, 575–596). In truth, the great majority of South Africans functioned under the laws of the various indigenous tribes. And these legal systems existed for centuries prior to Bartholomew Diaz's discovery of the Cape of Good Hope on February 3, 1488. Until the late twentieth century, historians, particularly of the white South African regime, persisted in an ethnocentric and limited exploration of the country's past.[1] Unfortunately, because this book focuses on the institutional progeny of these forces, little will be different here. The rules of the white man became the dominant force in the South African legal system. Nonetheless, the importance of the indigenous rule of law should not be equated with the space devoted to it here.

Arrival of the Dutch

Nine years after Diaz's discovery of the Cape of Good Hope, Vasco da Gama, under the egis of Portugal's King John II, rounded the Cape, eventually reaching India and proving the reality of a sea-going route. Subsequently, the Portuguese ignored the Cape, establishing ports on the eastern and western coasts. Eventually settlements were created on the eastern tip of South Africa in the area known as Table Bay by the Dutch East India Company as a way station for the Indian trade route (Riley 1991, 1).

In 1652, the Dutch East India Company established a settlement located on the Cape of Good Hope on the southern tip of the African continent. The Dutch brought their Roman-Dutch legal system, derived primarily from the works of Roman-Dutch jurists, judgements of the courts and provinces of the Netherlands, legal opinions of prominent jurists and applicable Dutch legislation (Du Plessis and Du Plessis 1995, 46).[2] Initially, legal disputes and criminal violations were resolved by the Court of Justice, comprised of the designated company commander and his "advisory council." The small hut in which this group met, decorated with animal skins and a stuffed zebra,[3] paralleled the stature of its jurists, who, without exception, had no legal training. The law reflected the interests of the company more than the rich Roman-Dutch law of the colonizers and was administered in an arbitrary and capricious manner (Sachs 1973, 17–19).

Initially there were no intentions to create a large colony at the Cape, and farming was limited to what was essential to provide for the passing ships and the small settler population. Increasing trade with passing ships and the growing friction with local farmers over access to grazing pastures and water necessitated greater articulation and precision in the language and application of the commercial law. The growing slave trade mandated similarly increased rigor in the coercive elements of the law, elements that were essential to maintaining control of the slave population that had burgeoned to 838 by 1700 (Worden 1985, 7).[4] While the Dutch law shaped the former, the latter was guided by the Digest of Emperor Justinian since slavery had been abolished in Holland (Sachs 1973, 22). The melding of the repressive and the formal law began in earnest.

Slavery represented not only the most repressive legal regime but also the extreme end of the social control continuum which requires extreme measures of coercion. Slaves who challenged their status by walking on a sidewalk reserved for whites or attempting to escape were dealt with harshly (Sachs 1973, 22–28). Minor offenses were punished with flogging, while those who physically harmed a master were put to a cruel and arduous death. One such penalty declared that the defendant be:

Bound on a cross, when his right hand shall be cut off, his body pinched in six places with red-hot irons, his arms and legs broken to pieces, and after that to be impaled alive before the Town House on the Square, his dead body afterwards to be thrown on a wheel outside the town at the usual place, and to be left as prey to the birds of the air. Prisoner also to pay all costs (Sachs 1973, 26).

Despite the limited intentions of the Dutch East India Company, the small settlement at Table Bay began to expand to the north and to the east. Land was acquired from the indigenous populations through seizure and conquest. Some of the indigenous population was captured for indentured labor on the farms established by the *trekboers* or migrant farmers. The formal boundary lines of the colony followed these migrants, pushing the borders further into the lands of the Khoikhoi, San and Xhosa (Thompson 1990, 45–52; Worden 1985, 8–11).

Arrival of the British

The British arrived in 1795 and encountered an economically weakened Dutch trading company. The British quickly gained control of the Cape in 1795 but ceded authority to the Batavian Republic (the United Netherlands) in 1803. European hostilities motivated the British to regain control of the Cape in 1806, but the Roman-Dutch law was allowed to continue to develop. However, Du Plessis and Du Plessis note that at the time the British gained control in 1806, the development of the Roman-Dutch law in the Netherlands was ending, leaving South African law without a foreign source. Thus the law "became purely indigenous" (Du Plessis and Du Plessis 1995, 48). This became particularly true as the indigenous Roman-Dutch traditions began to meld with those aspects of the law that were informed by the British. The British introduced English legal traditions in certain areas of the law via both legislation and judicial precedent. Criminal procedure was imported in 1819 and finally accepted in 1828 as was the English law of evidence in 1830. English law invaded aspects of company law, insurance law and the law of negotiable instruments. The Dutch court structure was replaced with an essentially English infrastructure in 1827 (Du Plessis and Du Plessis 1995, 47–51).

By 1850, the government began appointing colonial-born judges in the Cape, maintaining a balance between British and colonial judges until the late 1800s. While it was possible to qualify for the Bar in the Cape, the majority of those who pursued the legal profession did so after completing their education in Britain (Sachs 1973, 46–49).

The British Charter of Justice, adopted in 1827, and subsequent ordinances took steps to ensure the equality of races in both civil and criminal courts. Slavery was prohibited throughout the British Empire in 1834 (Worden 1993, 11; Sachs 1973, 39). According to an ordinance passed in 1828, "Hottentots[5] and other free persons of colour are . . . entitled to all the rights of law to which any other of His Majesty's subjects . . . are entitled" (Sachs 1973, 39).

Despite the equality of the races theoretically, the former slave population remained entirely subjugated to that of the white. Lack of skills and education left former slaves with little recourse but to take whatever menial employment was offered to them. While the law recognized the equality of the races, political reality created white domination. The Cape courts recognized the local tribal customs and folkways when not in basic conflict with British legal procedures (Sachs 1973, 62)

The *Voortrekkers*

The original Dutch settlers, or Afrikaners, resisted the changes in the legal status of blacks. The British emancipation of black slaves in the Cape significantly reduced the labor supply for the Afrikaner farmers. In 1840 some six thousand Dutch settlers, approximately 9% of the white population of the Cape, and their servants began the "Great Trek" northeast to establish new settlements free of British influence among the flat plains of central South Africa (Thompson 1990, 67). By the 1850s, these Dutch migrants, who became known as the *Voortrekkers,* or "vanguard *trekkers,*" had established the Orange Free State with its constitution and legal system based on the Roman-Dutch law, and subsequently the South African Republic (later to be known as the Transvaal) (Van Schoor 1975, 233–251; Du Plessis 1975, 252–292).

The relationship between the *Voortrekkers* and the indigenous populations was marked by "conflict, cooperation and complex interaction" (Worden 1993, 13). The legal machinery of the new Boer republics was crude at best, but by the 1870s, appellate courts were established in both the Orange Free State and the Transvaal, and these were staffed by well-trained legal minds. Though the courts utilized the Roman-Dutch law, the British rules of evidence were used in criminal cases (Sachs 1973, 72–73). Unlike the British Cape and Natal Colonies, the Afrikaners never recognized tribal customs and used Roman-Dutch law in all suits, regardless of the race of the litigants (Sachs 1973, 75). Indeed, the Constitution of the South African Republic stated that "the people desire to permit no equality between colored people and the white inhabitants."

The Emerging Republics

Meanwhile, the British had seized control of the short-lived *Voortrekker* republic of Natalia, to the east of the Cape, in 1843. Despite the British seizure, the Roman-Dutch law remained the recognized law of the land even after Natal became a separate colony in 1856. Because the British had outlawed slavery, Natal imported thousands of indentured servants from Madras and Calcutta, ultimately creating three distinct and overlapping populations that were black, white and Indian (Thompson 1990, 87–100).

The Cape, Natal and Boer republics overlay the various autonomous chiefdoms which existed throughout the country. The tribal political units varied in population and size with periphery units controlled by the center through the hereditary chief (Thompson 1990, 24–25). Initially, hunters and herders controlled the majority of the land, but by the late eighteenth century, these groups were eventually supplanted by farmers who also hunted and herded sheep and cattle (Thompson 1990, 15–30). Both intra- and intertribal conflicts emerged, developing cleavages that white settlers were able to exploit (Thompson 1990, 71).

The tribal justice system was a community process in which conflicts that could not be resolved were settled by the chief, advised by his council. The chief performed the legislative, executive and judicial functions within the tribe (Myburgh 1985, 5). There were no advocates for those either bringing the charges or being accused nor any formalized rules applied in a neutral fashion. Nonetheless, the tribal adjudicative system, like its British and Dutch counterparts, utilized rational procedures to reach a legal resolution (Sachs 1973, 95–99).

The tensions between the British and Dutch settlers and the black population escalated by the 1840s. Both the British expansion in the east and the Afrikaner expansion to the north and east met with black resistance. Eventually, the technology of the white man, along with the diseases he brought, led to the subjugation of the African chiefdoms and the integration of many black South Africans into the white-controlled regions (Thompson 1990, 70–109).

The discovery of the diamonds of Kimberly in 1867 and the gold of the Witwatersrand in the 1880s had a number of important consequences. It expanded the need for attorneys and the salaries of those attorneys. Thus many of the Cape lawyers traveled to the region, expanding further the Cape's impact, and thus the British legal influence (Sachs 1973, 48). It also increased the value of the South African colonies to the British empire, and the British now sought control over the entire tip of the continent. The British gained control over the diamond-rich territories near Kimberly and attempted to force union with the interior republics by encircling the territory with British-controlled protectorates and colonies. The discovery of the gold in the Transvaal allowed the Boer Republics to resist British control, and a growing Afrikaner nationalism contributed to the opposition (Van Zyl 1975, 293–323).

The economic bounty of the gold mines fed the fears of the British that the Boers would indeed gain first economic and then political superiority in the region. Unsuccessful attempts at negotiated union, understood by the Boers to mean British dominance, failed in the latter 1800s. Ultimately, the tensions between the British and Boer Republics erupted in war on October 11, 1899, a war that would continue for almost three years until the Orange Free State and the Transvaal accepted the "acts of peace" negotiated by both sides (De Kock 1975, 324). The terms of the Peace of Vereeniging, signed in Pretoria, gave absolute authority to the British monarchy, which was recognized as sovereign. The Roman-Dutch law was to remain a part of the judiciary if necessary for effective administration. The status of the indigenous population with regard to the franchise was postponed until representative government could be established (Van Zyl 1975, 356).

Union

Lord Alfred Milner, the British High Commissioner for South Africa and the Governor for the Transvaal and the Orange Free State, became the architect for unification following the war. Milner, an ardent Imperialist, envisioned a united South Africa under British domination. To achieve this, Milner made concessions to the Afrikaners, including deference to the color bar for the franchise in both the Orange Free State and the Transvaal, and subsequently these territories were granted autonomous rule. These concessions proved fatal to the British interests. Milner had hoped for a large influx of British immigrants into the territories to supplant the Afrikaner majority, and through the influence of the immigrants, he had hoped to weaken the Afrikaners' nationalism. Neither objective was achieved. The brutality of the war and fear of racial equality strengthened the nationalist movement among the Afrikaner population. Moreover, only a few thousand pro British moved into the territories, and the Afrikaners won the post-war 1907 elections in both the Orange Free State and the Transvaal. Even within the Cape, the anti-imperialist party secured control in the elections. Only within the Natal did the British maintain a majority, and only there did the British gain electoral control (Spies 1975, 358–371; Thompson 1990, 143–148).

Following the elections, the Afrikaners moved quickly to unite the four provinces and gain autonomy from Britain. In February 1909, delegates from the four provinces met to draft a constitution, completely ignoring the black, Indian and "coloured," or mixed-race, populations.[6] A delegation of black South Africans traveled to Britain seeking removal of the color bar for the franchise. The British Parliament, despite the sympathy of several members, ignored their request. Shortly thereafter, the British government passed the South Africa Act of 1909, creating a self-governing British dominion. The act mirrored almost exactly the document drafted by the South Africans, and on May 31, 1910, exactly eight years to the day after he had surrendered to the British as leader of the Boer rebellion, Louis Botha was elected Prime Minister of the newly formed South African Republic (Thompson 1990, 152–153).

The South Africa Act of 1909 created a unitary form of government with a bicameral legislature in a parliamentary system. The four colonies became the Union's four provinces though Parliament was sovereign. A Governor-General was appointed by the Crown to govern on the advice of the Cabinet, which was to be composed of not more than 10 ministers. The legislature was comprised of the 40-member Senate[7] and the House of Assembly of 121 representatives.[8] The franchise requirements of each province remained intact, but only British subjects or persons of "European descent" were eligible for election. In the Transvaal and the Orange Free State, all white males were allowed to vote; some minimal property requirements were associated with the franchise for white males in Natal, and practice and law excluded almost all people of color. Only in the Cape were voting rights theoretically nonracial, though only men who possessed some property and were minimally literate could vote.[9] In reality by 1909, 85% of the registered Cape voters were white, 10% coloured and 5% black (Thompson 1990, 150). To secure the voting rights of the black and coloured populations of the Cape, an "entrenched" clause, Section 152, was added to the Act of 1909, which required a vote of at least two-thirds of the Parliament to remove the franchise from the nonwhite voters. An additional entrenched clause was added that protected both English and Afrikaans as official languages. All other amendments to the Act of Union could be passed with a simple majority vote of Parliament.

Where to establish the seat of government became a hotly contested issue with Cape Town and the Transvaal's Pretoria battling for the anointment. Ultimately, the South Africa Act of 1909 provided for the three separate branches to be located in three separate places. The Parliament was to be located in Cape Town. The executive was housed in Pretoria. And the highest court, the Appellate Division, was to reside in Bloemfontein in the Orange Free State.

Black, Indian and coloured opposition to their secondary legal status began to organize in earnest around the turn of the century. The Natal Indian Congress, under the direction of Mohandas K. Gandhi, was formed in the 1890s (Beinart 1994, 90). The Cape coloureds established the African Political Organization in 1902 (later the African People's Organization) (Worden 1993, 83–84). The South African Native National Congress (renamed the African National Congress (ANC) in 1923) was formed in 1912 (Worden 1993, 81). The Industrial and Commercial Workers' Union was formed in 1920 (Davenport and Saunders 2000, 276), alongside the South African Communist Party, which emerged about the same time (Worden 1993, 50–57). However, in a pattern repeated throughout the remainder of the century, their concerns were ignored.

The Legal System

The legal system was comprised of the South African Supreme Court and local and regional magistrates. The Supreme Court included the Appellate Division, the highest court of appeal and the focus of this study, and lower courts known as Local and Provincial Divisions (Corder 1984, 20–21). The Provincial Divisions were both trial courts and courts of appeal. Local magistrates served in trial courts limited to misdemeanor and minor civil cases, and regional magistrates were restricted to criminal cases of limited jurisdiction.

Decisions from magistrates could be appealed to the Provincial Divisions. Appeals from Provincial Division decisions, were heard in the Appellate Division. Appeals alleging procedural irregularities in Provincial Division criminal trials could proceed directly to the Appellate Division. As a result, the Appellate Division entertained appeals from both intermediate and trial courts. Moreover, these appeals could involve civil or criminal cases with procedural or substantive challenges based on common law or statutory grounds (Dugard 1978, 10–13, 280–287; Du Plessis and Kok 1989, 29–40; Pitts 1986, 63–65).

The Appellate Division functioned as an appeal court but lacked discretionary control over its docket. Cases were certified to it from the lower courts. Petitioners denied leave to appeal in the lower courts could seek reprieve from the Appellate Division, but this was the atypical route to the Court. Until 1950, decisions of the Appellate Division could be appealed to the British Judicial Committee of the Privy Council, a relic repugnant to the newly elected apartheid government. After 1950, the Appellate Division was the court of last resort (Dugard 1978, 10).

Sitting judges on the benches in the four provinces at the time of appointment retained their positions. The Chief Justices of the colonies became the Judge Presidents of the Provincial Divisions. The Appellate Division consisted of a Chief Justice and a number of Appeal Court judges. Prior to the adoption of the 1961 Constitution Act,[10] judges on the Supreme Court (Appellate and Provincial Divisions) technically were chosen by the Governor-General, but in reality by the Cabinet. After 1961, judges were appointed by the State President in consultation with the Cabinet, specifically the Minister of Justice (Corder 1987, 95). In practice, the Chief Justice played a prominent role in suggesting potential nominees. Judges served on the Supreme Court until retirement at age seventy. Although the constitution allowed Parliament to remove a judge on grounds of misbehavior or incompetence, no judge was ever removed in this manner (Dugard 1978, 10; Pitts 1986, 64).

In 1950, the first year of this study, the Appellate Division had six judges. In 1990, the last year of the analysis, there were 18 Appeal Court judges. In addition, Acting Appeal Court judges could be appointed for short periods, usually a few months, to serve during illnesses, absences or interim periods between appointments.

Judges on the Appellate Division sat in panels to hear and decide cases. Decisions from a single judge were to be heard by panels of three Appellate Division judges; decisions from lower courts involving more than a single judge were heard by panels of five Appellate Division judges.[11] In criminal cases the quorum was generally three, though five-judge panels could be utilized in particularly complex cases. For civil cases the typical quorum was five.

Following the English practice, the South African Bar was (and still is) divided into advocates who appeared in court and attorneys who were largely confined to drafting documents and providing support for advocates. Traditionally, advocates attended law school, while attorneys began as apprentices. Judges on the Supreme Court were chosen nearly exclusively from among the senior advocates. No black served on the Supreme Court during the period of this study from 1950 to 1990 (Dugard 1978, 11; Pitts 1986, 64; Dugard 1987, 485).

This constitutional structure became the crucial foundation from which the repressive law, and thus ultimately apartheid, was able to emerge. The dominance of the white minority was assured through the "whites-only" Parliament. While nonwhites were allowed to vote in the Cape, their influence remained intentionally limited. In 1936, Parliament, in conformance with the two-thirds unicameral requirement of Section 152, disenfranchised the blacks in the Cape Colony. Thus, throughout the Union, the will of the majority of South Africans was silenced in the representative process, except for the few white South Africans who lent voice to their plight. The lack of judicial review and the absolute power of Parliament greatly restricted the capacity of the courts to challenge the inequities that would escalate with the victory of the National Party in 1948.

The Foundations of Apartheid

More repressive laws were established by the National Party[12] in 1948, but many earlier laws codified the second-class status of nonwhites. For example, the Bantu Land Act of 1913[13] prohibited the purchase or lease of lands by blacks outside the designated "reserves." These reserves constituted 7% of the land initially but increased to 14% by 1936 (Worden 1993, 49–50). These reserves formed the basis of the future "homelands" of apartheid. The Immorality Act,[14] passed in 1927, prohibited intercourse between whites and blacks. This served as the forerunner of the 1950 Immorality Act,[15] which prohibited sexual relations between whites and nonwhites, and the 1949 prohibition of mixed marriages.[16] The "pass laws," which restricted the movement of blacks in urban areas and required all blacks to carry a pass, were inherited from the pre-union period (Dugard 1978, 55). As previously mentioned, the franchise had always been limited by either law or practice to whites.[17]

When developing the diamond and gold mining industries, the cheap black labor was used extensively to offset rising capital costs. To ensure the stability of the labor force, variations on the pass-law theme were instituted in which blacks were forced to sign long-term employment agreements, the default of which was criminal. Skilled and semi-skilled positions were reserved for whites only (Dugard 1978, 85–89). Efforts to move cheaper black labor into these ranks resulted in massive and sometimes violent resistance by white labor. Ultimately, this "industrial apartheid" was statutorily instituted for the diamond and gold mines at the turn of the century (Fredrickson 1981, 205–234; Hindson 1987, 15–51).

With the onset of industrialization, the pass laws were used to establish a similar economic superiority for whites in the urban areas. Blacks and other people of color were allowed to enter and remain in cities only with employment. Those jobs that were unacceptable to the white population were reserved for nonwhites (Hindson 1987, 52–79). Without employment, nonwhites faced various punishments over time including being "ordered to return to his or her native reserve or 'homeland,' imprisoned, subjected to forced agricultural labor under conditions resembling the southern convict-lease system, or . . . sent to remote 'resettlement' camps of villages where 'superfluous' blacks [could] be gathered until the government decide[d] how to dispose of them" (Frederickson 1981, 242–244).

Throughout the history of apartheid South Africa, the government's motivation was in part to provide a large pool of cheap forced labor while simultaneously inflating the wages of the white workers by reserving higher-paying positions for them (Frederickson 1981, 244–249). Industrial apartheid enhanced the wages of the white workers at the expense of the black population (Dugard 1978, 85–89).

The National Party and the Constitutional Crisis

With the victory of the National Party in 1948, these earlier segregation statutes were followed by more extreme and systematic measures. The National Party, led by Prime Minister Daniel Malan, gained control of the South African Parliament in the 1948 election after running primarily on a two-prong, interrelated platform. First, the National Party was intent on returning control of the government to its Afrikaner heritage. This goal was pursued through strategic placement of Afrikaners in the bureaucracy and on the bench to replace, for the most part, English-speaking government officials. Second, a policy of apartheid, or separate development, was instituted, which was to assure the capacity of each race to develop "independently," thereby fulfilling its own destiny and potential. It should be noted that both Indians and coloureds were basically ignored in the homeland design (Leach 1986, 33–34). After winning the election, the National Party passed a series of laws, and governmental programs were instituted to initiate each of the prongs.

Initially, the courts, and especially the English-dominated Appellate Division, provided hope for those who sought to challenge the inherent inequality of apartheid. A number of cases in the early 1950s bolstered these expectations. In a series of decisions, the Appellate Division indicated that, in the absence of explicit statutory authority, segregation in public accommodations was impermissible unless the separate facilities were substantially equal. Using the British common law definition of unreasonable,[18] the Court struck down a number of regulations that violated this "separate but equal" doctrine.[19] In reaction, the National Party enacted the Separate Amenities Act of 1953,[20] which explicitly authorized separate and unequal public facilities for the different races. The swiftness with which Parliament reversed the Court's decisions made the inability of the courts to run interference painfully clear.

A second attempt by the Court to confront the engine of apartheid was provoked by the National Party's effort to remove the franchise from the coloured residents of the Cape by a simple majority vote. The National Party was committed to the franchise only for white South Africans throughout the entire Republic. While the two-thirds majority constitutionally required to remove black voters had been achieved in 1936, no such super majority existed in Parliament for a similar disenfranchisement of the coloured voters. Despite this, Parliament passed the Separate Representation of Voters Act of 1951[21] by simple majority vote. The Voters Act removed the coloured voters from the common voters' roll, placing them on a separate voters' roll from which they were to elect four "coloured representatives."

The Voters Act was in direct conflict with the entrenched clause of the South Africa Act of 1909 which required a two-thirds vote to remove the Cape coloured voters. Previously, the actions of the South African Parliament were required to conform to all provisions passed by the British Parliament, such as the South Africa Act of 1909. However, British passage of the 1931 Statute of Westminster, which repealed the Colonial Laws Validity Act of 1865, no longer required South Africa's Parliament to conform with such so-called "Imperial" acts. It provided autonomy to the actions of the dominion Parliaments such as South Africa; the South African legislature could act as it wished—or so the government's law advisors told it. Thus the legitimacy of the removal of the voters by a mere majority vote was "widely believed" to be beyond legal challenge (Forsyth 1985, 63). Still, the action of the Parliament was contested in *Harris v. Minister of the Interior* (1952).[22]

In *Harris,* the Appellate Division held that despite the 1931 Statute of Westminster, the dictates of the entrenched clause of the South Africa Act of 1909 remained in force. That Act had constituted the South African Parliament as a bicameral institution, functioning by simple majority for most matters, but a unicameral institution, functioning for the purposes of the entrenched clauses. The Court then rejected the argument of the government that no voters had been removed from the voter rolls but were merely placed on *different* voter rolls. While the Court deemed the argument "plausible," the Court rejected it as contrary to the spirit of the South Africa Act of 1909. The Court did not, however, condemn the substance of the act itself, merely its form (Forsyth 1985, 66–67).

In response, Parliament passed the High Court of Parliament Act of 1952[23] in which a "high court" consisting of the members of Parliament was able to review all judgements of the Appellate Division in which legislation was declared invalid. In the High Court's subsequent review of the Appellate Division's *Harris* decision, it reversed the Court and declared the Separate Representation of Voters Act valid. This decision of course was challenged, and in *Minister of the Interior v. Harris* (1952),[24] the Court found the High Court of Parliament Act against the dictates of the Act of Union, which clearly delineated the role and function of the legislative and judicial branches. As the Court noted, the High Court of Parliament "is simply Parliament functioning by another name."[25] While these actions increased the perceived independence of the judicial branches among the population in general (Dugard 1978, 288), Parliament was not impressed.

In retaliation, Parliament, under the orchestration of the National Party, increased the size of the Appellate Division from five to eleven and required a quorum of eleven where the validity of an act of Parliament was at issue and a quorum of five for all other cases.[26] It then increased the size of the Senate from 48 to 89, which doubled the National Party's majority in a single stroke (Lapping 1986, 98–103).[27] The reconstituted Parliament with the now requisite two-thirds support removed the voters and specifically rejected the power of judicial review for South African courts. The newly constituted, now predominantly Afrikaner, Appellate Division[28] upheld the actions of Parliament in *Collins v. Minister of the Interior* (1957),[29] with only one dissenter. Even the judges who had struck down the earlier attempts considered that Parliament's actions passed legal muster.[30]

The Appellate Division, therefore, was rebuffed in its attempt to exercise common law and constitutional review of legislative actions. As a result of these decisions in the 1950s, the English-dominated Appellate Division became known as "a liberal institution in an illiberal community" (Dugard 1978, 279). More importantly, however, the lack of judicial review created a legal system in which "Parliament [was] able to ride roughshod over individual liberty without fear of judicial obstruction" (Dugard 1978, 35).

Implementing the Grand Scheme

Removing the voters was a largely symbolic achievement. As stated earlier, the Cape coloured voters had little if any effect on electoral outcomes. The National

Party marched forward, but other aspects of the grand apartheid scheme were more complicated. In particular, Prime Minister Malan had less enthusiasm for implementing the "native policy." It was Malan's Minister of Native Affairs, Hendrik Frensch Verwoerd, who enthusiastically embraced his assignment to create a system of total separation of the races. His ambition was aided by the government's passage of the Population Registration Act of 1950[31] that created a system in which the Secretary of the Interior classified all South Africans by race.[32] This classification was then used in applying all other apartheid statutes. Passes identifying individuals by race, technically called "reference books," were required at all times for blacks.[33] The Bantu Land Act of 1913[34] and the Bantu Trust and Land Act of 1936[35] set aside some 87% of the most desirable land for whites, despite the fact that blacks comprised some 75% of the population (Pitts 1986, 53). The subsequent Group Areas Act of 1950[36] established designated areas for whites, blacks and coloureds who were further divided into Indian, Chinese, Malay and "other." Forced removals from "white" areas followed[37] (Dugard 1978, 80).

The Bantu Education Act of 1953[38] provided public education at last for the nonwhite population but did so, of course, in segregated facilities. Verwoerd insisted that the "Bantu," as he referred to black South Africans, needed only minimal education for the basic manual labor that he or she was destined to perform (Mallaby 1992, 18–19). Eventually, the Extension of University Education Act of 1959[39] created a segregated higher education system, which unintentionally created a fertile ground for the Black Consciousness movement among the educated black youth (Lapping 1986, 157–158). The resource differential between the higher education facilities of the white and nonwhite students was as profound as its end results (Dugard 1978, 84–85).

Verwoerd also courted the tribal leaders to entice their cooperation in the grand apartheid scheme which would return millions of urban and suburban blacks to the rural territories. The government began its forced removal policies focusing on townships such as Sophiatown, outside Johannesburg, which in a cruel twist of apartheid triumphalism it renamed in Afrikaans "Triomf."[40]

Conversely, the industrial machinery demanded a constant supply of cheap black labor. The government drew from the "homelands" the necessary supply of urban, mining and agricultural workers. The Bantu Urban Areas Act,[41] along with the other pass and labor laws, limited where the individual could work, the wages that could be paid, the promotions that could be earned, the areas where the individual could reside, and the time of the day the individual could traverse the designated area (Beinart 1994, 149–153).

Once inside the white area, South Africans of color, under the Reservation of Separate Amenities Act,[42] could not sit on the same park bench; ride in the same taxi, bus or railcar; visit the same zoo, restaurant, swimming pool, library, museum, concert or post office as whites. Drinking fountains were separated as were the restroom facilities. If a black South African became ill, a separate ambulance was required for transport to a separate hospital. And if the treatment failed, a separate burial ground was required. In sum, the apartheid system was "an immense edifice of discriminatory and oppressive law" (Ellmann 1989, 389). Verwoerd would eventually be rewarded for his efforts with the prime ministership in 1958 following the death of Prime Minister J. G. Strydom (Davenport and Saunders 2000, 406).

Opposition

Those who sought to change the system faced an insurmountable problem. The South Africa Act forbade the election of any nonwhite. Blacks had no vote. Group organizations such as the multiracial Communist Party were forced to go underground or disband by the Suppression of Communism Act of 1950,[43] which authorized the executive to arrest and incarcerate political opponents without judicial supervision. Racially mixed parties were ultimately outlawed[44] and the Liberal Party disbanded, while the Progressive Party was required to remove its nonwhite members (Dugard 1978, 101; Beinart 1994, 149; Barber 1999, 144–145).

Political organizations such as the ANC and the Pan-Africanist Congress[45] began massive defiance campaigns throughout the country. In 1955 the National Action Council[46] drafted the "Freedom Charter," which supported nonracial equality of rights and economic changes which were sufficiently imbued with socialist rhetoric to inflame white fears (Lodge 1983, 68–74; Terreblanche and Nattrass 1990, 13–15; Worden 1993, 105–106). In 1956, the government used the Suppression of Communism Act to arrest 156 people on charges of treason, among them, ANC leaders Albert Luthuli and Nelson Mandela, then head of the Youth League. The trial lasted almost six years. Ninety-one were initially brought to trial with only 30 surviving to its end. Eventually, all were found not guilty. The treason trials brought world attention to the South African government's policy of suppression and oppression. By 1961, the trial became a focal point for the world as well as the country and provided a platform for the opposition leaders to espouse their own doctrines in the courtroom (Leach 1986, 110). Moreover, the 1960 Sharpeville incident, in which South African police opened fire to disperse an estimated crowd of 15,000 to 30,000 black demonstrators protesting the pass laws, marked the climax of several years of both domestic and international opposition to apartheid (Thompson 1990, 210). One-hundred and eighty people were wounded and 69 died (Davenport and Saunders 2000, 413). The debacle became known as the Sharpeville massacre and gained worldwide attention and sympathy.

International condemnation followed.[47] The government responded by extending the powers of the police to detain individuals without charges for 12 days. This was extended to 90 days in 1963, 180 days in 1965, and to an indefinite period by 1966 if authorized by a judge. By 1976 the necessity for judicial authorization was removed (Davenport and Saunders 2000, 422).

Verwoerd responded to the increasing violence by banning the PAC and the ANC. It was illegal for banned organizations to operate. Individuals who were banned were prevented from meeting with more than one individual at a time, participating in or even possessing material related to an outlawed organization.[48] Punishment was one to ten years imprisonment (Dugard 1978, 164–165).

The Constitution Act of 1961

Ironically, while passing repressive law after repressive law, Parliament consolidated its emphasis on the formal *rules* of law by passing the Constitution Act of 1961,[49] marking South Africa's departure from the Commonwealth. The new constitution symbolized the overlapping nature of a legal structure dedicated to procedural rigor and yet substantively devoid of fairness.

Among other things, the 1961 Constitution Act warned that:

> (1) Parliament shall be the sovereign legislative authority in and over the Republic, and shall have full power to make laws for the peace, order and good government of the Republic.
> (2) No court of law shall be competent to enquire into or to pronounce upon the validity of any Act passed by Parliament, other than an Act which repeals or amends or purports to appeal or amend the provisions . . . [which entrenched the equal status of both the English and Afrikaans language].[50]

Verwoerd persisted in establishing ten bantustans or "homelands," which were given nominal authority over the residents. In a faux internal colonization scheme, these were eventually to be granted independent status.[51] Following this "improvement" on the tribal system, the white representatives elected to represent black interests in Parliament were abolished (Lapping 1986, 132–135).

After the 1966 assassination of Verwoerd, Balthazar Johannes Vorster, the former Minister of Justice, became Prime Minister. Vorster began an intense campaign to complete the tribal relocation program that "resettled" hundreds of thousands of blacks to desolate, essentially uninhabitable "homelands." Many had lived in townships for generations and knew nothing of their tribal ancestors. Descendants of those originally imported as slave labor had no true "native" homeland in the Republic of South Africa. Mixed-raced South Africans were essentially ignored within these designations and assigned to the most ethnically appropriate homeland (Thompson 1990, 193). Through massive force and cooptation of the bantustan governments, it is estimated that Vorster successfully moved approximately 3.5 million blacks to the homelands (Lapping 1986, 154).

Increasing Tension—Soweto and Biko

Though the South African economy had seen an economic boom in the 1960s, foreign capital began to leave the South African economy by the 1970s. Moreover, in response to the increasing cost of living for black workers, widespread strikes ensued affecting almost every sector of the economy (Stadler 1987, 30–31; Terreblanche and Nattrass 1990, 15). International economic pressure further increased following the 1976 Soweto uprising (Terreblanche and Natrass 1990, 16; Jenkins 1990).

In June of 1976, 15,000 students demonstrated against the requirement that math and social studies be taught in Afrikaans. In the initial confrontation with the police two protesters were killed and many injured. Subsequently, violence erupted nation-wide ultimately resulting in at least 575 deaths and 2,389 wounded according to official estimates, estimates which Lapping argued were surely underestimated (Lapping 1986, 160). Compounding the chaos was the death of Steve Biko, a thirty-year old popular and magnetic leader of the Black Consciousness movement. He was respected not only within South Africa, but had established external ties, including those to the United States. Biko, like many before him, died in prison, the result of blows to the head during an "interrogation." Unlike the fates of the many anonymous prisoners who died before him, his death caused a firestorm of international attention (Lapping 1986, 160–161). The repressive and oppressive nature of apartheid became highly visible and again international condemnation was near universal.

Amidst the increasing internal turmoil, the National Party became embroiled in a governmental scandal involving the misappropriation of public funds, the so-called "Muldergate affair." In the maelstrom of the late 1970s South Africa, P. W. Botha succeeded Vorster as Prime Minister, and began his tenure which would end just shortly before the demise of apartheid itself.

As Nonet and Selznik (1978) and Hund and Van der Merwe (1986) argue, the need for continuity and security in commercial interactions spurs the development of the formal law based on fair and consistent treatment. Economic investors worldwide found it difficult to continue to invest in South Africa because of both political pressure from stockholders, and concerns for the political instability within the country. The removal of foreign investments pressured

South Africa to retreat from its concept of separate development of the races. South Africa had become dependent upon foreign capital and the refusal of a number of banks to continue loans made it clear to many leaders that the domestic economy was too closely tied to the world community to ignore their concerns (Jenkins 1990).

The Beginning of the End—the Constitution Act of 1983

In deference to the pressure externally and the violence erupting internally, South Africa adopted a new constitution in 1983 with elections held under it in 1984. The Constitution Act of 1983[52] created a tricameral legislature, with separate chambers for whites, individuals of mixed race and Asians, but with no representation for blacks. The House of Assembly was comprised of 178 white members representing some five million whites. Three million coloureds were represented by 85 coloured members of the House of Representatives, while the nearly one million Indians were represented in the House of Delegates by 45 Indian members (Dugard 1992, 5–6). Representation was based on the proportion of the population in each group, giving the white population a 4 to 2 to 1 ratio and clear control (Lapping 1986, 170–171). Only 20% of the eligible coloured and Indian voters participated in the 1984 election (James and Du Pisanie 1987, 39).

Concomitantly, the government established African Community Councils,[53] or elective governing bodies for blacks in the townships. These Councils remained under the direct control of the white authorities. Again, some 80% of the black population did not participate in the elections (James and Du Pisanie 1987, 46–47).

The 1983 Constitution Act was clearly seen as an attempt by the National Party to counter the onslaught of its apartheid critics. While the new constitution provided no new rights or liberties, it marked the turning point in the eventual capitulation of the regime.

In reality, the new constitution did little to change the status quo, and did nothing to address the concerns of the majority black population. Violence continued throughout the country, and the violence escalated in the townships. The police and the army were incapable of maintaining order (Greenberg 1987; James and Du Pisanie 1987, 47).

The inability of the National Party government to maintain order, much less to govern, became increasingly evident in the 1980s. Despite the National Party's rhetoric that "apartheid is dead" and that the economy would have to be "deracialized" (James 1987, 2), the government's actions spoke louder than its words. On July 21, 1985, the government declared a state of emergency for part of South Africa. Though lifting the state of emergency in March of 1986, the government returned to a nation-wide state of emergency on June 12, 1986, unleashing unprecedented repression. In 1986 alone, some 26,000 people were detained. The notorious government sponsored hit-squad is suspected of hundreds of incidents of violence against anti-apartheid activists or their organizations, including the assassination of leaders, in the mid- to late 1980s (Haysom 1992).

President[54] P. W. Botha's declaration of the state of emergency was renewed annually for the next three years. The state of emergency simply expanded the already extensive internal security powers available to the South African regime. These statutory provisions provided for detention without trial, limited or nonexistent access to detainees, banning of political organizations as well as individuals, press censorship, and significantly limited access and review of these actions by courts. The South African regime in the mid- to late 1980s represented a most repressive legal order. Despite this, every "i" was dotted and every "t" was crossed in the formal legal process, though the government's shadow encompassed a wide variety of extra-legal violence and repression.

Ironically, at the same time the government was increasingly repressive in certain areas of the law, it was removing various aspects of social apartheid, or the so-called "petty" apartheid laws. The prohibitions against interracial marriage and sexual relations were repealed in 1985;[55] the pass laws were repealed in 1986;[56] job reservation was ended and black trade unions were recognized and allowed to bargain and litigate for collective and individual fairness in a labour court;[57] statutory segregation in public facilities such as libraries and parks as well as segregation in sports, hotels and restaurants was eliminated;[58] universities were permitted to integrate;[59] and some racially integrated suburbs were allowed to develop[60] (Dugard 1992, 16–21).

The election of President F. W. de Klerk in September of 1989 signaled the demise of apartheid. De Klerk realized the impotence of the apartheid philosophy, and he was willing to negotiate with blacks for some share of power. As signs of his sincerity, in February of 1990 De Klerk lifted the 30-year ban on the ANC and subsequently on the Communist Party and the PAC.[61] De Klerk then suspended the death penalty, limited the detention without trial of the accused to six months, lifted some restrictions on the press, and he culminated the reforms with the release of Nelson Mandela after 27 1/2 years of imprisonment on February 11, 1990. For all practical purposes, it became clear that apartheid was a failed experiment.

Through lengthy and often rancorous negotiations between the ANC, the government and other political and business interests, free elections in which all South Africans voted for the first time in the history of the Republic were held in 1994. Nelson Mandela was elected President of the new democratic Republic of South Africa, and the new South African constitution was signed into law on December 10, 1996.[62]

Courts and Repressive Regimes

Undoubtedly, most analysts would have predicted a future of extreme turbulence fraught with violence preceding any significant change in South Africa's political structure. What has made South Africa of even more interest is that events of the late 1980s and 1990s confounded those analysts. In a largely peaceful transition, South Africa has moved to democratic majority rule. Though the emerging democracy certainly is still troubled,[63] the new Republic of South Africa is nonetheless very different indeed from the previous, white-dominated apartheid regime. As South Africa has embarked on its transition to democracy, its courts have played an increasingly important role. Scientific study of those courts, their history and behavior, assumes even greater importance than it might have previously. Indeed, there has been increasing recognition of the importance of courts generally in what has been termed the "global expansion of judicial power" or the increasing policy authority delegated to the courts (Tate and Vallinder 1995). Analyses of these events are not lacking (see Tate and Vallinder 1995; Jackson 1997), but systematic comparative analyses of court behavior based on replicable data over lengthy periods are still scarce, though impressive exceptions exist (see for example, Schubert 1985; Epp 1998).

Political regimes, it may be said, emerge because of new distributions of resources. For South Africa, the new black majority rule has dramatically altered the power structure and the ultimate allocation of "who gets what, when and how"(Lasswell 1936). The apartheid state allowed white domination of political, social and economic resources. Much criticism was directed at the courts' legitimation of the nondemocratic rule with its attendant rights abuses (Cameron 1987a; Dyzenhaus 1998; Marcus 1985). There was no institutional independence for courts in South Africa. As evidenced in several of the high profile cases discussed previously, direct challenge to the government's wishes was met quickly with constitutional or statutory changes that reversed the Court's affront. In addition to the ever present power of parliamentary supremacy, critics asserted that the courts were in fact staffed by ideologically-driven Afrikaner sympathizers who consistently supported the government and its racist policies. In the triad of conflict resolution, critics argued that the courts, and the Appellate Division in particular, represented a mere extension of the National Party. It was criticized for its lack of both independence and impartiality. No doubt the mere functioning of courts in an authoritarian regime legitimates such criticisms, but judging in an oppressive regime is an intriguing dilemma largely ignored in judicial research.

The history of the South African legal system demonstrates the overlaying of the typologies suggested in Chapter 1. The government insisted on a formal law system with its emphasis on order and rationality. But such a system proved problematic for a regime based on unequal and disparate treatment of the majority of its population. The repressive nature of the apartheid system required elaborate statutory provisions to ensure that the repressive component of the law could exist within the recognized formal law mechanisms.

The Appellate Division was required to apply this formalistic heritage found in its British and Roman-Dutch legal traditions to the repressive apartheid edifice. As subsequent chapters will note, apartheid permeated the whole of the laws of South Africa. Even within the Court's interpretations of tort and contract laws, which one might presume devoid of the repressive nature of the apartheid philosophy, inequality emerged.[64]

These judges, the equivalent of the brightest legal minds in the world, were asked to walk a legal tightrope of sorts; they were trained to respect equality and protect the individual and yet required to apply repressive laws. They appreciated the formal law as the foundation of the legal system, emphasizing rationality, neutrality and impartiality. The threads of the formal law became intertwined with the repressive laws of a segregated social system. The weaving of these two legal types resulted in a fabric that was impossibly weak and untenable.

This book evaluates the decisions of the South African high court during the weaving and unraveling of the apartheid fabric. This chapter has provided a highly condensed history of the Court and its background. The following chapters will provide empirical assessments of the behavior of the Court in the apartheid era.

CHAPTER THREE

Winners and Losers in Cases Before the Appellate Division, 1950–1990

On August 26, 1985, the Catholic Archbishop of Durban, Dennis Hurley, a staunch oppositionist to apartheid, received a phone call informing him that the Security Branch of the South African Police was searching the offices of Diakonia, an organization of a number of Christian churches in the Durban area. Diakonia was established "to encourage and facilitate Christian social concern among the congregations of its member-churches."[1] While such a purpose would be thought a worthy goal in most parts of the world, for South Africa, such an ambition was deemed a potential threat to the status quo. Thus the police arrived to search for incriminating materials that would indicate the intent to foster not only social concern but social unrest. In addition to the search of the building, Colonel Coetzee had ordered the arrest of one Gerald Patrick Kearney, the director of the organization and the occupant of the premises under scrutiny.

Archbishop Hurley grew alarmed at the "detention" of Mr. Kearney. Kearney had been arrested not under an ordinary criminal statute but under the provisions of the Internal Security Act of 1982,[2] which gave the police virtually unfettered capacity to arrest without warrant, to detain and to interrogate individuals presumed to be a threat to internal security. Moreover, these individuals were not allowed outside contact and could be refused bail. When the Commissioner of Police deemed their detention to no longer serve any useful purpose, then, and only then, could the individual be released. The 1982 Act was the progeny of earlier security statutes developed shortly after the National Party's victory to suppress oppositionist groups[3] (Mathews and Albino 1966; Mathews 1971, Ch. 11; Mathews 1986, Ch. 6).

The archbishop, along with Kearney's wife, filed a petition with the Durban and Coast Local Division to force the release of Mr. Kearney. The state thought the action superfluous. After all, Section 29 of the Internal Security Act contained an infamous "ouster clause:"

> (6) No court of law shall have jurisdiction to pronounce upon the validity of any action taken in terms of this section, or to order the release of any person detained in terms of the provisions of this section.[4]

At first blush, the "ouster clause" appears to be a fatal blow to any legal remedy for those detained under statutes protected by these clauses. Under such clauses, the courts had no capacity to review actions under the affected legislation, to demand the release of the detainee or otherwise to interfere. If Kearney's detention fell under the aegis of such an ouster clause, why would the archbishop seek judicial relief? Hurley's hope was that while courts could not review actions that fell within the definitions of the statute, courts could determine which actions were and which actions were not taken "in terms of" the section. The archbishop argued that the statute required the police officer to have "reason to believe"[5] that the detainee had committed an offense which fell under the scope of the jailable offenses delineated in the act or was withholding relevant information from authorities. Further, Hurley argued that he was "appalled that any person having had the slightest acquaintance with Kearney or his activities could have any reason to believe that his conduct could fall within the section."[6] Hurley's contention was that the police officer's reasons for believing Kearney should be detained *were* objectively justiciable. Thus, the state must articulate the "reason to believe" Kearney guilty of subversive action for the detention to be legally within the statute and the review of the Court removed.

By asserting the South African common law rule of *audi alteram partem*—the requirement to hear the other side—some relief could be available even in statutes which included an ouster clause. Considered a bedrock of the legal traditions embodied in fairness and equal treatment, the rule requires that any individual detained by the government had the right to be given information or facts relating to his or her detention and the right to controvert the state's position. Essentially, if Hurley prevailed, the Court could require that the state articulate the grounds for the officer's belief that Kearney's detention fell within the statute. Kearney would be given the opportunity to rebut. If the detention was legally within the statute, then the ouster clause was in effect, and court review was not possible.

The state argued that the intent of Parliament was to allow the widest possible discretion in preventing rebellion and violence. To require disclosure of the reasons for the arrest could be harmful to security. In particular, the state did not want to allow any review of its actions by the ordinary courts. The whole intent of the ouster clause was to allow the police to detain at will. To argue that the ouster clause was intended to authorize court review of administrative action, even to determine which actions were ousted, was a perversion of legislative intent.

Previous Appellate Division rulings on internal security detentions did not provide much optimism for Mr. Kearney. The Appellate Division had generally supported the government on numerous occasions determining that detentions could be renewed based on the discretion of the arresting officer;[7] that detainees could be denied access to reading and writing materials;[8] and that courts could not intervene even in cases of alleged physical or mental torture.[9]

The lower court ruled that courts were ousted only if the action had been taken in terms of Section 29. The judge was free to examine whether or not the officer "had reason to believe" that the detainee had contravened the law.[10]

In evaluating the lower court's decision, the Appellate Division supported the finding that the phrase "reason to believe" was objectively justiciable. Moreover, the Court ruled that the onus to prove that the detention was legally "in terms of" Section 6 rested with the state. Since Colonel Coetzee refused to proffer any proof that the arrest was justifiable under the section, the Appellate Division held the state had not fulfilled its responsibility to prove that the arrest legally fell within the confines of the Internal Security Act. Mr. Kearney was to be freed.[11]

An extension of the *Hurley* question followed in *Omar and Others v. the Minister of Law and Order and Others* (1987).[12] A state of emergency had been declared in July of 1985 according to Section 2 of the Public Safety Act.[13] This section authorized the State President to suspend the ordinary law of the land if in his opinion the "safety of the public, or the maintenance of the public order is seriously threatened."[14] The last week of October, Abdulah Mohamed Omar[15] was arrested under the state of emergency regulations which read:

> 3 (1) A member of a Force, may without warrant of arrest, arrest or cause to be arrested any person whose detention is, in the opinion of such member, necessary for the maintenance of public order or the safety of the public or that person himself or for the termination of the state of emergency, and may, under a written order signed by any member of a Force, detain or cause to be detained, any such person in custody in a prison.
> 3 (2) No person shall be detained in terms of subreg (1) for a period exceeding 14 days from the date of his detention, unless that period is extended by the Minister in terms of subreg (3).
> 3 (3) The Minister may without notice to any person and without hearing any person, by written notice signed by him and addressed to the head of a prison, order that any person arrested and detained in terms of [the regulation], be further detained in that prison for the period mentioned in the notice, or for as long as these regulations remain in force.[16]

Mr. Omar had been detained beyond the 14 days by order of the Minister of Law and Order. Mr. Omar argued that under the rule of *audi alteram partem,* he should be allowed a hearing prior to an extension of the detention. Mr. Omar also argued that access to a legal adviser should not require permission. The Minister of Justice had refused to grant the legal advisors access to the detainees unless it was approved by either the Minister of Law and Order or the Commissioner of the South African Police.[17] The case was initially heard in the Cape Provincial Division, which refused to grant the hearing or to allow access by the legal advisers so that the detainee could exercise his right of *audi alteram partem* and present the other side. Judge Friedman dissented from the Cape Provincial Division's decision, arguing that the State President in issuing regulation 3(3) had not appropriately applied his mind, but had "applied incorrect principles."[18] The regulation accordingly was *ultra vires*.[19] Despite Judge Friedman's dissent, the majority opinion upheld regulation 3(3) and that the right of *audi alteram partem* was excluded. Mr. Omar remained in jail, and he appealed the decision to the Appellate Division.

The specificity of the language certainly suggests that Parliament intended to negate the long-standing *audi alteram partem* rule. The state argued that the *audi alteram partem* rule is a part of the ordinary law of the land, which is superceded during states of emergency because the ordinary law has been incapable of maintaining public order. It is therefore essential that wider latitude be provided to the executive. Courts are not free to question whether the executive has properly exercised the very broad discretion provided to it under the statute. Courts simply cannot question an *opinion* or its formulation.

Mr. Omar argued that South African jurisprudence required that the State President must "properly apply his mind" to the matter.[20] If the State President's action is "grossly unreasonable," then he has misconstrued his authority and the action was not properly authorized by Parliament.[21] If the State President has properly applied his mind to the matter, then the state of emergency is valid as are the regulations that flow from it. However, if the State President acted *male fide*, the extension of the detention without a hearing and the limitations on access to counsel are *ultra vires*.

Again, the Court was faced with a very clear choice between supporting the regime or providing some minimal adherence to a rule of law for those suffering the abuses of the rules of the law. *Omar* contained a set of circumstances very similar to *Hurley*, brought during a very similar period of time, but led to a different result. This time, the Court behaved as critics predicted and supported the government. The Court ruled that the State President had not acted with "gross unreasonableness" in declaring the state of emergency. Therefore, Sections 3(1), 3(2), and 3(3), which essentially negated the *audi alteram partem* rule, were valid. No hearing was required prior to the extension of the detention. Moreover, the Court upheld the limitations on access to the detainees by their legal representatives.

Hurley and *Omar* are excellent examples of the government's attempt at social control. Under the apartheid regime, the majority of the population was without voice. For the minority white population to maintain control, the South African government had to silence and subjugate the black population. Only through the most repressive means could that be achieved. Thus to maintain social control, the government created repressive statutes that enabled them to silence the opposition. However, because the government espoused fidelity to the rule of law, it was required to dictate such measures in formal mandates. Thus, the repressive laws were embodied in formal or positivist legal rhetoric. The interpretation of these laws, of course, was delegated to the courts. However, by limiting the jurisdiction of the courts, the government attempted to prevent the judges from intervening. The ouster clauses are excellent examples of the government's effort to limit or control the discretion available to the judges. *Hurley* and *Omar* offer opportunities to examine the use of judicial discretion. In one decision the Court favored the individual; in the other decision the Court favored the government.

Hurley and *Omar* are predictable uses of judicial discretion. In these high-profile cases, courts cannot consistently defy the state. The courts will not oppose the regime in those areas where the will of Parliament is resolute. Internal security concerns represent precisely those types of issues. If courts limit the state's authority, as it did in *Hurley,* Parliament can overturn a court's decision by simple statute. Courts do not want to damage their institutional health by enduring repeated reversals. While reversals favoring the rule of law can increase the perceived independence of the courts, if Parliament consistently negates the decisions of the court, then the Court will be seen as powerless and irrelevant. Courts will avoid constant frontal clashes. This, of course, assumes that courts are not ideologically aligned with the executive branch, an empirical question to be sure, and one to be examined in this chapter. This also assumes that the courts are not consistently ideologically opposed to the regime. An imaginative court, or judge, if sufficiently determined, can oppose the regime, as Judge Friedman did in the *Omar* decision.

For South Africa, the nondemocratic nature of repressive laws, such as the Internal Security Act and the Public Safety Act, limited the amount of discretion, independence and impartiality that could be afforded the judiciary in performing their social control function. While the formal law, such as the common law *audi alteram partem* requirement, demands a certain amount of independence to achieve the perceived neutrality equated with judicial decision making, the repressive law requires centralization of authority and little or no true independence for courts. Judges in South Africa contended with the diametrically opposed forces of the repressive and formal law.

For democratic regimes with basic guarantees of rights and liberties, courts are generally provided various avenues to protect their autonomy: tenure, separation of powers, checks and balances, budget protections and, of course, judicial review. These protections allow the judiciary the potential to be independent; that is they reside within a political framework that provides for and protects their independence and the presumed impartiality that follows.

Corder (1984, 242–244) argued that the independence of the South African judiciary was limited in three major ways. Constitutionally, he argued, the Court was the weakest of the three branches. Absent enforcement powers, the Court required the willing cooperation and support of the legislative and executive powers, particularly the bureaucratic structures, to implement its decisions. Absent judicial review, Parliament could overturn any judicial decision with legislative enactments. Absent constitutional protection, Parliament could, and did, limit the Court's jurisdiction, restricting the types of disputes that could be resolved by them. Corder also argued that the mere threat of these actions must certainly have influenced the behavior of the Court.

Second, Corder suggested that the appointment system for the Court, in which judges were essentially appointed by the Cabinet from among similar elites, ensured "a close alliance of character" between judges and Parliament (Corder 1984, 243). The judges enjoyed security of tenure until age 70,[22] and their salaries could not be reduced. "It should not be a surprise that a male judge, comparatively advanced in years, an adherent of the dominant religion and a product of the elite educational institutions, should identify with similar men in the legislature" (Corder 1984, 243).

Last, Corder noted that these judges were the products of the social milieu from which apartheid emerged. A conservative ideology emerged among the individual judges reflecting their own individual experiences in and evaluations of "contemporary social circumstances and needs" (Corder 1984, 243).

Corder thus argued that constitutional, functional and ideological reasons created a situation in which the "judges were locked into a role supportive of the political status quo" (Corder 1984, 243). Moreover, he found in his evaluation of the Court until 1950, they were not unwilling adherents.

Forsyth (1985) came to similar conclusions in his evaluation of the more modern era of the Appellate Division. He asserted that the Court selected more conservative and harsh choices in apartheid-era cases resulting in pro-executive interpretations not required by statute.

These authors suggested that the South African Appellate Division was often influenced by factors other than the facts and the law. These assertions are not unique to courts in nondemocratic South Africa. Shapiro (1981) argued that courts in general are never truly independent of the parties before them because courts exist as a component of the government enforcing the government's laws. Thus, in a way similar to Corder's arguments, the structure and function of courts within the broader governmental framework negated the capacity for true independence.

Courts in these systems cannot be fundamentally averse to avowed governmental goals, and in this sense "independent," in those cases that represent a significant threat to the government. In those cases, the Court may challenge Parliament on occasion, as in *Hurley*, but by and large, the Court will ultimately defer to the wishes of the executive and legislative branches as evidenced in *Omar*. But *Hurley* and *Omar* represent only two decisions of the apartheid-era Appellate Division. Evaluating the Court by only the one or the other or only by these two decisions is, of course, absurd. Only if the winners and losers over the whole of the docket are evaluated will a more complete picture of the Court's behavior emerge.

Facts, Law, Politics and Outcomes

As evidenced in Chapter 2, it quickly became apparent to the National Party following its rise to power in the late 1940s that it could not overlook the importance of the judges of the South African courts in the implementation of its vision of separate development of the races. The predominant English make-up of the Court led to Afrikaner concerns for judicial opposition, and the Appellate Division initially seemed unwilling to acquiesce in the new regime's stampede of legislation differentiating South Africans by race. As discussed in Chapter 2, while the South African courts had no power of judicial review, in a number of cases in the early 1950s, the Appellate Division used both the common law and the doctrine of *ultra vires* to nullify a series of governmental actions. However, Parliament's rebuttal to the "separate but equal" cases,[23] and particularly the Cape voters' case,[24] made clear the commitment of the National Party to end any pretense of equality between the races.

The expansion of the size of both the Parliament (from 48 to 89) and the Court (from 5 to 11) following the Court's rejection of the High Court of Parliament Act in 1952,[25] in particular, resulted in several tactical victories. The newly expanded Parliament removed the mixed-raced voters; they removed any possibility of judicial review; and they packed the expanded Appellate Division with Afrikaner appointees. The percentage of Afrikaners on the Court rose from 34% in 1950 to 68% by 1955.

The supremacy of Parliament becomes particularly painful as the legitimacy of the regime suffers. As Mathews noted, in repressive systems like South Africa, the "legitimacy crisis is not a true emergency but rather a fundamental social malaise requiring political responses from those in power" (1986, 193). These societies exist in a perpetual crisis state from the denial of basic political rights and liberties, the result of which is the declaration of a state of emergency. The state of emergency then allows the government to exacerbate the denial of basic political rights and liberties even more.

Both *Hurley* and *Omar* dealt with the capacity of courts to check arbitrary executive power. In one the Court provided some protection; in the other the Court did not. Critics asserted that the Court had neither the power nor the will to undermine the government. The Court argued that it possessed no will independent of Parliament. *Hurley* was the product of Parliament's text which did not specifically prevent the evaluation of the police officer's "reason to believe." In *Omar* the statute carefully articulated the denial of the Court's jurisdiction. The discretion available to judges always provides choice. The positivist premise always provides credence to their decisions. Decisions must be examined empirically to determine systematic evidence of support for one party or another.

Omar and *Hurley* empirically suggest that the Court was not consistent in its deference even in the high-profile cases, those that the government is most likely to win. The following analysis provides greater insight into the winners and losers before the Appellate Division in the whole of its decision making. This chapter empirically assesses the published outcomes of cases argued before the South African Appellate Division from 1950 to 1990.

A Deferential Division?

The bulk of the criticism of the courts generally, and the Appellate Division specifically, focused on the perceived allegiance, or at minimum deference, of the courts to the apartheid state following the early challenges. Indeed, among the major questions South African judicial scholars debated was the capacity of the courts to be anything but a rubber stamp for the apartheid regime. Within the Afrikaner-dominated government, judicial independence seemed unlikely at best and impossible at worst. While professing allegiance to Western legal traditions, the Appellate Division became a part of an oppressive political order that denied basic rights to the vast majority of its population (Dugard 1987, 487).

On the one hand, scholars like Corder suggested that politically, the courts were incapable of challenging a regime in which Parliament is supreme, and there is no power of judicial review. Others argued that the "pro-executive" nature of the Appellate Division and the legal system more broadly was the result of the positivist philosophy of the judges (Dugard 1971), which embodied the concept that the primary function of the courts is to "apply the law—any law" that

Parliament elects to pass, whatever the nature (Van Blerk 1988, 155). Thus, the black and white of the formal law perspective provided the cloak for upholding the regime.

Still others suggested that sympathetic judicial ideologies were the better explanatory variable. Millner asserted that "the selection and promotion of judges on the basis, primarily, of allegiance to a reactionary political creed reduce[d] the status of the court, just as surely as the constant legislative sapping of judicial power emasculate[d] it" (Millner 1962, 891). This sentiment echoed that of Forsyth (1985), discussed at length in Chapter 1.

Thus South African legal scholars were fairly consistent in their assertions that independence for courts with strong repressive law is not feasible. The regime will structurally limit the capacity of the courts to authoritatively determine winners and losers. As Budlender noted "there was clearly no possibility of success if the legal attack threatened the very foundations of the system" (Budlender in Abel 1995, x). Without judicial review and constitutionally protected institutional independence, these courts will fail in any direct challenge to critical regime preferences. Moreover, sympathetic judges can be strategically appointed to ensure that challenges do not arise because regime preferences and the preferences of the judicial decision makers will coalesce. Judges' decisions supporting the regime are the result of ideological and structural biases.

Ellmann's study of the decisions of the Appellate Division during the late 1980s state of emergency certainly provided support for this viewpoint (Ellmann 1992). A case study of the political trials in the Black Consciousness era came to a similar conclusion (Lobban 1996). But Abel's study of the legal challenges to apartheid suggested that the courts were, in fact, responsive to those who challenged the regime in some cases (Abel 1995). And Abel's work suggested that the irony of the apartheid state is that the law represented the only real political alternative for the oppressed. The leaders of the National Party realized that the courts were a necessary component of the apartheid system with its respect for the rules of law but no respect for the rule of law. Thus Abel asserted that the commitment of the apartheid regime to carefully defined legal procedure allowed the courts to provide some protection.

There is no question that the South African Appellate Division's independence was structurally limited. Parliament was supreme with the capacity to reverse court decisions through mere statute. Even if the Court desired to limit the abuses of apartheid, it must surely have recognized its limitations, particularly in high-profile cases like *Hurley* and *Omar*.

What is less clear is a broader evaluation of the Court's decision making over the entire course of its docket. Did the Court provide consistent support for the regime, or can the formal law provide at least some refuge for the less powerful in systems with pervasive repressive law?

Previous research for American courts, with established institutional independence, found that, in general, the government fared consistently better than other parties before appellate courts (Galanter 1974; Owen 1971; Sheehan, Mishler and Songer 1992; Songer and Sheehan 1992; Wanner 1975; Wheeler et al. 1987). This success was presumably the result of advantages at both the system and individual level. At the macro level, the system is generally structured to protect the interests of the haves. At the micro level, those with greater financial resources to invest in litigation on a repeat basis and to hire more experienced counsel when they do fare better than those who enter court on a "one-shot" basis. Thus in general, corporations, businesses and associations and, of course, the government, repeatedly access the courts to resolve disputes and should fare better than individuals with far less experience and resources (Galanter 1974).

A study of the U.S. Supreme Court found that the ideology of the justices was more closely associated with winning. However, the government, with its essentially unlimited resources, consistently fared well (Sheehan, Mishler and Songer 1992). In the English Court of Appeal, success was related to greater capability among the parties in terms of various resources (Atkins 1991). McCormick's study of the Canadian Supreme Court found a strong correlation between presumed resources and success. The government had the highest rate of success followed by businesses. Individuals were the least successful litigants (McCormick 1993).

These results, for countries that are structurally independent, suggested that the government and powerful economic interests have a significant advantage. Very little research has been done on nonindustrialized, developing countries with limited independence. Some research suggested that in an effort to balance the interests of the "haves" and the "have nots," appellate courts in developing countries may use at least portions of their dockets to "redistribute" resources to those who have less. However, for the handful of critical cases that challenge the regime or those in power, the court will defer to the "haves." The judges can then increase their legitimacy in the aggregate without challenging the powerful elites directly (Haynie 1994). These assertions were supported in a regional analysis, which demonstrated that individuals who challenged corporations or the government and resided in the least developed regions of the country were significantly more likely to succeed for certain economic cases (Haynie 1995).

None of the studies cited previously were directly related to explaining litigation outcomes for a nondemocratic, racially polarized developing country, and thus our theoretical expectations are somewhat unclear. South Africa is not an advanced industrial nation, the modal category of the previous research, nor during the period of investigation was South Africa democratic, again the predominant category studied. South African courts lacked the power of judicial review of legislation and established constitutional boundaries that limit statutory and administrative abuses of rights (Davenport 1996; Keith 1999; Lijphart 1999). Parliament was supreme, and the courts were in many respects impotent in substantive powers to challenge the government.

So what should we have expected for the South African Appellate Division? Did its behavior mirror the results for the United States and England, or did the judges engender a sympathy for those with less with an eye to increasing the perception of the legitimacy of the courts? Did the dominance of Afrikaner judges translate into distinct advantages for the government mirroring the ideologically driven outcomes of the United States Supreme Court? (Sheehan, Mishler and Songer 1992). Given the previous discussion of the Court's critics, one might anticipate that the government would be the overwhelming winner, given the government's resources, the lack of review for courts, the lack of rights for citizens and the nondemocratic polity within which the courts resided.

However, the Appellate Division was certainly aware of its critics. For South Africa, millions of individuals fell under the umbrella of the "law" and never embraced its legitimacy or that of the government that created it. For those whose skin color was insufficiently white, the courts represented an artificial edifice created to perpetuate white rule. Among the disenfranchised, there was no perceived independence and no perceived impartiality among either the rules or the judges who enforced them. South African judges were well aware of the criticism directed at them.[26]

The Court was also aware that it could not ultimately win against the National Party in the major challenges, given its lack of power to review statutes or actions for constitutional validity. Indeed, as the earlier examples demonstrate, the few times that the Court did engage in a frontal attack, it ultimately lost. Nonetheless, the bulk of the docket was not concerned with these major challenges. Table 3.1 provides an examination of the major issue presented in each of the published decisions of the Appellate Division during the period from 1950 to 1990.[27] A large portion of the docket is devoted to criminal cases.[28] The second largest category concerns private economic conflicts,[29] though challenges to various public laws[30] comprise a significant component of the Court's docket. Family law cases are not often brought before the Appellate Division, and those that are generally involve probate and estate questions. A fairly significant number of tort decisions are challenged before the Appellate Division. Excluding criminal cases, the numbers of civil rights and liberties[31] challenges are negligible. This is not surprising considering that no bill of rights or indeed any constitutional guarantees of liberties existed during the period examined. An average of 74 cases per year was published with a low of 54 in 1969 and a high of 99 in 1978.

TABLE 3.1

Decisions of the South African Appellate Division by Issue, 1950–1990

Year	Criminal Cases	Civil Liberties	Private Economic	Torts	Public Law	Family Law	Procedural & Other	Annual N
1950	23	1	8	5	15	1	3	56
1951	23	1	13	1	21	6	0	65
1952	22	2	16	3	14	7	2	66
1953	37	3	11	3	10	6	0	70
1954	15	0	19	7	16	3	0	60
1955	27	0	19	5	20	8	3	82
1956	37	2	13	4	14	5	3	78
1957	23	3	13	5	16	6	2	68
1958	32	0	10	4	18	2	1	67
1959	45	0	8	4	18	5	2	82
1960	29	1	21	10	15	2	2	80
1961	14	2	14	6	21	1	1	59
1962	30	2	20	7	11	2	0	72
1963	26	1	20	6	10	3	3	69
1964	17	4	17	6	15	2	0	61
1965	28	2	15	10	12	1	2	70
1966	24	2	13	12	7	2	2	62
1967	16	2	25	7	7	1	6	64
1968	30	1	11	7	8	3	3	63
1969	18	1	15	6	12	2	0	54
1970	18	1	18	10	12	0	0	59
1971	19	2	22	8	12	2	0	65
1972	30	1	18	14	14	2	4	83
1973	18	1	24	12	8	1	4	68
1974	16	0	23	10	13	1	3	66
1975	31	4	21	11	15	6	3	91
1976	30	1	26	21	13	2	2	95
1977	26	1	29	15	11	1	6	89
1978	37	2	27	19	9	4	1	99
1979	26	3	18	24	9	3	2	85
1980	31	3	16	14	11	0	6	81
1981	31	0	27	16	9	7	4	94
1982	25	2	26	16	17	1	2	89
1983	15	0	19	14	11	2	3	64
1984	21	1	26	4	2	3	2	59
1985	17	1	35	8	13	4	4	82
1986	18	5	28	9	13	2	2	77
1987	33	5	27	9	10	5	0	89
1988	36	12	27	3	16	1	2	97
1989	24	9	26	4	9	3	2	77
1990	21	5	26	8	21	1	3	85
Total	1,039	89	810	367	528	119	90	3,044

Analysis

To assess the advantages of the various parties before the Appellate Division, all 3,044 reported cases were coded according to whether the primary appellant was an individual, a business or the government. If the pro-executive critics are correct, the government should fare better than at least its American counterpart. Further, given the presumed resources of the parties, corporations should fare better than individuals.

Appellants in the cases examined in this analysis have already lost at least once in the courts below. If one assumes that appellate decisions are driven by the formal law and litigation resources are irrelevant, one would expect that respondents would prevail in the majority of appeals if the formal law also drives the decisions of the lower courts. One presumes courts will interpret the law more often correctly and the need for reversal to be less, particularly in systems like South Africa, where there is no discretionary control over the docket. However, the respondent enjoyed only a slight advantage.[32]

In order to assess whether the hypothesized advantage of the government and business (those with presumed greater resources) actually exists, it is not enough to know which class of litigants won more often in an absolute sense. The overall success rate of a given class of litigants can be influenced by how frequently they appeared in the Appellate Division as the appellant rather than the respondent. It is important to know whether or not a given class of litigants was better able to overcome the basic tendency of appellate courts to affirm. To control for this aspect of relative advantage several studies have utilized an "index of net advantage" (Wheeler et al. 1987; Songer and Sheehan 1992; Haynie 1994, 1995; McCormick 1993). This "net advantage" is derived by taking the success rates of each class of litigants when they appear as appellant and subtracting the reversal rate (the success rate of their opponents) when they appear as respondent. This measure is independent of both the frequency with which one appears as appellants versus respondents as well as the propensity of appellate courts to affirm the lower courts. It is, therefore, a stronger measure of success

TABLE 3.2
Net Advantage of Parties Before South Africa's Appellate Division, 1950–1990 (%)

Type of Party	Success Rate as Petitioner	When Respondent, Opponent's Success Rate	Net Advantage	Averaged Success Rate as Petitioner & Respondent
Individual	39	41	−2	49
Corporation	37	38	−1	49
Government	41	38	3	51

N = 2,825

TABLE 3.3
Petitioner Success Rates Against Different Respondents
Before South Africa's Appellate Division, 1950–1990 (%)

	Respondent					
	Individual		Corporation		Government	
	%	N	%	N	%	N
Petitioner						
Individual	42	346	41	263	38	1,071
Corporation	41	267	34	298	36	176
Government	40	230	44	138	33	15

than a simple measure of the proportion of decisions won by either the government, the business or the individual (Songer and Sheehan 1992, 241).

Table 3.2 provides the net advantages of the litigants.[33] Table 3.2 shows that the government maintained the highest success rate when petitioning the Court as well as the greatest averaged success rate but only by a few percentage points in each category.[34] The government enjoyed the only positive net advantage of the three petitioner categories.

Table 3.3 shows the likelihood of success of differing pairs of litigants. Individuals fared somewhat better when challenging corporations, winning 41% of the time as opposed to a success rate of 38% when challenging the government. When corporations faced individuals, the corporation won 41% of the time but won only 36% of the cases when challenging the government. When the government challenged an individual, it won only 40% of the time and won 44% of the time when challenging corporations. While the government fared better than either corporations or individuals, a clear advantage did not emerge.

Table 3.4 shows the net advantage for different combination of parties. The government fared best, though only marginally in disputes with individuals (2% net advantage) but more strongly with interactions involving corporations (8% net advantage).

Table 3.5 reports the success rates across differing issue categories. In criminal cases, the government managed a higher net advantage of 13 compared to -9 for individuals, and -33 for corporations, but the low N when corporations were

TABLE 3.4
Net Advantage for Different Combinations of Parties (%)

Combination of Parties	Net Advantage
Individual v. Corporation	No net advantage
Individual v. Government	Government by 2
Corporation v. Government	Government by 8

TABLE 3.5
Net Advantage for Party by Issue (%)

Type of Party/Issue	Success Rate as Petitioner (N)		When Respondent, Opponents' Success Rate (N)		Net Advantage	Averaged Success Rate as Petitioner & Respondent
Individual						
Criminal	39	(854)	48	(52)	−9	45
Apartheid Challenges	31	(35)	31	(16)	0	50
Civil Rights/Liberties	37	(35)	42	(43)	−5	47
Private Economic	42	(332)	44	(326)	−2	49
Torts	46	(163)	38	(182)	8	54
Public Law	28	(160)	33	(120)	−5	47
Procedural	24	(42)	33	(27)	−9	45
Corporation						
Criminal	27	(26)	60	(5)	−33	33
Apartheid Challenges	0	(5)	50	(8)	−50	25
Civil Rights/Liberties	35	(17)	57	(21)	−22	39
Private Economic	38	(419)	37	(420)	1	50
Torts	39	(133)	44	(117)	−5	47
Public Law	36	(124)	40	(98)	−4	48
Procedural	19	(21)	20	(35)	−1	49
Government						
Criminal	51	(55)	38	(879)	13	56
Apartheid Challenges	39	(23)	28	(39)	11	55
Civil Rights/Liberties	56	(32)	35	(20)	21	60
Private Economic	54	(24)	50	(28)	4	52
Torts	32	(40)	54	(37)	−22	39
Public Law	37	(219)	33	(285)	4	52
Procedural	31	(13)	18	(11)	13	56

respondents in criminal cases limits the utility of this figure. The government's averaged success rate in criminal cases as petitioner and respondent was 56% compared to 45% for individuals.

Surprisingly, there was no decisive advantage for the government in challenges to apartheid rulings,[35] certainly not the result one would have predicted. While the government did enjoy a higher net advantage of 11, its averaged success rate was only slightly higher than that of the individual, 55% compared to 50%. However, the limited number of apartheid challenges suggests that the vast majority of apartheid rulings by the lower courts went unchecked by the highest court of appeal. However, had individuals pursued these challenges, the results suggest that the Appellate Division was not predisposed to rule in the government's favor, though clearly the government won the prominent challenges to its racist laws (Ellmann 1992; Abel 1995).

For civil rights and liberties issues the government again fared better than either individuals or corporations with the highest averaged success rate of any category (60%) and a net advantage of 21 compared to individuals' averaged success rate of 47% and a net advantage of −5 and corporations' averaged success rate of 39% and net advantage of −22. The low success rate of corporations was fueled in large part by the restrictive defamation laws protecting individuals, such as elected officials, as opposed to the press.

The government had a fairly strong advantage over either individuals or corporations in private economic cases.[36] These involve government contract or property disputes. The Court appeared to favor the government's interests when the government was challenged by either individuals or corporations in basic private economic litigation.

For torts, corporations fared better than the government with an averaged success rate of 47% compared to the government at 39%. However, individuals fared better than either corporations or the government with an average success rate 15% higher than the government's. Moreover, individuals were the only category with a positive net advantage (8) that is almost four times that of the government.

While the government fared better than either individuals or corporations in public law cases, its advantage was hardly overwhelming. In procedural cases[37] the government fared better than individuals with a net advantage of 13 compared to the individual's −9 as well as corporations with a net advantage of −1. However, the low success rates of petitioners overall suggest that the Court did not provide threshold access in most cases.

These results suggest that overall, the decision making of the Appellate Division did not demonstrate distinct advantages for any party though the government fared slightly better than most and did best in the predictable categories of rights of the accused and apartheid challenges. However, even within these categories, the government faced a losing proposition some 40% of the time. This certainly undermines the predominant perspective, which asserted that the Court's structural dependence on the National Party limited its capacity to oppose the government.

Thus the government was not at an overwhelming advantage in litigation outcomes and actually fared only marginally better than individuals or corporations.[38] A portion of the Court's docket, cases seeking damages, did result in a significant advantage for individuals. Looking at the aggregate of the decisions of the Court, the Appellate Division clearly was not consistently ideologically driven. The Court's support of the government is similar to Wheeler's findings for state supreme courts in the United States (Wheeler et al. 1987). The Appellate Division's rulings in favor of the government are actually less than the success rate of the government demonstrated by the United States Courts of Appeals (Songer and Sheehan 1992) or the United States Supreme Court (Sheehan, Mishler and

Songer 1992). This may, in part, be a function of the Appellate Division's desire to increase its legitimacy by limiting its support of the regime in the aggregate because it could not do so in the few politically sensitive cases it heard each year.

When analyzing the overall results, the government, similar to its American and British counterparts, did enjoy better success rates than either individuals or corporations. But given the despotic nature of the apartheid regime, it is surprising that the government did not enjoy an even greater advantage in litigation. Previous research has focused overwhelmingly on the major disputes and resulted in a distorted picture of an institution with an inherently pro-executive bias (Dugard 1978; Dyzenhaus 1991; Ellmann 1992). That the South African Appellate Division's capacity to challenge the National Party was limited is not disputed. The Court resided in a polity in which Parliament was supreme, and there was no capacity for courts to void its actions or those of the executive. As noted above, many critics have suggested that the alleged pro-executive stance was less a function of the Court's structural dependence than a function of an Afrikaner-dominated Court particularly sympathetic to the apartheid philosophy. These results do not support such a simplistic evaluation when analyzing the full context of the Court's docket.

When studying the aggregate of the Court's decisions, a necessary evolution in the study of any court, a different picture emerges. Certainly the Court would not be considered an institution that consistently favored the individual in litigation outcomes, but neither would the Court be viewed as an overwhelming supporter of the regime even in such critical issues as rights and liberties. A more balanced picture emerges of a moderately pro-executive institution functioning within a nondemocratic, repressive regime.

Conclusion

The irony of the regulations delineated by the government in the Internal Security Act and the Public Safety Act should not be lost. The South African government wanted the appearance of the rule of law. Individual rights routinely guaranteed by the common law were sufficiently respected that the government negated them in writing. The capacity of judges to limit the abuse sufficiently threatened Parliament so that it limited their jurisdiction by statute. Limiting their purview was determined essential to maintaining the repressive legal order. The increasing need for repressive control necessitated the expansion of the formal law to achieve it.

The early challenges to the National Party indicate that in systems where Parliament is supreme and the will of the regime is resolutely against the position of the Court, statutes can be written to easily overturn decisions. Even in those constitutional cases, such as the challenges to the removal of the Cape coloured voters, parliamentary manipulation easily can remove judicial roadblocks to legislative wishes.

These tactics were revisited during the state of emergency between 1985 and 1990 as evidenced in the *Omar* challenge. Again, *Omar* represents a high-profile case in which the government supported an interpretation that favored dramatic limits on the rights of individuals. The Appellate Division adopted the conservative interpretation, negating the *audi alteram partem* rule and severely, if not completely, restricting any right for the detainee to a hearing. What is apparent from the aggregate analysis is that this capitulation was not a routine one for the Court across the whole of the docket.

This is not to argue that the decisions of the Court are equivalent across the whole of its docket. The hope inspired by a decision like *Hurley* or the desperation that follows a precedent like *Omar* cannot be compared to a tort case in which the Court ruled liberally that the common law required an expansion of the duty to care. Nor could one argue that decisions like *Hurley* and *Omar* were similar in impact to the Court's decision that a sentence of death was too harsh given the facts of the case and should be lessened to 30 years. *Hurley* and *Omar* and similar internal security appeals were seen as petitions that tested the capacity of the courts to provide any hope of protection against the onslaught of abuse that flowed from apartheid. The repressive laws of apartheid South Africa limited the capacity of courts to stem the inevitable tide of abuse that flowed from its framework, and politically the Court was not going to place itself in a wake that would destroy the Court as a political institution. The analysis of the Court's entire docket, however, suggests that the Appellate Division was not ideologically supportive in the whole of its decision making. If the Court was the legislature's lackey or at least comprised of individuals philosophically sympathetic to the apartheid regime, the support of the government should have been more systematically evidenced, and one would anticipate this conservative philosophy to have affected private economic decisions as well. That the data do not support this implies that the Court was not pro-executive *in toto*. This analysis, however, does not undermine the damage incurred to rights and liberties by decisions like *Omar*, nor should it lessen the volume of the critics of the Court for those choices.

While this chapter has focused on the aggregate decision making of the Appellate Division as a judicial body, the next chapter will focus on the individual decision makers. The outcome for any particular decision is the sum of the choices of the individual judges who sit on the panel that evaluates the conflict.

CHAPTER FOUR

Individual Voting Behaviors of the Appellate Division Judges, 1950–1990

Shortly after assuming control of the Republic of South Africa, the National Party passed the Population and Registration Act of 1950, which Dugard referred to as the "cornerstone of the whole system of apartheid" (Dugard 1978, 60). This statute required that:

> Every person . . . be classified as a white person, a coloured person or a native, as the case may be, and every coloured person and every native whose name is so included shall be classified by the Director according to the ethnic or other group to which he belongs.[1]

This compulsory racial classification was then used in applying all other apartheid statutes. The difference between being classified as white, coloured or black meant the difference between the potential for a decent life and condemnation to abject poverty.

There was no scientific approach to this process. Classification often was determined by a bureaucrat's evaluation of the individual's appearance, sometimes with disastrous results. In one case, an elderly gentleman of eighty-one was classified as "native" and his wife of 25 years as coloured. The couple contemplated divorce because the classification would have forced the wife to move to a black township with its accompanying hardships. In another family a brother was classified as "native" while his sibling was classified as coloured, threatening to divide the family. Each case required an appeal to alter the classification (Brookes 1968, 25).

Among those who faced such a challenge was Mr. Felton, who on November 28, 1966 was notified by the Race Classification Board that his classification had been changed from "white" to "coloured." Mr. Felton appealed the change before the Board. Difficulties in determining an individual's race had led the government to amend the Population Registration Act. The new Sec. 1 of Act 61 of 1962 provided that:

> "white person" means a person who
> (a) in appearance obviously is a white person and who is generally not accepted as a coloured person; or
> (b) is generally accepted as a white person and is not in appearance obviously not a white person,
> but does not include any person who for the purposes of his classification under this Act, freely and voluntarily admits that he is by descent a native or a coloured person, unless it is proved that the admission is not based on fact.

This definition proved problematic for individuals who were registered "white" because of their appearance, but whose parents, one or both, were not classified white. The government contended that if either parent, or indeed any blood relative was classified as coloured, it was impossible for the individual to be white regardless of appearance. The Cape Provincial Division had ruled that "a person who is admittedly of mixed blood cannot be said to be a member of the White race. . . . [T]hat is, that the person concerned must be of full-blood to qualify as a member of the White race. . . ."[2]

Implementation of this statute meant that the determination of one's race, and thus the political, economic and social freedoms available, was the arbitrary evaluation of skin pigment. If errors were made, the onus to prove the mistake resided with the individual inappropriately classified. For Mr. Felton, the change in classification from white to coloured meant the difference between the white man's world in South Africa and the second-class status of other citizens.

In his appeal to the board, Mr. Felton was queried concerning his "descent." When asked about his mother, he explained that he had always regarded his mother, a dressmaker, as a white person, as did the white ladies of the Cape for whom she sewed. Fatally, he conceded under cross-examination that his mother could be a Cape coloured.

> Q: But you knew that she was a coloured woman working for white people?
> A: Yes, well, let's put it that way, yes.
> Q: You say you were well aware of the fact that your mother was a coloured person?
> A: No, I wasn't.
> Q: I thought you said so just now?
> A: Well, after it was pressed to me.
> Q: You did know?

A: Yes.

Q: You did know that?

A: Yes.[3]

The Race Classification Board rejected Mr. Felton's request to retain his white classification. The appeal of the denial was heard in the Transvaal Provincial Division which upheld the board's decision.[4] On further appeal to the Appellate Division, the state contended that this exchange met the requirements of Section (b) and that Mr. Felton had "freely and voluntarily" admitted that he was by descent a coloured person. Mr. Felton argued that the admission was in no way voluntarily or freely given, and therefore his classification should remain white. Previous decisions by the lower provincial courts, like that of the Cape, placed the emphasis on the fact that an individual was not white if either parent was classified as nonwhite and disregarded the voluntary component of the section. If, after all, the intent of the statute is to correctly identify the individual, information that assists in that endeavor should be given judicial notice. Mr. Felton asserted that the means to that end was important. In his case, the facts were predicated upon information not freely or voluntarily given and thus had to be ignored. Based on the other aspects of the statute's definition, he appropriately should be classified as white.

The "facts" of the case would seem to support the state's assertion that Mr. Felton was indeed a person of mixed race if his mother was of mixed race. However, the interpretation of the statute provided the Court with the potential to focus on the manner in which this information was obtained. While Mr. Felton clearly was not tortured, the Court was required to interpret the terms "freely" and "voluntarily." This discretion, Dugard would suggest, provided the Appellate Division with the capacity to rule in Mr. Felton's favor, undermining the regime (Dugard 1971, 1978, 1984, 1989).

The Appellate Division ruled that Mr. Felton's admission that his mother "may be a Cape coloured person [was] clearly not an admission that she [was] in fact a Cape coloured,"[5] nor even could his concession that "there may possibly be colored blood in him"[6] be considered an unequivocal admission concerning *his* classification. The Court specifically noted that Mr. Felton had "never regarded himself" as anything other than white. Given this, there had been no intention to "freely and voluntarily" make an "unequivocal admission" that he was not white, "even though the evidence might suggest that he was in fact not a white person by descent."[7] The Court thus rejected the lower court's decision and ruled in Mr. Felton's favor.

A second case illustrative of the inherent discretion in judging was decided in 1985 by the Appellate Division, *Black Affairs Administration Board, Western Cape, and Another v. Mthiya*.[8] The Court was asked to determine whether Mr. Mthiya, a black South African, could remain in Cape Town following the revocation of his legal residence within this designated white area by one of the vast number of apartheid bureaucratic agencies, the Black Affairs Administration Board. Mr. Mthiya had obtained employment in the Cape with Chick's Scrap Metals in 1967. Like many black South Africans, Mr. Mthiya was forced by the soaring unemployment in his homeland to seek work in the city while his family remained in his place of birth at Engcobo in the former Transkei.[9] This forced separation was not by Mr. Mthiya's choice but the result of an apartheid system consumed by maintaining white superiority.

By statute, Mr. Mthiya was required to have permission to live and work in a designated white area. Indeed, the Native (Urban Areas) Consolidation Act[10] prohibited any black from remaining longer than 72 hours in an urban area without permission. Permission was assured only if he or she had resided in the area continuously since birth, had worked continuously in the area for the same employer for more than 10 years or lawfully resided in the area for more than 15 years. Even if employed, if the above conditions were not met, the employee could be returned involuntarily to his or her designated homeland.

Black South Africans were necessary for employers like those of Mr. Mthiya, but South African law required that these workers officially reside in a "designated homeland." The law required that Mr. Mthiya's employer justify the lack of requisite white laborers and request permission to "import" black labor from outside the designated white area. This permission was granted and forwarded to the Transkei. Mr. Mthiya was required to report to the local Transkei Labour Bureau, which provided the relevant documentation in his passbook. Mr. Mthiya then proceeded to the Cape to begin his employment. Like many workers, Mr. Mthiya was hired on a yearly contract. In order to maintain his employment with Chick's Scrap Metals, he arranged annually for his employer to forward again the justification and request for Mr. Mthiya's employment to the local Labour Bureau in the Transkei, and Mr. Mthiya would travel back to the Transkei to obtain the necessary documentation in his passbook. Many employers provided their employees with annual leave of a month or so to return for the required documentation and to visit family. After all, Mr. Mthiya's wife and children could not legally follow him to Cape Town; thus he was separated from them for 11 of 12 months every year, except for three occasions.

On three separate occasions it became necessary for Mr. Mthiya to remain in the Transkei to care for family or legal matters. The first of the three lengthier absences was the result of Mr. Mthiya's building a house for his family. The second was to recover two cows stolen from his land, precious property for Mr. Mthiya. The third separation, for a rather extended period of eight months, was necessitated by a government agricultural scheme which removed Mr. Mthiya from his land and required that he select a new plot for his family home. Mr. Mthiya was also arrested during this period, along with others, for the murder of a local headman despite the fact that the murder occurred before his return to the village. Several court appearances were required in the ensuing months before the charges were withdrawn.

On each of these three separations, Mr. Mthiya contacted his employer and was granted permission for the leave. When Mr. Mthiya was able to return, the employer notified the local Labor Bureau and forwarded the necessary paperwork to enable Mr. Mthiya to resume his employment in the Cape.

The government asserted that through these annual leaves, and particularly the rather lengthy eight-month absence, Mr. Mthiya violated Section 10 (1) (a) and (b) of the Urban Areas Act which read:

> No Black shall remain for more than 72 hours in a prescribed area unless he produces proof in the manner prescribed that–
> (a) he has, since birth, resided continuously in such area; or
> (b) he has worked continuously in such area for one employer for a period of not less than 10 years or has lawfully resided continuously in such area for a period of not less than 15 years, and has thereafter continued to reside in such area and is not employed outside such area and has not during either period or thereafter been sentenced to a fine exceeding R500 or to imprisonment for a period exceeding six months

For his violation, Mr. Mthiya, like thousands before and after him, was arbitrarily "repatriated" or deported to his tribal home in the Transkei. Like thousands before and after him, Mr. Mthiya had little hope of employment in the poverty-plagued Transkei. Mr. Mthiya elected to use the courts as an avenue to retain his job, the only means of supporting his family.

The government asserted that the legislation must be literally interpreted. Mr. Mthiya could not satisfy Section (a) because his family residence was in the Transkei, not the Cape. Of course, Mr. Mthiya's residence was *required by law* to be in the Transkei, so he could never satisfy Section (a), an irony lost on the government.

The government further asserted that Mr. Mthiya could not satisfy Section (b) either. Any absence from the employer would necessarily be a violation of the "continuous" work requirement of Section 10 (1) (b). If this interpretation were adopted by the Court, then no annually employed worker could ever satisfy this requirement. All workers employed on an annual contract were *required by law* to return to their homeland to obtain the necessary paperwork that allowed them to "continuously" work in designated white areas. The government's interpretation would create a catch-22 in which by following the law, it would become impossible to satisfy the law. The Appellate Division had ruled previously that annual leaves of a month's duration did not qualify as "breaks" in sufficient duration to negate "continuous" work.[11] The government contended that even if short breaks were allowed to obtain certification, Mr. Mthiya's absences were much too long to be considered an annual vacation or leave to obtain legal certification in his homeland.

Mr. Mthiya's attorneys claimed that he had more than satisfied the spirit of the law. He had been in the sole employ of Chick's Scrap Metal since 1967, some 14 years prior to the government's revocation of his pass. They noted the irony of the government's interpretation. It was the government's own actions that led Mr. Mthiya to this dilemma. He was not allowed by law to have his family with him. Economically there was no possibility of providing for his family in the Transkei. His employer, understanding and appreciating the difficulty of the separation, allowed a month each year for Mr. Mthiya to return home and reunite with his wife and children and to complete whatever family responsibilities had accumulated for him over the course of the year. Of course, he also would obtain the documentation for his passbook from the local Labor Bureau that would allow him to repeat the cycle, year after year after year. The lengthiest of the absences was necessitated, first, by the government's forced removal of Mr. Mthiya's family, and, second, from the government's false charges of murder. Mr. Mthiya's attorneys begged the Court to be cognizant of the fact that neither of these events were the fault of Mr. Mthiya but the result of government actions.

The lower court had applied the Court's previous ruling, which placed the emphasis on the work relationship rather than the contract, and ruled in favor of Mr. Mthiya.[12] The government appealed the decision to the Appellate Division.

In applying the formal law, the Appellate Division faced a clear choice between an interpretation that supported the repressive nature of the law or undermined it. A conservative, literal interpretation would lead to a pro-executive decision that doomed Mr. Mthiya and hundreds of thousands facing similar situations, to unemployment and greater poverty than that they already embraced. On the other hand, a more liberal interpretation of the law, equally justified and one Dugard would argue was required by the Roman-Dutch law and English common law traditions that emphasized individual liberty, would return Mr. Mthiya to the designated white area of the Cape and his job at Chick's Scrap Metal.

By 1985, the year in which the Appellate Division rendered its decision, the untenable nature of the pass laws had become evident. Abel noted that large employers favored relaxation of the influx control mechanisms to ensure continuity in their labor force (Abel 1995, 62). Moreover, the Riekert Report on Manpower Utilisation[13] had been issued in 1979 and called specifically for liberalization of labor markets (Hindson 1987, 80–96).

In its decision, the Appellate Division ruled that "literal continuity" was not required.[14] The Court emphasized the relationship between the employer and the employee rather than the contract itself. If the employer and employee realized an agreement for future work, then the absence would not be considered fatal under Section 10 (1) (b). Mr. Mthiya was able to return to his job at Chick Scrap Metal.

A final case for analysis, *More v. Minister of Co-Operation and Development and Another* (1986)[15] involves the infamous forced removal of the Bakwena Ba Magopa tribe from farms of approximately 20,000 acres. The tribe had purchased the land in 1916 and 1931 in the district of Ventersdorp in the Western Transvaal, south and west of Pretoria and Johannesburg. The National Party's apartheid platform required that the races be completely separated and allowed to "develop" independently and individually. The reality of this fiction required that millions of individuals, mostly black, be uprooted and resettled in the appropriately "white" or "black" areas. Many South Africans were required to return to areas they had never seen before nor had members of their families, who had left their "native" villages decades or even centuries earlier. These individual tragedies were played upon the apartheid stage repeatedly.[16] Even more devastating were the forced removals of entire black communities like those of the Magopa people.

As early as 1969 the rumors of the Magopa resettlement began to surface, but nothing concrete followed. The tribe flourished and by the early 1980s consisted of more than 420 families, their schools, churches, clinic, shops and several hundred stone houses, some of which rivaled those of any white middle-class South African suburb.[17] Unfortunately, the green rolling grasslands of the Magopa tribe were considered a "black spot" in the government's designated white area. The grand scheme of apartheid could not allow the Magopa to remain. The government bureaucracy determined that the tribe would be moved to Pachsdraai, described as "dry and primitive [with] no food, no grazing—and no water" (Abel 1995, 389).

Not surprisingly, the Magopa tribe refused to move. The government allied itself with Jacob More, a former tribal leader whom the Magopa had lawfully removed from his headmanship. The tribe had lawfully selected Isaac More, the plaintiff in the case, to represent them. The tribe sought redress in court to remove Jacob More from his negotiations with the government and was told by a regional magistrate, "I am a white man and as magistrate of this district I am telling you that Jacob More will rule until he dies."[18] The irony of this should not be lost. Apartheid was philosophically based on the concept that blacks should not participate in white governance because they were empowered to develop within their own local political traditions; the government then ignored their attempt to do just that.

The Magopa sought an order restraining the government from executing the forced removal. In the trial before the Transvaal Provincial Division, Judge Van Dyk dismissed the application and refused the leave to appeal. Absent the leave to appeal, the tribe was removed as soon as leave was refused.

The Appellate Division subsequently granted the leave to appeal. In its appeal before the Supreme Court, the tribe did not stress the interactions between Jacob More and the government, which they considered illegitimate, but stressed that the government had not met the requirements of Section 5 (1) (b) of the Black Administration Act of 1927,[19] which in amended form read:

The Governor-General (State President) may—

> (b) whenever he deems it expedient in the general public interest without prior notice to any person concerned order that, subject to such conditions as he may determine after consultation by the Minister with the Black Government concerned, any tribe, portion of a tribe, Black community or Black shall withdraw from any place to any other place or to any district or province within the Republic and shall not at any time thereafter or during a period specified in the order return to the place from which the withdrawal is to be made or proceed to any place, district or province other than the place, district or province indicated in the order, except with the written permission of the Secretary for Plural Relations and Development: Provided that if a tribe which is resident on land referred to in s 25 (1) of the Development Trust and Land Act 18 of 1936, refuses or neglects to withdraw as aforesaid, no such order shall be of any force and effect unless or until a resolution approving of the withdrawal has been adopted by both Houses of Parliament.

The government contended that following the issuance of the removal order, both houses of Parliament in May of 1975 adopted a resolution that approved the withdrawal as required by Section 5 (1) (b) when a tribe refused to move. The appellants argued that Parliament's approval was not valid because it did not designate the place to which the tribe was to be moved. Without such information, Parliament could not fully evaluate the tribe's refusal to move, and the approval could not be considered legitimate but merely a rubber stamp of the State President's order, an action that abdicated Parliament's responsibility envisaged by the legislature when the statute was adopted.

Again, the Appellate Division was provided with two alternative interpretations of the statute. The more conservative interpretation would favor the government's view that Parliament clearly supported the removal and noted such, as required by the statute, thus legitimizing the forced removal. The more literal and liberal interpretation would argue that Parliament could not legitimately have approved the forced removal since the information to reach a rational decision was incomplete.

The Appellate Division ruled that Parliament could not sufficiently have evaluated the appeal of the Magopa tribe without knowledge of the site to which they were to be moved. The Court declared the removal illegal acknowledging the necessity for the thorough evaluation of decisions that result in such hardship. Nonetheless, the Court declared the issue moot since the removal and expropriation had already occurred. Though the Court set aside the order of the lower court, the Magopa were not able to return to their land.[20]

Both Mr. Felton's and Mr. Mthiya's disputes are excellent examples of the melding of the repressive and formal law within the social control and conflict resolution function of courts. To separate individuals by race required some definition of black and white, a difficult task as evidenced by the verbiage of the Population Registration Act. The Urban Areas Act was similarly indicative of the detail required by the formal law to implement the repressive law thus increasing social control. Inevitably the determination of what constituted continual residence or sufficient "whiteness" required the judgement of authorized individuals. Conflicts over those determinations must be resolved. Courts were designated that responsibility, and with it came the discretion to determine the winner and the loser.

In each of these cases, the Court was presented with alternative interpretations of statutes. The positivist or mechanistic approaches of more traditional jurisprudential treatises would suggest that either legislative intent, plain meaning or strict construction would require one interpretation over another. But how does the judge determine the plain meaning of the words "freely and voluntarily" in Mr. Felton's case? Surely no individual in South Africa challenging a racial classification would ever freely or voluntarily concede to facts that would prejudice the case against him. On the other hand, responding to questions absent torture or other pervasive coercion would surely constitute voluntary evidence.

Similarly, if legislative intent is essential, surely the legislature would not have created a right to legal residence in a designated white area for Mr. Mthiya while at the same time making it impossible for him to meet the requirements by having to return to the Transkei for paperwork. However, the legislature wrote both statutes, and, given the history of apartheid legislation, such intention was easily within the realm of possibility.

In both the case of Mr. Felton and Mr. Mthiya, the Appellate Division ruled in their favor. Mr. Mthiya was able to return to his position in Cape Town, and Mr. Felton was able to retain his classification as white. In the millions of injustices perpetrated in apartheid South Africa, these are minor victories, but for these individuals they were significant.

The tragedy of the Magopa tribe represents the flip side of the coin. While critics of the Appellate Division argued that the Court should use its discretion to favor the underdogs in oppressive legal systems, such choices can be of limited utility in systems with parliamentary supremacy. Thwarting the will of a determined legislature can be feasible for only so long. Such was the case of the Magopa. While the Appellate Division did side with the Magopa people, the victory was largely symbolic. Unlike either Mr. Felton or Mr. Mthiya, this was a case that had garnered not only national attention but international scrutiny as well. Moreover, the Magopa people had been able to gain support from sympathetic interest groups, among them Black Sash, a black oppositionist group, and the

South African Council of Churches. Despite the international and national pressures, the government eventually forcibly removed the tribe. Thus the Court's ruling that Judge Van Dyk erred in dismissing the petition was entirely academic. As Able noted, the Appellate Division's "rebuke was a politically cheap form of sympathy; the Appellate Division could be generous with rhetoric precisely because it was stingy with results" (Abel 1995, 430). Certainly this was not the outcome the Magopa wanted, but politically the decision was exactly what judicial scholars would have anticipated.

Dugard would argue that the judges in cases like that of Mr. Felton and Mr. Mthyia should adhere to the interpretation that was most favorable to individual freedoms and human rights. Judges are able to do this because of the discretion inherent in determining legislative intent and the plain meaning of statutes. Dugard hoped, however, that judges inherently wish to rule in such a liberal manner. In other words, the judge's attitude or preference favors the individual over the government. Dugard and others criticized the Court for adhering to conservative ideologies which provided support and credibility for the regime. Dugard asserted that the courts became increasingly "establishment minded" and consistently advanced a "loyalty to the status quo" (Dugard 1978, 380). As in most evaluations of judicial behavior, these assertions are based on a few of the more politically charged cases, like that of the Magopa. While these cases form a critical component of the core by which the Appellate Division must be analyzed, they are a component and not the bulk or even the large majority of the Court's decisions.

Courts in legal systems with a strong repressive law component, like that of South Africa, are not capable of Dugard's strategy in the few high-profile, politically important decisions determined annually, regardless of preferences or ideologies. These cases represent the greatest institutional threat for the Court.

However, these particularly high-profile cases represent a small portion of the Court's docket. Appellate courts on occasion can challenge the regime successfully even in the high-profile cases but not consistently so. The remainder of the docket, in cases like that of Mr. Felton and Mr. Mthyia, provides judges with the opportunity to decide cases in opposition to the regime. This, of course, assumes a preference among the judges to do that.

Some evaluations of the South African courts suggested that judges whose home language was Afrikaans were presumed more likely to support the apartheid regime than the English-speaking judges (Forsyth 1985, 44–45). Afrikaans-speaking judges were presumed to be more likely to share the apartheid philosophy and to support the government in legal challenges.

These assertions have been made based on evaluations of the high-profile cases and have ignored the fact that language is not a surrogate for ideology; moreover, the language dichotomy is problematic. All judges were bilingual, but even evaluation of the "home" language as indicative of general policy positions is too simplistic. The more critical divide was between Afrikaner Nationalists who supported apartheid, and other Afrikaners who did not, some of whom were staunch opponents such as J. C. Kriegler[21] or the academic Barend van Niekerk.[22] This analysis will test the assertion that differences existed among the Afrikaans-speaking and English-speaking judges.

There has been no systematic evaluation of the voting patterns among the Appellate Division judges over the whole of the apartheid era. As the three cases demonstrate, judges are provided with "choice" in the performance of their functions to resolve the dispute and control behavior. This chapter attempts to evaluate variation in that choice among individual judges.

Analysis

As evidenced in Table 4.1 a high level of consensus existed on the Court. In almost 90% of the cases, no dissenting opinion emerged. Moreover, another judge joined the dissenting opinion in just less than 3% of the cases. A slightly higher level of concurring opinions existed, but again, in just over 2% of the cases did another judge vote with a concurring opinion. Figure 4.1 suggests that while there was greater dissensus in the early 1950s, the Court's unanimity was fairly constant over the time period examined, with an apparent trend toward increasing dissenting behavior in the latter 1980s.

There are several potential explanations for this high level of agreement. The first echoes the sentiments of mechanical jurisprudence suggested by Wacks (1984) and Van Blerk (1988). South African judges merely interpreted the law adhering appropriately to legal construction and arrived at consistently similar opinions. This would suggest that the United States legal system may be an anomaly with its ideologically driven judges.

A second possibility involves the lack of control of the Court over its agenda. The Appellate Division's docket was largely comprised of leaves to appeal which they were required to hear. Thus it may be that these disputes represented routine

TABLE 4.1
Concurring and Dissenting Opinions and Votes
of the South African Appellate Division, 1950–1990[a]

Concurring Opinions		Concurring Votes		Dissenting Opinions		Dissenting Votes	
424	(13.9%)	67	(2.2%)	339	(11.3%)	87	(2.9%)

[a]Percentages calculated on total number of cases (3,044).

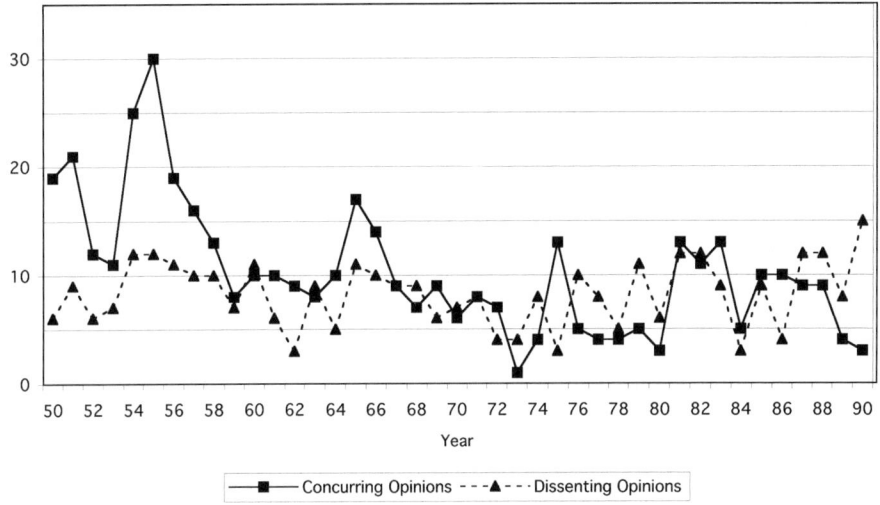

Figure 4.1 Concurring and Dissenting Opinions, 1950–1990.

legal challenges easily disposed of by the Court rather than major constitutional and statutory disputes that were more likely to engender disagreement. It should be noted though that lower court judges were expected to refuse to grant leave to appeal in cases which lacked substantive questions of law. Nonetheless, if individuals differed in their interpretations, some variation in voting patterns should emerge.

A third possibility involves the existence of a strong consensus norm. Expectations about behaviors arise within institutions. These expectations become institutionalized and affect outcomes. One effect of a strong consensus norm is the reluctance of judges to disagree through written opinions.

Fourth, decision making in groups of only three and five constrains dissensus in terms of small-group behavior and logistically. The group decision-making process itself creates greater potential for agreement. Judges met directly after oral argument to discuss the decision to be crafted and subsequently the draft opinion itself. The personal interaction of the judges required by this process, no doubt, lent itself to greater unanimity. Logistically there were simply few individuals within the group to potentially dissent or concur. Research on the United States Courts of Appeals, where decisions are made in panels of only three, also found high levels of consensus (see Songer 1982).

Most voting behavior analyses for the United States Supreme Court depend upon a lack of consensus to establish evidence of individual voting differences. "Liberal" votes are associated with judges who favor the underdog in the case, and "conservative" votes are associated with those who favor the upperdog. For example, judges whose votes would support Mr. Felton, Mr. Mthiya or the Magopa tribe would be considered supportive of the underdog, a liberal position. Those votes favoring the government in the three cases would be considered as favoring the upperdog or the conservative position. Similarly, judges whose votes support economic underdogs, such as an individual hurt in an automobile accident, a debtor to a large shipping firm or a small tenant farmer battling a plantation landlord, would be considered liberal and the opposite would be conservative votes.

Judges are analyzed for their support for the underdog or upperdog in each case. Judges in appellate courts that sit *en banc* hear the same set of facts, read the same statutes or constitution and yet reach different conclusions. Voting coalitions and patterns are used to place judges along a voting continuum. This presumes two things: judges hear the same disputes, rather than sitting in panels, and dissents exist. But many national high courts use panels, and when such a strong consensus norm exists, an analysis of dissenting votes may indicate little difference among judges. While the dissenting behavior in the South African judges will be explored, the small number of dissents limits its utility. How then can voting behavior be explored?[23]

In a system with a strong consensus norm, one can explore the differences among voting behavior between judges' overall voting pattern and their votes as majority opinion writers. In the South African system, the assignment of the majority opinion writer has changed over time. Initially, the opinion writer was determined after oral arguments at conference. During Chief Justice Rabie's tenure this was altered so that the majority opinion writer was assigned prior to oral argument by the most senior judge on the panel. This tradition continued under Chief Justice Corbett.[24] Though this assignment was considered "provisional," the majority opinion writer was not altered unless the opinion did not garner support from the other two or four judges serving on the panel. If this happened, the opinion that garnered majority support became the new majority opinion. As evidenced by the low numbers of dissents and concurrences, this rarely occurred.

The majority opinion writer was assigned primary responsibility for the analysis of the legal issues raised in the briefs and comprehensive review of the records of the case though all judges were presumed to have read the record. The control of the majority opinion writer was limited. The judges met in conference immediately following oral arguments and collegially determined the major points to be included in the opinion. The judges generally met at least one additional time, if not more, once the draft opinion was prepared to discuss its final form. Nonetheless, majority opinion writers did have some control over the language and direction of the opinion as it developed under their supervision.

The majority opinion might have been indicative of the author's individual ideology under both the pre- and post-oral-argument assignments. Under the post-oral-argument assignment system, individuals who feel particularly strongly about an issue might be more likely to express their preferences at conference and perhaps be assigned the majority opinion. Under the pre-oral-argument assignment system, the majority opinion writer may have had greater influence to some degree since he has responsibility for drafting the language that will ultimately resolve the conflict at law. If there was a consensus norm that constrained disagreement, and if the majority opinion writer had some greater level of influence on the outcome, then there should be differences evident between the general votes of judges and the votes of judges as majority opinion writers. For example, if the majority opinion writer assigned to the Magopa decision was ideologically sympathetic to the underdog, I anticipate that he would favor the tribe and find that Parliament could not have genuinely evaluated the Magopa's appeal when no destination had been determined. The consensus norm would then enhance the likelihood that the other members of the panel would adhere to the majority opinion. If, in fact, the opinion is a truly collaborative effort of equal influence, then I should not find significant differences between the voting patterns of the individual as majority opinion writer and the overall voting patterns of the individual.

Judges also may vary in their voting behaviors according to particular issues; thus another avenue of analysis is to examine the differences among voting patterns across issue categories. If a judge adheres to a consensus norm, one anticipates that the judge would be most likely to abandon that norm over particularly salient issues or those issues the judge feels most strongly about. For example, one could imagine that a truly conservative ideologue would find it more difficult to adhere to a consensus norm if the majority of the panel supported reinstating Mr. Mthiya's work permit. This would be a particularly salient issue to a supporter of the National Party given the importance of influx control to the apartheid regime. I anticipate support for or against the underdog to be particularly evident in apartheid and related political disputes.

If there are no ideological differences among the judges, and the consensus represents not a norm but merely a reflection of a common understanding of the legal rules, I expect consensus to be maintained across issue categories and across various judges. In other words, there should not be evidence of systematic variation in the voting patterns of individual judges. If, on the other hand, judges do maintain individual differences in their attitudes, I anticipate significant differences among the voting patterns of judges, and I would anticipate that to be most evident in the more sensitive issue areas.

Last, the long-held but little explored assertion that Afrikaans-speaking and English-speaking judges maintain differing ideologies should be explored.[25]

Common understanding, as noted above, asserted that English-speaking judges were considered to be less conservative than their Afrikaans-speaking brethren.

To create a measure of judicial attitude, I follow the standard approach to understanding judges' voting patterns developed by judicial behavioralists over the last 50 years. Appendix D provides a full explanation of the coding and operationalization of the individual voting variable. Table 4.2 reports the percentage of votes supporting the traditionally defined underdog for each judge. A few caveats should be noted. Given the nature of the apartheid regime, traditional categorization of support for the government in economic regulation as pro-underdog is problematic. In fact, any support for the government categorized as pro-underdog would be enigmatic. Therefore, cases involving the government were excluded in calculating the overall pro-underdog score for each judge, except for health, safety and environmental issues in which votes supporting the government were considered pro-underdog. Votes against the government in public employment and benefits cases, as well as apartheid, rights of the accused and civil rights and liberties cases were coded as pro-underdog. All other traditional public law categories, such as regulation of business and land use unrelated to apartheid, were excluded from the analysis. Other cases were excluded where no underdog was present. Because of these exclusions, some judges, particularly Acting Appeal Court judges who usually served only for a few months when necessary,[26] may not be included in the tables. For example, Judge Preiss, who served for a short period of time in 1990, actually voted in five cases, but all of these were excluded. The minimum number of votes is recorded by Judge Newton-Thompson appointed as an Acting Appeal Court judge for a short period during 1952 to the maximum number of 341 votes by Judge Wessels who served from 1961 to 1984.[27]

Not surprisingly, there is substantial variation in the support for the underdog demonstrated by the voting records among the 76 judges who served during the 1950 to 1990 period. The lowest score is that of Judge H. H. W. de Villiers (1955–57) at 17% of 23 votes. Judge Reynolds (1955–58) voted in favor of the underdog in only 32% of his 62 votes. Judge Klopper (1977–78) supported the underdog in 32% of his 19 votes; whereas, a number of judges have fairly high support for the underdog: Judge A. S. Botha (1979–) at 64%; Judge Nicholas (1982–) at 57%; Judge F. H. Grosskopf (1987–) at 73%; Judge Smalberger (1984–) at 59%; Judge Kumleben (1987–) at 68%; Judge Friedman (1989–) at 68%; and Judge Goldstone (1990–) at 67%.[28] The average score for the Court is 47%, quite moderate overall, especially given the general presumption of conservatism in the South African apartheid regime. However, it must be kept in mind that this was a judiciary in a system in which the vast majority of the population had no voice, no rights, no equalities and little freedom, and the extent to which they existed was strictly at the whim of Parliament. Nonetheless, this certainly suggests that the Court was not an overwhelmingly conservative institution. Moreover, there appear to be more judges who vote significantly pro-underdog than those who voted significantly pro-upperdog.

Table 4.2 also assesses the support for the underdog when the judge was the majority opinion writer. There were a number of judges who became either more supportive or less supportive of the underdog when writing the majority opinion than in their overall voting patterns. For example, Judge Corbett (1974–) voted for the underdog in 48% of all votes, but supported the underdog in 58% of cases when he was the majority opinion writer. Similarly, Judges Van den Heever (1948–56) and Jansen (1968–88) voted more often for the underdog as majority opinion writers (46% and 55% respectively) than in their overall voting (38% and 48% respectively). This pattern is especially striking for some judges. Judge A. S. Botha (1979–) voted for the underdog in 64% of all votes, but voted for the underdog in 74% of the cases in which he wrote the majority opinion. Of the 8 opinions Judge Boshoff (1985–88) wrote, 12% of them favored the underdog; whereas, in his overall voting pattern, he favored the underdog in 48% of cases in which he participated. Judge Smalberger (1984–) was much more supportive of the underdog in his majority opinions (79%) than in his overall voting (59%), as were Judges Beyers (1955–67), Trengove (1977–87) and Kumleben (1987–). Conversely, Judges Holmes (1959–77), Rabie (1969–88), Hofmeyer (1974–79), Nicholas (1982–), E. M. Grosskopf (1983–), Boshoff (1985–88), Nestadt (1986–), Milne (1988–) and M. T. Steyn (1987–) all became less supportive of the underdog as majority opinion writers. These results demonstrate that there was some differentiation between the votes of judges when they were the majority opinion writer and the other votes cast by these judges.

Particularly interesting are the voting patterns of the Afrikaans-speaking judges appointed in the early 1950s as well as those appointed with the expansion of the Court in 1955. Judge Van den Heever was the first appointee following the victory of the National Party in 1948. His score of 38% is well below the Court average of 47%. A second appointee, Judge Fagan, is also at 38%, suggesting that these government appointees did not disappoint.

Of the core of the 1955 appointees only Judge De Beer is above the Court average of 47% (at 49%). The other four 1955 appointees are all below the Court average, some well below it: Brink (35%), De Villiers (17%), Hall (40%) and Reynolds (32%). The overall mean for these judges is 35%. The overall voting patterns of the sitting judges at the time were conservative as well, ranging from 25% for Judge Watermeyer to 41% for Judge Greenberg. However, support for the underdog among the judges sitting at the time of the 1955 expansion was considerably higher for civil rights and liberties cases. These voting patterns exceed the mean of the Court even during the waning years of apartheid ranging from Judge Van den Heever's 80% to Judge Fagan's low of 50% (Table 4.3). This suggests that the concerns over the potential for the Court to undermine the National Party's

TABLE 4.2

Percent of Votes Favoring the Underdog, All Cases, 1950–1990

Judge[a]	%	Total Votes	Majority Opinions %	Majority Opinions N	Dissenting Votes %	Dissenting Votes N
Watermeyer, E. F. (1937–50) Eng	25	8	50	2	0	0
Centlivres, A. v d S. (1939–56) Eng	38	170	37	82	50	4
Greenberg, L. (1943–55) Eng	41	123	49	35	100	1
Schreiner, O. D. (1945–60) Eng	40	281	43	122	13	15
Van den Hever, F. P. (1948–56) Afr	38	154	46	37	78	9
Hoexter, O. (1949–64) Afr	40	261	37	69	80	5
Fagan, H. A. (1950–59) Afr	38	155	33	36	75	4
Murray, J. M. (1950) Eng	50	4	0	0	0	0
De Villiers, H. H. W. (1955–57) Afr	17	23	0	0	0	0
Newton-Thompson, C. (1952) Eng	50	2	0	2	0	0
Brink, C. P. (1955–57) Afr	35	34	0	2	0	0
Hall, C. G. (1955–58) Eng	40	53	25	4	100	1
Ramsbottom, W. H. (1955–60) Eng	46	28	50	8	0	1
Reynolds, F. G. (1955–58) Eng	32	62	0	0	67	3
Steyn, L.C. (1955–70) Afr	41	276	39	87	27	11
De Beer, E. M. (1955–60) Afr	49	113	100	3	0	6
Beyers, D. O. K. (1955–67) Afr	47	160	65	20	0	1
Van Blerk, P. J. (1956–76) Afr	51	299	50	54	50	8
Malan, A. C. (1957–60) Afr	49	74	50	4	100	1
Price, N. (1957–58) Eng	48	33	50	2	100	1
Ogilvie Thompson, N. (1957–73) Eng	42	278	39	74	78	9
Smit, A. J. (1957–59/61/66–67/70–71) Eng	55	20	50	2	0	0
Beyers, A. B. (1959) Afr	54	13	100	1	0	1
Botha, D. H. (1959–75) Afr	44	238	47	72	0	2
Holmes, G. N. (1959–77/81–82) Eng	47	336	40	97	40	10
Rumpff, F. H. L. (59–83) Afr	38	329	40	125	46	13
Van Wyk, J. T. (1959/60/63/64/67) Afr	45	20	67	3	0	0
Van Winsen, L. d V. (1960–62/64–69/72/76–83) Afr	49	106	40	20	100	2
Dowling, W. (1961) Eng	33	6	0	1	0	0
Jennett, A. G. (1961/67) Eng	42	12	0	1	0	0
Wessels, P. J. (1961–84) Afr	46	341	45	64	58	12
Williamson, A. F. (1962–68) Eng	47	110	41	22	50	8
Potgieter, H. J. (1964–73) Afr	46	107	50	22	0	0
Marais, J. F. (1965) Afr	67	3	0	0	0	0
Trollip, W. G. (1965–82) Eng	49	206	45	51	60	5
Bekker, S. (1967) Afr	60	5	0	0	0	0
Jansen, E. L. (1968–88) Afr	48	325	55	60	42	19
De Villiers, J. N. C. (1970–71/76–77) Afr	53	36	33	6	0	0

Table 4.2 *(continued)*

Judge[a]	%	Total Votes	Majority Opinions %	Majority Opinions N	Dissenting Votes %	Dissenting Votes N
Rabie, P. J. (1969–88) Afr	43	255	34	71	86	7
Muller, W. G. (1970) Afr	40	5	0	1	0	1
Muller, G. v R. (1968/1971–82) Afr	47	184	50	36	83	6
Corbett, M. M. (1970–72/74–) Eng	48	254	58	62	33	6
Hofmeyer, S. (1974–79) Afr	43	82	31	13	0	1
Van Zijl, J. W. (1974–75) Afr	58	12	100	1	0	0
Galgut, O. (1975–86) Eng	51	135	48	27	0	2
Kotze, G. P. (1971–72/75–86) Afr	56	166	61	33	40	5
Miller, S. (1970–72/76–86) Eng	49	135	47	30	0	2
Diemont, M. A. (1971–72/77–82) Eng	58	103	54	26	67	3
Viljoen, G. v N. (1976–88) Afr	48	148	57	28	33	6
Joubert, C. P. (1976–) Afr	42	197	41	32	0	2
Klopper, H. W. O. (1977–78) Afr	32	19	50	2	0	0
Trengove, J. J. (1977–87) Afr	54	124	73	22	50	2
Hoexter, G. G. (1978–) Afr	52	106	58	26	0	2
Botha, A. S. (1979–) Afr	64	141	74	31	78	9
Cillie, P. M. (1980–85) Afr	43	49	17	6	50	2
Nicholas, H. C. (1982–) Eng	57	95	47	19	50	4
Smuts, F. S. (1982–84) Afr	56	18	40	5	50	2
James, N. (1983) Eng	83	6	0	0	0	0
Howard, J. A. (1983–84) Eng	86	7	0	0	0	0
Van Heerden, H. J. O. (1980–) Afr	52	118	51	39	33	6
Hefer, J. J. F. (1983–) Afr	47	76	56	16	100	1
Grosskopf, E. M. (1983–) Afr	51	81	45	22	0	1
Eloff, C. F. (1984–85) Afr	54	13	33	3	0	0
Smalberger, J. W. (1984–) Eng	59	75	79	19	0	2
Vivier, W. (1984–) Afr	60	58	64	14	100	1
Boshoff, W. G. (1985–88) Afr	48	42	12	8	75	4
Jacobs, H. R. (1986–87) Afr	52	21	0	4	0	0
Nestadt, H. H. (1986–) Eng	51	51	36	14	100	1
Kumleben, M. E. (1987–) Eng	68	50	75	12	100	2
Steyn, M. T. (1987–) Afr	53	60	40	10	100	2
Grosskopf, F. H. (1987–) Afr	73	22	50	2	0	0
Milne, A. J. (1988–) Eng	49	47	30	10	12	8
Eksteen, J. P. (1988–) Afr	70	30	100	3	100	2
Friedman, G. (1989–) Eng	68	19	80	5	0	0
Goldstone, R. J. (1990–) Eng	67	12	75	4	0	0
Nienaber, P. M. (1990–) Eng	58	12	67	3	0	0
Total	47	7,832	46	1,847	49	240[a]

[a] The numbers in parentheses refer to the years of service for the judge. Periods of interrupted service beyond the typical single session leave are indicated with slash marks.

apartheid agenda were not without foundation. The voting patterns of the so-called "second team" 1955 appointees suggest that the National Party's faith in their conservatism was well placed.

Table 4.2 also assesses dissenting votes. Dissents are often presumed to be more indicative of a judge's policy preferences; constructing a dissent purposively delineates the judge's individual attitude from that of the others on the panel. There were only a few judges who had sufficient numbers of dissenting votes for meaningful analysis; however, of these a number show remarkable differences. For example, Judge Schreiner (1945–60) voted in support of the underdog in 40% of cases but supported the underdog in only 13% of his dissents. Judge Wessels (1961–84), by contrast supported the underdog in 46% of his 341 total votes but supported the underdog in 58% of his dissenting votes. Judges L. C. Steyn (1955–70), Holmes (1959–77) and Van Heerden (1980–) became increasingly less supportive of the underdog when their overall voting is compared to their dissenting votes. However, Judges Ogilvie Thompson (1957–73), Williamson (1962–68), G. v R. Muller (1971–82), Rabie (1969–88), A. S. Botha (1979–) and Cillie (1980–85) all became increasingly more supportive of the underdog in their dissenting behavior than in their overall voting pattern.

Individual voting patterns across issues are presented in Table 4.3. According to the means across each issue, the judges are least supportive of the underdog in apartheid cases, only 39%, while most supportive of the underdog, 55%, in tort cases. Some interesting variations are also evident in the voting patterns of the judges. For example, Judge Schreiner's (1945–60) overall score was 40%, but his support for the accused in criminal cases was 33%. However, his support for the underdog in the 10 civil rights and liberties cases in which he participated was 70%. If the government's primary concern was support for the government in rights and liberties issues, then its usurpation of seniority to elevate Judge Steyn to the Chief Justiceship seems prescient. He supported the underdog in only 25% of the 16 civil rights and liberties cases he heard.

The individual differences among Afrikaans-speaking and English-speaking judges can be evaluated in Tables 4.2 and 4.3. However, Table 4.4 suggests that significant differences existed for only certain issue areas. Afrikaans-speaking judges clearly voted differently from English-speaking judges in civil rights and liberties cases. English-speaking judges, on average, supported the individual in 50% of cases; whereas, Afrikaans-speaking judges supported the individual in only 41% of cases. Similarly, in tort cases Afrikaans-speaking judges were much less supportive of the individual claiming harm (52% of the cases) than were English-speaking judges (60%). However, for both sets of judges, the person claiming harm was likely to win over 50% of the time. For apartheid cases, the overall patterns of voting do not support the suggestion that Afrikaan-speaking judges were more conservative than their English-speaking brethren. The voting

TABLE 4.3
Percent of Votes Favoring the Underdog by Issue, 1950–1990

Judge[a]	Criminal %	N	Civil Rights %	N	Torts %	N	Econ %	N	Apartheid %	N
Watermeyer, E. F. (1937–50) Eng	20	5	0	0	0	1	0	1	0	0
Centlivres, A. v d S. (1939–56) Eng	30	106	67	6	53	19	51	33	37	8
Greenberg, L. (1943–55) Eng	32	85	67	6	53	15	71	14	60	5
Schreiner, O. D. (1945–60) Eng	33	179	70	10	58	41	45	38	43	14
Van den Heever, F. P. (1948–56) Afr	33	95	80	5	43	21	50	30	33	6
Hoexter, O. (1949–64) Afr	36	148	54	11	61	39	33	54	20	10
Fagan, H. A. (1950–59) Afr	35	96	50	4	56	18	39	28	25	8
Murray, J. M. (1950) Eng	33	3	0	0	100	1	0	0	0	0
De Villiers, H. H. W. (1955–57) Afr	21	14	0	1	0	3	20	5	0	1
Newton-Thompson, C. (1952) Eng	0	1	0	0	0	0	0	0	0	0
Brink, C. P. (1955–57) Afr	33	21	50	2	60	5	20	5	33	3
Hall, C. G. (1955–58) Eng	33	30	50	4	64	11	29	7	33	3
Ramsbottom, W. H. (1955–60) Eng	50	18	0	0	40	5	67	3	0	1
Reynolds, F. G. (1955–58) Eng	19	32	33	3	50	12	50	12	40	5
Steyn, L.C. (1955–70) Afr	36	145	25	16	51	47	46	63	40	20
De Beer, E. M. (1955–60) Afr	47	70	50	2	46	13	50	18	62	8
Beyers, D. O. K. (1955–67) Afr	45	76	29	7	56	39	48	31	30	10
Van Blerk, P. J. (1956–76) Afr	43	122	33	12	63	79	55	69	37	19
Malan, A. C. (1957–60) Afr	42	43	50	2	69	13	36	11	33	3
Price, N. (1957–58) Eng	37	19	0	0	75	4	67	3	67	3
Ogilvie Thompson, N. (1957–73) Eng	31	144	44	9	69	52	50	64	21	14
Smit, A. J. (1957–59/61/66–67/70–71) Eng	45	11	0	0	100	3	0	1	0	0
Beyers, A. B. (1959) Afr	43	7	0	0	100	2	0	0	67	3
Botha, D. H. (1959–75) Afr	37	100	31	16	53	57	54	59	26	19
Holmes, G. N. (1959–77/81–83) Eng	33	145	25	12	64	84	53	84	39	15
Rumpff, F. H. L. (1959–82) Afr	32	169	33	18	50	93	39	54	18	18
Van Wyk, J. T. (1959/60/63/64/67) Afr	20	10	100	1	100	2	57	7	0	0
Van Winsen, L. d V. (1960–62/64–69/72/76–83) Afr	42	38	67	3	70	23	47	34	25	8
Dowling, W. (1961) Eng	0	1	0	1	67	3	0	2	0	0
Jennett, A. G. (1961/67) Eng	33	3	0	0	100	4	0	5	0	0
Wessels, P. J. (1961–84) Afr	44	119	30	10	50	111	48	93	33	12
Williamson, A. F. (1962–68) Eng	32	53	0	4	65	26	57	30	0	0
Potgieter, H. J. (1964–73) Afr	37	40	33	3	50	28	50	30	43	7
Marais, J. F. (1965) Afr	50	2	0	0	0	0	100	1	0	0
Trollip, W. G. (1965–82) Eng	44	78	38	13	50	72	61	44	44	9
Bekker, S. (1967) Afr	50	2	0	0	100	2	0	1	0	0
Jansen, E. L. (1968–88) Afr	33	126	33	15	58	96	60	89	33	12
De Villiers, J. N. C. (1970–71/76–77) Afr	56	9	33	3	36	14	67	12	0	0

Table 4.3 *(continued)*

Judge[a]	Criminal %	N	Civil Rights %	N	Torts %	N	Econ %	N	Apartheid %	N
Rabie, P. J. (1969–88) Afr	36	92	33	21	48	77	51	75	37	8
Muller, W. G. (1970) Afr	67	3	0	0	0	2	0	0	0	0
Muller, G. v R. (1968/1971–82) Afr	43	68	60	5	47	62	56	48	25	4
Corbett, M. M. (1970–72/74–) Eng	45	92	60	20	53	85	51	67	25	4
Hofmeyer, S. (1974–79) Afr	40	30	20	5	36	28	54	22	0	0
Van Zijl, J. W. (1974–75) Afr	67	3	0	0	60	5	67	3	0	1
Galgut, O. (1975–86) Eng	57	42	33	3	50	44	47	47	50	2
Kotze, G. P. (1971–72/75–86) Afr	48	56	80	5	54	63	70	40	57	7
Miller, S. (1970–72/76–86) Eng	42	38	25	4	56	46	46	43	50	6
Diemont, M. A. (1971–72/77–82) Eng	45	44	100	2	78	32	58	26	0	1
Viljoen, G. v N. (1976–88) Afr	47	55	29	14	52	62	39	28	50	2
Joubert, C. P. (1976–) Afr	42	64	20	20	44	71	37	56	40	5
Klopper, H. W. O. (1977–78) Afr	37	8	0	0	17	6	40	5	0	0
Trengove, J. J. (1977–87) Afr	44	43	75	4	59	51	56	27	100	1
Hoexter, G. G. (1978–) Afr	56	34	44	9	53	32	42	33	100	1
Botha, A. S. (1979–) Afr	63	63	88	8	72	32	55	38	100	3
Cillie, P. M. (1980–85) Afr	33	21	0	1	50	12	50	16	0	0
Nicholas, H. C. (1982–) Eng	57	30	75	4	68	22	56	36	33	3
Smuts, F. S. (1982–84) Afr	37	8	0	0	80	5	75	4	0	0
James, N. (1983) Eng	100	1	0	0	80	5	0	0	0	0
Howard, J. A. (1983–84) Eng	75	4	0	0	100	1	100	2	0	0
Van Heerden, H. J. O. (1980–) Afr	48	48	58	12	57	37	50	30	100	2
Hefer, J. J. F. (1983–) Afr	44	34	39	18	44	27	50	12	100	2
Grosskopf, E. M. (1983–) Afr	38	26	42	12	40	25	67	24	100	3
Eloff, C. F. (1984–85) Afr	43	7	100	1	67	3	67	3	0	0
Smalberger, J. W. (1984–) Eng	64	36	67	6	60	10	52	27	100	1
Vivier, W. (1984–) Afr	62	21	60	15	50	22	69	13	100	2
Boshoff, W. G. (1985–88) Afr	53	15	0	4	36	14	45	11	100	1
Jacobs, H. R. (1986–87) Afr	42	12	0	0	50	4	75	4	0	0
Nestadt, H. H. (1986–) Eng	39	18	25	4	61	13	61	18	0	1
Kumleben, M. E. (1987–) Eng	67	27	67	3	71	7	75	12	50	2
Steyn, M. T. (1987–) Afr	60	35	33	6	38	13	50	10	0	0
Grosskopf, F. H. (1987–) Afr	86	7	50	4	50	4	75	8	0	0
Milne, A. J. (1988–) Eng	47	17	75	4	58	12	44	16	0	0
Eksteen, J. P. (1988–) Afr	83	12	67	3	57	7	70	10	0	0
Friedman, G. (1989–) Eng	71	7	50	2	50	4	71	7	0	0
Goldstone, R. J. (1990–) Eng	100	1	0	0	75	4	87	7	0	0
Nienaber, P. M. (1990–) Eng	50	4	0	1	0	2	80	5	0	0
Total	40	3,491	43	419	55	2,009	51	1,869	39	302

[a]The numbers in parentheses refer to the years of service for the judge. Periods of interrupted service beyond the typical single session leave are indicated with slash marks.

TABLE 4.4
Afrikaans-Speaking and English-Speaking Voting Patterns

Judges' Home Language	All Votes		Criminal		Civil Rights		Torts		Apartheid	
	%	N	%	N	%	N	%	N	%	N
Afrikaans-Speaking	47	6,436	41	2,217	41	298	52	1,369	39	202
English-Speaking	48	3,650	38	1,273	50	120	60	637	39	100
χ^2	1.267		2.396		3.076		9.299*		.000	

*$p < .01$

patterns among the judges are identical. However, it is interesting to note that Afrikaans-speaking judges cast 202 apartheid-related votes while English-speaking judges cast only 100. This is a greater rate of participation than in the overall distribution of cases between Afrikaans-speaking and English-speaking judges. The Chi-Square statistic for each issue area suggests that only in tort cases did English-speaking and Afrikaans-speaking judges vote significantly differently when the entire period is evaluated.[29]

Ellmann's study of the decision making of the Appellate Division during the state of emergency in the late 1980s suggested that those cases that involved state of emergency issues were assigned by the Chief Justice to panels strategically selected from the so-called "emergency team" to ensure government support (Ellmann 1992, 57–114). Despite reaching the mandatory retirement age of seventy, Chief Justice Rabie was appointed by the National Party government to serve as "Acting Chief Justice" which enabled his continued service. It was widely presumed that Rabie was asked to continue because the most senior Judge of Appeal on the Court at the time, Michael Corbett, was considered too liberal to be appointed Chief Justice as the seniority norm dictated (Cameron 1987b, 345). Chief Justice Rabie, on the other hand, was considered to be supportive of the government. According to Ellmann, the so-called emergency team was comprised of

TABLE 4.5
Percent of Votes Favoring the Underdog by Issue:
The "Emergency Team"

Judge	All Votes		Criminal		Civil		Torts		Apartheid	
	%	N	%	N	%	N	%	N	%	N
Rabie, P. J. (1969–88) Afr	43	255	36	92	33	21	48	77	37	8
Hefer, J. J. F. (1983–) Afr	47	76	44	34	39	18	44	27	100	2
Joubert, C. P. (1976–) Afr	42	197	42	64	20	20	44	71	40	5
Viljoen, G. v N. (1976–88) Afr	48	148	47	55	29	14	52	62	50	2
Vivier, W. (1984–) Afr	60	58	62	21	60	15	50	22	100	2
Emergency Team Avgs	48	734	46	266	36	88	48	259	65	19
Overall Court Averages	47	7,832	40	3,491	43	419	55	2,009	39	302

TABLE 4.6
Percent of Votes Favoring the Underdog by Issue:
Select Members, 1985–1990

Judge	All Votes %	N	Criminal %	N	Civil Rights %	N	Torts %	N	Apartheid %	N
Corbett, M. M. (1970–72/74–) Eng	48	254	45	92	60	20	53	85	25	4
Galgut, O. (1975–86) Eng	51	135	57	42	33	3	50	44	50	2
Trengrove, J. J. (1977–87) Afr	54	124	44	43	75	4	59	51	100	1
Botha, A. S. (1979–) Afr	64	141	63	63	88	8	72	32	100	3
Hoexter, G. G. (1982–) Afr	52	106	56	34	44	9	53	32	100	1
Van Heerden, H. J. O. (1980–) Afr	52	118	48	48	58	12	57	37	100	2
Grosskopf, E. M. (1983–) Afr	51	81	38	26	42	12	40	25	100	3
Boshoff, W. G. (1983–88) Afr	48	42	53	15	0	4	36	14	100	1
Jacobs, H. R. (1986–87) Afr	52	21	42	12	0	0	50	4	0	0
Smalberger, J. W. (1984–) Eng	59	75	64	36	67	6	60	10	100	1
Nestadt, H. H. (1986–) Eng	51	51	39	18	25	4	61	13	0	1
Kumleben, M. E. (1987–) Eng	68	50	67	27	67	3	71	7	50	2
Milne, A. J. (1988–) Eng	49	47	47	17	75	4	58	12	0	0
Eksteen, J. P. (1988–) Afr	70	30	83	12	67	3	57	7	0	0
Steyn, M. T. (1987–) Afr	53	60	60	35	33	6	38	13	0	0
Non-Emerg Team Avgs	55	1,335	54	250	49	98	54	386	75	21
Emergency Team Avgs	48	734	46	266	36	88	48	259	65	19
Overall Court Averages	47	7,832	40	3,491	43	419	55	2,009	39	302

Judges Rabie, Joubert, Viljoen, Hefer and Vivier. The presumption is that these judges were more conservative and thus more likely to support the regime than other judges serving on the Court at the time, and further, the assumption is that Rabie hand picked the panels to hear the emergency challenges to ensure government victory. Table 4.5 provides the voting behaviors of these individuals.

These judges were less supportive of the individual in their voting patterns in rights and liberties questions, where the emergency cases would fall in this analysis. Their overall mean in civil rights and liberties cases is 36% compared to 43% for the Court overall. The voting patterns were actually more supportive of the individual for criminal cases (46% to the overall Court average of 40%), and interestingly, these judges voted against the government in 65% of the 19 apartheid cases they heard,[30] far more supportive of the individual than the Court average over the entire period of 39%.

Table 4.6 provides the voting behaviors of the judges who served sufficient amounts of time during the state of emergency to have been reasonable alternative selections for Chief Justice Rabie. The overall mean for these judges is 49% in civil rights and liberties cases, significantly above the emergency team. The mean for criminal cases is 54% for the alternative judges and 46% for the emergency team. While the emergency team's average for apartheid issues is lower than the alternative judges, 65% compared to 75%,[31] only Chief Justice Rabie and Judge Joubert were supportive of the individual less than half the time.

Conclusion

Regimes that establish a formal law system to resolve conflicts and control behaviors must delegate some authority to individuals who interpret the laws. The capacity to interpret the law is embedded with the discretion to determine who is or is not black, who is or is not a lawful resident. This chapter specifically explored the individual use of discretion in the decision making of the judges of the Appellate Division in the performance of their dispute resolution and social control functions. Of particular interest is the response of judges in systems that profess allegiance to the formal law but have strong repressive law components.

The findings suggest that a number of the Appeal Court judges during the apartheid era of South Africa were not overwhelmingly and consistently conservative. The major political challenges brought to the Court did not represent opportunities for the Court to challenge the National Party. Inevitably, in those high-stakes cases, Parliament would reign supreme. However, the numbers of cases involving individuals like Mr. Felton or Mr. Mthiya represented opportunities for the Court to use its discretion more independently. These were cases that did not represent high-stakes decisions in the overall grand scheme of apartheid but did create important precedents for others. And it should not be forgotten that these were cases involving real individuals in the midst of very real tragedies. For Mr. Felton and Mr. Mthiya, the individuals who comprised the bench mattered a great deal. Their concern was not in the significance of the lofty legal debate concerning plain meaning or legislative intent but in the outcome for their individual dispute. Of course, the one is necessarily related to the other, and as scholars, our understanding of the Court as a political body and its judges as political actors can affect the lofty legal debates that potentially affect where a man may work or live or how the government classifies his race.

These results support the assertion that judges have and exercise discretion in their choices and that the use of that discretion can vary across time and across individual judges. The results do not seem supportive of a mechanistic, formal law approach to judging for South African Appellate Division judges. If we accept that judges utilize their discretion differently, then the individuals who comprise a court at any given time significantly affect the policies or choices that drive legal doctrine for these systems. For those who reside in these systems, like Mr. Felton, Mr. Mthiya, and the Magopa tribe, the individuals who comprise the court and their attitudes toward the use of their discretion are particularly significant.

Developmental theory suggests that courts progress from more repressive to more formalized systems. Judges' decisions should reflect more independence and impartiality as the courts move away from coercion and brute force to the application of neutral rules required under the positivist approach. South African judges existed within a legal system where both the repressive law and the formal law exited.

While the previous chapters have evaluated the Court's decisions in the aggregate and at the individual level, it is also critical to evaluate the behavior of the Court over time. The following chapter will analyze the decisions of the Court over the entire 41-year period.

CHAPTER FIVE

Longitudinal Analysis of the Outcomes Before the Appellate Division, 1950–1990

In the early 1960s, Ennerdale South Township was a minor suburb of Johannesburg, consisting of approximately 2,000 whites and 3,000 coloureds. It was a poor rural town populated by a few farmers, with the majority of the employed adults traveling daily by train to Johannesburg for work. Alongside a small post office and a few stores were the butchery and the gas station; a hundred telephones dotted the city. In November of 1962, one Ms. Kuhn applied to the Johannesburg Liquor Licensing Board for a liquor license to open a "bottle store" in Ennerdale South.[1]

Ms. Kuhn was the only applicant seeking a liquor license for South Ennerdale. The police report on the application noted that she was experienced in operating a bottle store. Both she and the proposed premises were deemed suitable. Moreover, the police acknowledged that the liquor store was "reasonably required for the convenience of the public."[2]

The role of the board was to determine the reasonable needs of the community, including convenience for those who wanted access to liquor. This was the crucial issue to be determined; the board was not to consider the morality of either the sale or the consumption of alcohol. Since Parliament had sanctioned the sale of alcohol, it was not within the prerogative of the board to evaluate the license beyond the suitability of the licensee and the needs of the community in terms of reasonable access to alcohol for those who wished to consume it. The decisions of the board were reviewable under Section 29 (1) of the Liquor Act of 1928[3] to determine if the board, in either its conduct or in its proceedings, acted arbitrarily, grossly unreasonably or with substantial prejudice to the applicant. While the act did not specifically define these terms, the Court had determined that "arbitrariness connotes caprice, or the exercise of the will instead of reason or principle, without a consideration of the merits."[4] And reasonableness was defined as "considering the matter as a reasonable man normally would and then deciding as a reasonable man normally would decide."[5] This of course begs the question of who is a "reasonable" man and what is a "normal" decision of this "reasonable" man. Defining one term simply leads to the ambiguities of the second. Even the Court agreed that "Grossness of unreasonableness is a matter of degree, and cannot be precisely gauged. . . . It depends upon the facts of each case. It follows . . . that a gross irregularity, as showing any of the specified grounds, coupled with prejudice, would also warrant interference by the Court."[6]

Thus, the Court agreed that decisions are case by case evaluations of "reasonable" or "gross unreasonableness." One judge's determination of "reasonable" may differ significantly from another, and Ms. Kuhn's case demonstrates just this.

At the hearing, the board allowed a number of those in opposition to the license to speak. Among them was the Reverend Prangley who objected on moral grounds. First, the church urged sobriety, and second, he asserted that the residents "cannot afford to spend their money on liquor."[7] The representative of another church echoed Reverend Prangley's sentiments, while Mrs. Skinner, the representative of the temperance union, "stressed the misery caused by drink."[8]

Ms. Kuhn's attorney then replied "at length" to the objectors, after which the chair of the board queried him, "We have heard this morning that this is a very poor area, that Coloured people predominate, and that they are also very, very poor. Who is going to buy . . . liquor at this bottle store?"[9]

To which Ms. Kuhn's attorney replied, "The people who are drinking it now."[10]

"Who are they?" responded the chair. "The poor people."[11]

The board determined that both Ms. Kuhn and the premises were suitable but decided to personally inspect the area to determine the fitness of the proposed location for the bottle store. After doing so, the board refused the application. The board asserted that "the license was not reasonably required to meet the convenience of the public, and would not be in the public interest. . . . "[12]

On appeal, the defense argued that morality was not a consideration in the licensing process since Parliament had established the legality of bottle stores. Clearly, the major objections to the liquor store were not secular in nature. Even the objections concerning the inability of poor people to either afford or to handle alcohol stemmed from paternalistic concerns extrinsic to the record, which should not be a part of the board's deliberative process according to the legislative act. Moreover, Ms. Kuhn had not been informed about the concerns of the board following its inspection of the area, and she was thus afforded no opportunity to respond to them. Under the *audi alteram partem* rule, the requirement to hear the other side, Ms. Kuhn should have been provided the opportunity to rebut the board's concerns.

The board contended that its objections were based not merely on the moral grounds raised by the objectors but on the non-necessity of the license for a poor rural area. The board had debated factors not extrinsic to the application but on those issues specifically placed before it, particularly, the suitability of the area for the bottle store, which was within its discretion in evaluating the reasonableness of the request for the new license. Ms. Kuhn certainly was aware of these issues and bore the responsibility of rebutting them, which she did not do.

Thus, the Appellate Division's decision turned on the interpretation of the board's actions as those of a reasonable man. In making the determination of whether the board acted reasonably, the Court had to interpret what the statute required of those seeking a liquor license and whether the board's evaluation of the statutory requirements were in accordance with the intentions of Parliament. Certainly the answer was not black or white. Both the board and Ms. Kuhn made reasonable arguments. The lower court had reversed the decision of the board, agreeing with Ms. Kuhn's attorneys that the police report had been ignored and that the decision of the board was based on factors extrinsic to those that should have been lawfully considered.

In its decision, the Appellate Division agreed with the board and held that "it had not been shown that the Board had come to its conclusions on inadequate grounds or drawn inferences without proper investigation" and further, that the board had been right in regarding "the question of poverty as one of the factors amongst several others which fell into relevant consideration."[13] Ms. Kuhn was denied the requisite license to open her bottle store.

A similar licensing case presents another example of the discretion available to judges. In 1948, after dutifully obtaining a certificate to trade in meat as required by the Livestock and Meat Control Scheme, one Mr. Garda, governmentally designated as Asian, opened a butcher's shop in Vrededorp, Johannesburg, a designated Malay or Asian community. Mr. Garda's clientele, however, was derived almost entirely from a large black population living in a nearby township. For some ten years Mr. Garda maintained his business successfully, but in the fall of 1958 the government relocated the black population, removing them from the Vrededorp area and demolishing their homes. The loss of his black clientele proved fatal to Mr. Garda's enterprise, and he was forced to seek a new location for his butchery. To that end, he leased new premises in Ferreiras Town, Johannesburg, which was not a "defined" Asiatic area. As such, it was necessary for Mr. Garda to obtain a permit from the Group Areas Board, which authorized him to occupy the premises. Subsequently, Mr. Garda applied with the Livestock and Meat Industries Control Board for the transfer of his license to the new location and, as required, advertised his intention to transfer his business to the Ferreiras Town location in both the *Goverment Gazette* and the *Vaderland* newspapers. No objections were lodged in response to these publications.

In his application to the Livestock and Meat Industries Control Board in March of 1959, Mr. Garda explained that the resettlement scheme had created an unprofitable situation forcing him to relocate his business some mile and a half from the previous Vrededorp location. He noted that there were eight other butcher shops in the area but that none of these had articulated any opposition to the transfer.

Several months passed without any response from the board. Mr. Garda's attorney learned upon contacting the board that the original certificate permitting Mr. Garda to open the butchery in Vrededorp was in jeopardy. The board was considering the withdrawal of his certificate because of the lack of compliance with clause 11 (e) of the conditions of registration initially noted on his certificate. Under the terms of clause 11 (e), "This certificate may be canceled if the holder does not offer meat for sale from the premises specified in this certificate for a period reckoned from Monday to Saturday inclusive."

Mr. Garda had violated clause 11 (e) by closing his shop following the government's removal of his clientele. The irony of the situation was somehow lost on the board. Mr. Garda's attorney requested that the board explain why they were refusing the transfer and to note if the board had "information unfavourable to the application before it when considering the application for a transfer."[14] In response, the board refused to disclose its reasons for denying the application of transfer, reiterated clause 11 (e) as the reason for canceling the original certificate and stated that it had received no information unfavourable to the *applicant*. Last, the board suggested that it would reconsider the cancellation of the original certificate if Mr. Garda were to be in compliance with 11 (e). Again, the Board seemed to be ignoring the fact that there was no business to entertain at the previous location.

In response, Mr. Garda's attorney again reiterated that the effects of the forced removal of his black clientele compelled Mr. Garda to close his business at the original location. The board then countered with a proposal that Mr. Garda's registration as a butcher would be reinstated for a period of six months at the original location, contingent upon Mr. Garda's "obtain[ing] other premises acceptable to the board in an Asiatic area proclaimed under the Group Areas Act, within the specified period of six months."[15] This proposal was clearly beyond the discretion of the board which did not have the power to "prescribe where applicants for a license [were] to trade."[16] After this was brought to its attention, the board withdrew the requirement that a defined Asiatic premises be located, but it still refused the transfer.

After additional pressure, the board finally proffered a new reason for the refusal of the transfer: that the area in question was "adequately and conveniently catered for by the existing butcheries in the area."[17] The board asserted that the large number of butcheries already located within literally yards of the proposed site were sufficient. The nearest butchery was only 60 yards away, a second only 130 yards, and the furthest was a mere 800 yards away.[18]

Mr. Garda countered that "[t]he right to trade is a right given to every citizen" and that he had "a vested right which should not be taken away except for special reasons."[19] Necessity was never raised as a concern by either the existing butchers in the area or previously by the board and thus could not be considered a sufficient reason. Moreover, the board's discretion in considering transfers did not include concerns for necessity, he argued. There was no onus on an applicant seeking a new license to prove necessity; requiring such for a simple transfer, which already implies vested rights, was unreasonable and beyond the powers of the board detailed in the enabling statute creating it. Additionally, he argued that in terms of fairness and reasonableness, under the *audi alteram partem* rule, if the board were going to consider necessity, Mr. Garda should have been notified of that and allowed the opportunity to respond, which he was never permitted to do.

Mr. Garda essentially claimed that because he was an Asian who was seeking to do business in an area not specifically designated for Asians, he was refused the transfer. When the board realized this was not a lawful reason for denial, the board, needing an alternative excuse, claimed that the transfer would create an overabundance of butcheries for the area. Mr. Garda believed that the latter excuse could not be realistically excised from the former, and as such, the board had no proper reason for the refusal. Neither the requirement that the new premises be located in an Asiatic area nor the requirement of necessity was a valid, legal claim for the denial of the transfer.

The board countered that the enabling statute provided that:

> The Board may refuse any registration or grant registration for such period and on such conditions as it may determine and may cancel any such registration if the person registered has contravened or failed to comply with any condition so determined.[20]

This discretion, the board contended, was virtually unfettered, and certainly it was reasonable for the board to consider whether "a reasonable need" existed for the butchery. There was no duty for the board to inform Mr. Garda of the degree of importance with which necessity would be considered. When an applicant knew, or should have known, that a factor would be considered by the board, it was incumbent upon the applicant to address these factors. Regardless of necessity, Mr. Garda had clearly violated clause 11 (e), and that alone was sufficient to refuse the transfer.

The Appellate Division restored Mr. Garda's license. The Court found that the "powers conferred upon the Livestock and Meat Industries Control Board ... do not include one which suggests that the Board can restrict the number of butcheries in a given area."[21] The board should not have refused Mr. Garda the transfer, and rather than remitting the matter to the board to reassess the matter in light of the Court's ruling, the Court required the board to transfer the registration in concern for "fairness" to both parties.

The cases of Ms. Kuhn and Mr. Garda are concrete examples of specific sets of facts from which a decision must be rendered, the conflict must be resolved. These disputes are excellent case studies for several reasons.

First, one of the major functions of courts as noted in Chapter 1 is to resolve conflicts. When disputes arise concerning the meaning of the statutes, judges must "interpret" both the statute and the facts to determine the winner. Both of these cases involve questions surrounding the limitations, or lack thereof, on licensing boards and what factors should and should not be considered under the statute.

Second, both cases are indicative of the ways in which the repressive nature of the law is articulated in the formal law. If judges are to apply the formal law, that inevitably demands that they enforce the repressive nature of its dictates.

Third, these cases, as well as the previous ones presented in Chapters 3 and 4, demonstrate the inevitable discretion available to judges. The statutes that created the licensing requirements for both Ms. Kuhn and Mr. Garda were inevitably vague and ambiguous. Conflicts arise, and judges are delegated the responsibility to determine the meaning of "arbitrary" and "unreasonable" and "necessity."

In the case of Ms. Kuhn, the Appellate Division supported the decision of the administrative board to deny the license. Mr. Garda, on the other hand, had his license restored. Why was Ms. Kuhn unable to obtain her license and Mr. Garda able to succeed in getting the transfer of his? Certainly the decisions of the administrative agencies involved were guided by different statutes. Moreover, the discretion available to each was utilized differently; in other words, the facts of the cases differed. Thus it may be simply that differing statutes were applied to differing sets of facts.

This chapter suggests that decisions are affected by more than simply the facts and the law and that specifically the external environment may play a factor in the outcome. Why would we presume that Ms. Kuhn's opening her bottle store or Mr. Garda's capacity to sell meat in a non-Asiatic area would be affected by the adoption of a new constitution? Why would decisions of judges be altered by apartheid tragedies such as the death of Steve Biko? These external events are unrelated to the specific facts of the case and are irrelevant to the formal law statutes that should theoretically govern the outcome. This chapter argues that courts, as political bodies, are inherently affected by the particular political context within which they emerge and persist.

While this argument will not be novel to judicial politics scholars, for judges and scholars imbued in the positivist or formal law traditions, such as Wacks, Van Blerk and others, the notion of macro-level politics affecting micro-level decisions will seem dubious, if not absurd. But even positivists would agree that the social, political and economic conditions within which cases arise affect not only the law, but the evaluation of the facts and the outcomes that flow from the application of the former to the latter.

Why should one anticipate that the decisions of judges will be affected by external political influences? The formal law tradition would argue that there is a marked distinction between politics, particularly popular social perspectives, and legal outcomes. While the laws are clearly the products of popular will, judging is the resolution of conflicts that arise relative to those regime rules.

However, the law, as a compilation of rules bound in leather and placed carefully on library shelves, is derived from a broader political context. Outcomes are driven in part by the mandates of the law as positivists would suggest. However, the law can remain static for lengthy periods of time or change only incrementally. Presuming a stasis in the law, what does change in each case? The facts are certainly unique in each scenario, and the subsequent interpretation of those facts as well as the interpretation of the leather-clad statute may vary in each decision. Inevitably, interpretation is affected by the discretion of the judges. The discretion of the judges is affected by their own understanding of the facts and the law. Judges' perceptions are affected by the social and political forces surrounding them. Judges are not automatons programmed with statutory construction, legal canon and constitutional doctrine to be mechanistically applied to conflict. Judges are human decision makers who are products of particular social and political milieus. The context that envelops the individual during his or her life affects the values and attitudes with which the law and the facts are judged.

Moreover, the social and political context is responsible for the election of the government officials who determine who will sit on the bench. As the social and political context changes, the composition of the bench will change as well. As discussed in Chapter 3, the National Party initially staffed the Appellate Division, as they did the entire judiciary, indeed the entire government, predominantly with Afrikaners presumed to be loyal to the regime. The results of the previous chapters suggest that while the government won the significant legal challenges, overall, it did not succeed in placing majorities of conservative ideologues on the bench.

If judges' decisions are affected by external factors, I argue that we should see significant changes in the aggregate of the Court's decision making over time. Moreover, I argue that certain interventions, which represent important social or political events, can shift the context and affect the individual judge's perceptions. These shifts affect how each case is evaluated and thus ultimately affect the overall decision-making pattern for the Court. These effects may not be evident in any single case like that of Ms. Kuhn or Mr. Garda, but if one aggregates the whole of the Court's docket, then trends or patterns should emerge over time, and I argue these trends would be attributable in part to important events, which may alter the social and political context in significant ways, as opposed to the usual incremental shifts that generally occur.

This is certainly not a novel assertion. Dahl's classic 1957 evaluation of the United States Supreme Court as a national policy maker suggested exactly this. Courts will not long be removed from the social context within which they exist. Shifts should be anticipated because of external changes in the political and social context as well as internal changes resulting from the shifting composition of the membership of the court (Helmke 2002). Thus in terms of the United States Supreme Court, the Warren Court was more likely to favor the underdog in part because of the more liberal appointees to the Court and in part because of the more liberal attitudes emerging within society broadly. Concomitantly, as social attitudes in the United States became more conservative in the 1980s and 1990s, more conservative members emerged on the Court, and more conservative decisions followed. Disentangling the effects of court composition versus changing social context is no easy task, but this chapter attempts to assess this in part.

How would we expect a court to exercise its functions of social control and conflict resolution in a political environment where the rights of the majority of the population were denied? By the late 1950s, the Appellate Division was comprised of a majority of Afrikaans-speaking judges, who presumably appreciated the apartheid philosophy yet were legal scholars trained in the law to respect equality and personal freedom. Moreover, the Court sought to be above the political fray through its defense of "merely interpreting the law." The lack of judicial review certainly limited the institutional power of the South African Appellate Division, but there continued to be important policy choices made by the Court on a regular basis. The major legal challenges that attracted the attentions of the regime represented a handful of decisions. The bulk of the docket generally involved lesser controversies, like that of Ms. Kuhn and Mr. Garda, that garnered much less public attention from government elites than the cases of Mr. Hurley and Mr. Omar. Thus courts largely impotent in frontal clashes nonetheless can use those portions of their docket that remain to challenge the regime if they choose. It may be, however, that judges wish to support the government, even at the expense of their own perceived legitimacy among the population at large. Sachs (1973) argued that the Court's capitulation in the 1950s had less to do with Parliament's machinations and more to do with justices whose ideologies reflected those of the National Party. While Chapters 3 and 4 provided some support for this, the aggregate support for the government *over time* has not been evaluated. Chapter 2 provided a cursory exploration of the highlights of the rise and fall of apartheid in South Africa and introduced three interventions to be explored in this analysis: the 1961 creation of the Republic of South Africa, the 1976 Soweto uprising and the passage of the Constitution Act of 1983. These three interventions will be considered in more detail below.

Before turning to the analysis, the following caveat should be noted. I have selected three interventions that I believe have the potential to be sufficiently important politically to significantly affect the trend of court outcomes. These are not the only events in the apartheid era that may have been influential, nonetheless, these are events of sufficient magnitude that their effect *should* be evaluated.

Assessing the Interventions

If we accept the premise that courts as political institutions respond to the external political environment, we must determine what sorts of variables can affect their choices. Clearly, the individuals who comprise the court affect the outcomes. It is after all the aggregate of their preferences and perceptions that determines outcomes. No direct measure of the preferences of the justices that is independent of the votes exists for the entire period. As previously noted, a common understanding of the Appellate Division has assumed Afrikaans-speaking judges to be more supportive of the government than their English-speaking colleagues (Forsyth 1985), but as noted previously, the empirical evidence in Chapters 3 and 4 provided modest support for this. To further evaluate this division, I include a measure of the annual percentage of the Court comprised of Afrikaans-speaking judges.[22] The presumption is that the greater the percentage of Afrikaans-speaking judges on the Court, the greater the support for the government. Figure 5.1 provides these annual percentages, which clearly demonstrate the dramatic increase in Afrikaans-speaking judges serving on the Court following the rise of the National Party.

The National Party serves as a constant over the course of the series. This constant is measured by the inclusion of the series counter, which is given a value of 1 in the first year of the study, 2 in 1951, 3 in 1952, etc. The party gained power and was never seriously in jeopardy of losing it throughout the period studied. However, the passage of the two constitutions chronicles the major legal positions of the National Party. Thus, the position of the National Party is measured by two interventions. The first is the Constitution Act of 1961, which is *prima facie* evidence of two things that are particularly important signals for the members of the Court. First, the government was not going to respond to the criticisms of the international community. The Constitution Act created a supreme Parliament with the capacity to rule with an iron fist. Second, and relatedly, the regime intentionally limited the capacity of courts generally, and the Appellate Division in particular, to review any legislation. The Constitution Act represented the power of the National Party to consolidate the white minority population behind the

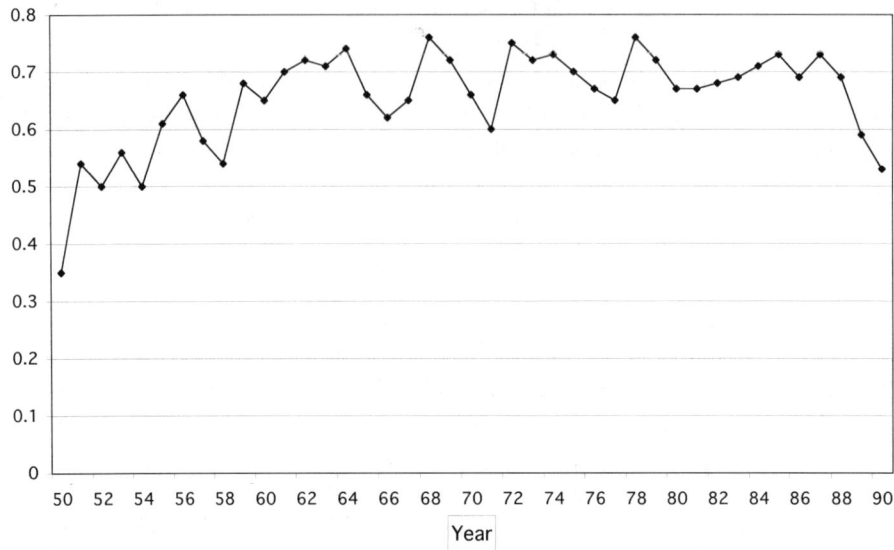

Figure 5.1 Percentage of Afrikaans-Speaking Judges Serving on the Court, 1950–1990

apartheid scheme and to separate itself fully from its British past. Thus, despite the rising tide of international concern following the 1960 Sharpeville massacre, I expect the Court to increase its support for the government following the passage of the Constitution Act of 1961.

Some fifteen years later, the futility of establishing a segregated South Africa was becoming apparent. The violence erupting in the townships was becoming increasingly costly to suppress. The increased repression led to greater violent resistance. Moreover, the suppression resulted in greater exposure of the massive repression required by apartheid, which led to even more international condemnation. The collision of apartheid theory and apartheid reality manifested in the Soweto uprising. Combined with the death of Steve Biko in 1977, whose international recognition and popularity gave a specific face to the poison of apartheid, near-universal criticism of the Republic of South Africa followed. I expect a significant decline in the likelihood of the government winning a case before the Appellate Division following the 1976 Soweto uprising and Steve Biko's death.

Subsequently, the passage of the Constitution Act of 1983[23] signaled a decline in the power of the National Party's policy of separate development. The new constitution changed very little in the power and structure of the courts and the Appellate Division, in particular. The Constitution Act of 1983 did not significantly shift power away from the white population, but its passage signaled a dramatic shift away from the grand design of separate development. Moreover, the party was struggling to maintain the expensive edifice of apartheid. The Constitution Act of 1983 symbolized the recognition of the regime that the Republic could not survive the economic costs, both internally with lost labor potential and externally through international economic pressure. Moreover, the escalating violence made it evident that the black majority was not going to accept apartheid, and the government had to explore alternatives. Thus, I anticipate that support for the government in case outcomes will decline significantly following the passage of the Constitution Act of 1983.

Figure 5.2 shows the overall annual success rates of the government in all cases. The government was winning 65% of cases even during the period when English-speaking judges dominated the Court in the early 1950s. Following the successful appointment of a majority of Afrikaans-speaking judges during the 1950s, a sharp increase in support for the government occurs during the early 1960s. Success rates for the government clearly begin declining in the 1970s, with the lowest success rate, a mere 38%, occurring in 1984. The series ends with the government winning less than 50% of the time in 1990.

Figure 5.3 suggests a similar trend for the success of the government in challenges to civil rights and liberties abuses, including criminal cases and challenges to apartheid legislation. The government fared much better generally in this category, as one would expect in a country with no delineated protections for individual rights. The government's success rate began at an impressive 70% and increased

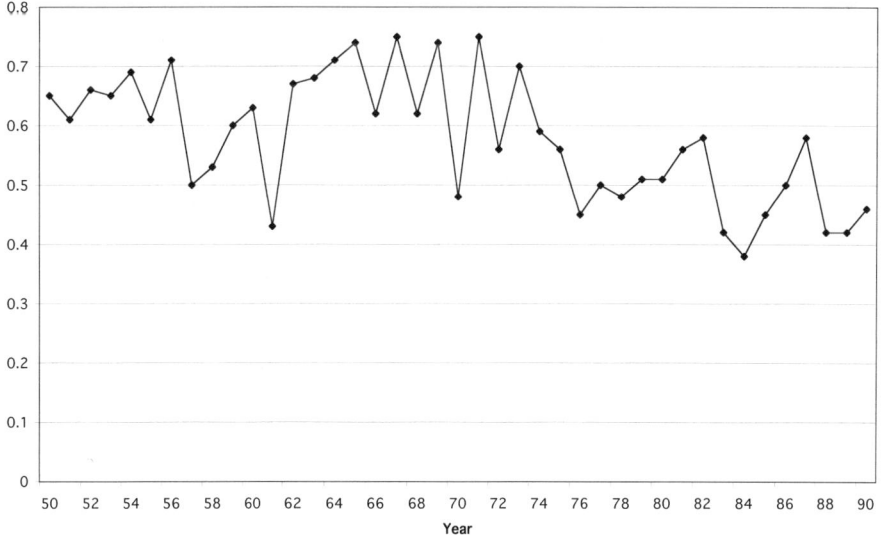

Figure 5.2 Percentage of Cases Favoring the Government in All Decisions, 1950–1990

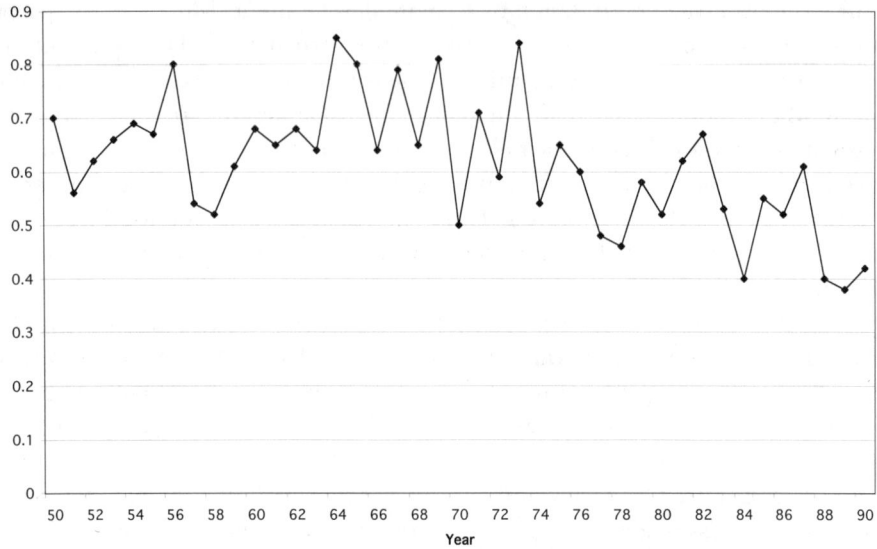

Figure 5.3 Percentage of Cases Favoring the Government in Civil Rights and Liberties, Criminal and Apartheid Cases, 1950–1990

during the 1960s to a high of 85% in 1964. This level of support declined during the 1970s, to only 40% in 1984 and an even lower 38% by 1989.

Figure 5.4 mirrors the patterns emerging in the previous two issue categories with a steady decline of support for the government in public law cases over the 41-year period.[24] In several years there were noticeably low percentages of cases or even no cases in which the government succeeded. However, it should be noted that there are often very few cases in those years. For example, the government won only 12% of cases in 1983, but there were only 8 cases decided in that term, and some of the cases were technical copyright and taxation questions. Moreover, the government did not win a single case in 1984, but only 2 cases were decided. By the end of the series in 1990, the government succeeded in just half of its 18 public law cases decided by the Court that year.

Multiple interrupted times series analysis was used to assess empirically the response of the Appellate Division to its political environment in the three issue areas presented in Figures 5.2, 5.3 and 5.4. This type of statistical analysis compares the Court's support for the government prior to the particular point in the series where the intervention occurs, with the Court's support for the government following the intervention. If the particular event has an influence on the support for the government, the estimated parameters will demonstrate significant increases or decreases following the intervention. Thus if the Soweto uprising and the death of Steve Biko *(Soweto/Biko)* are significantly related to a decline in the support for the government, there will be an immediate drop in decisions in which the government wins. Counter variables are included for each intervention and are given the value of 1 the first year of the intervention, and 2 in the second year following the intervention, 3 in the third year following the intervention, etc. If the counter variable associated with this intervention *(Soweto Counter)* is significant and positive, then decisions supporting the government gradually increased following the initial drop after 1976. If the counter variable is significant and negative, then the decisions supporting the government gradually declined over the remaining years of the series following the initial drop. If the counter variable is not significant, then the intervention (if significant) had an immediate and permanent effect on the series. The overall series counter provides the same information for the series as a whole. For variables such as the annual percentage of Afrikaans-speaking judges on the Court, the parameters will indicate statistically significant negative or positive relationships to government support.

The results are presented in Table 5.1 and suggest that the Court did respond to its surrounding environment. For all decisions in which the government was a party, the passage of the Constitution Act of 1961 positively and significantly affected the support for the government; however, the Soweto uprising significantly decreased the support for the government, as predicted, with approximately a 20% initial decline. The counter indicates that the Court's support increased following the initial impact almost 2% annually, suggesting a return to the status quo of support once the furor subsided. The passage of the Constitution of 1983 also abruptly and significantly decreased the support of the National Party by almost 17%. The counters for both the 1961 and 1983 Constitution Acts suggest that

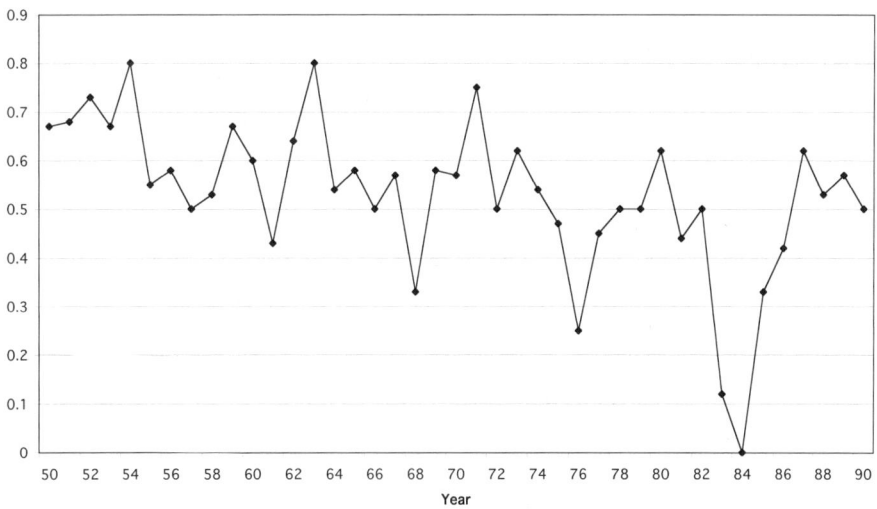

Figure 5.4 Percentage of Cases Favoring the Government in Public Law Cases, 1950–1990

TABLE 5.1
Multiple Interrupted Times Series Results for Percentage of Cases Favoring the Government[a]

Variable	All Cases		Civil Rights & Liberties		Public Law	
	Estimate	Std. Err.	Estimate	Std. Err	Estimate	Std. Err
Intercept	.555	.108***	.473	.130***	.483	.178***
Series Counter	−.016	.007**	−.012	.009*	−.039	.012***
1961 Constitution	.093	.045**	.104	.055**	.039	.074
1961 Counter	.014	.008**	.007	.009	.036	.013**
Soweto/Biko	−.198	.058***	−.185	.070***	−.117	.094
Soweto Counter	.023	.011*	.028	.014*	.023	.019
1983 Constitution	−.165	.066*	−.111	.079*	−.540	.107***
1983 Counter	−.009	.014	−.029	.017**	.074	.023**
% of Afrikaans-speaking	.282	.230	.421	.276*	.673	.378**
	N=41 *Adj R²* =.67		N=41 *Adj R²*=.69		N=41 *Adj R²*=.62	
	Durbin-Watson 1.94		Durbin-Watson 2.01		Durbin-Watson 2.13	

*p < .10, one-tailed; **p < .05, one-tailed; ***p < .01, one-tailed
[a] Parameter estimates for this model were obtained using Prais-Winsten time series autoregression procedure.

the interventions resulted in permanent increases and decreases respectively. The percentage of Afrikaans-speaking judges on the bench was not significant, suggesting that Afrikaans-speaking majorities did not affect government success in the overall docket.[25]

The results for the civil rights and liberties cases mirror almost identically the results for the series overall. The passage of the Constitution Act of 1961 correlates with an increase in the Appellate Division's support of the government permanently by 10%. The Soweto uprising again significantly decreased the government's success rate by 18.5%, with a statistically significant shift in the slope or counter following the decline, suggesting an increase of almost 3% annually in government support. The passage of the Constitution Act of 1983 again significantly and negatively affected the support for the government in rights and liberties cases; there was a gradual decrease in support of 11% annually, as predicted, following its passage. The 1983 Counter suggests that this decrease was permanent. The percentage of Afrikaans-speaking judges serving on the Court was significantly related to the probability of the government winning in rights and liberties cases. Thus as the percentage of Afrikaans-speaking judges increased on the Court, the likelihood of the government winning increases slightly as well, though this variable is only significant at the .10 level, suggesting the effect is not as robust as that of the interventions.[26]

For public law cases, the series counter declined significantly, at a rate of just under 4% annually over the 41-year period. The passage of the Constitution Act of 1961 was again positively related to the government's success. The Soweto demonstration and Steve Biko's death were not significant. However, the passage of the Constitution Act of 1983 was highly significantly related to a decline in the support for the government. The coefficient for the Constitution Act of 1983 suggests that support for the government declines abruptly by 54% and then increases gradually over the remainder of the series by approximately 7% annually. As noted earlier, these numbers must be interpreted tentatively because of the low number of cases for some years, where the loss of a single case can affect the percentages by 20% or 30%. Nonetheless, the analysis clearly demonstrates the downward trend of the Court's support for the government over the series as well as its response to the interventions included in the analysis.[27]

Discussion

The results of this analysis support the obvious conclusion that judging is affected by more than merely laying the facts of the case beside the statute and applying the latter to the former. If that were true, there should be no significant effects from the variables assessed here. In fact, analyzing the aggregate or macro-level decision making of the South African Appellate Division suggests that it was affected by both the individuals who comprised the bench and external events. For the aggregate of the Court's docket, all of the interventions statistically affected the decisions of the Court, and all estimates are in the predicted direction. The Soweto uprising brought international attention externally and increased opposition and violence internally. It decreased the support for the government, as did the passage of the Constitution Act of 1983, which many saw as the beginning of the end of the National Party's grand scheme of apartheid. While the coefficient for the percentage of Afrikaans-speaking judges on the Court is positive, it demonstrates no statistically significant relationship.

When the National Party gained control in 1948, it began immediately appointing Afrikaans-speaking judges to the previously English-dominated bench. The initial surge in support for the government parallels the initial increase of Afrikaans-speaking judges on the Court. However, as the regime begins to lose its support internally and becomes an international pariah, the support of the Afrikaans-speaking judges declines as well. Because judges serve essentially for life, it makes sense that concern for institutional legitimacy should drive the Court's decisions, at least in part. Continuing to support a regime that is clearly losing power would not be likely to enhance the long-term political health of the court. These judges were also drawn from a South African elite that increasingly recognized the futility of the apartheid enterprise both morally and logistically. Interviews conducted with judges of the Appellate Division noted that they "hated" the apartheid cases, hoping to avoid them. The judges found ruling in cases involving the apartheid regime awkward, perceiving the Court as a liberal institution in an illiberal setting. The results support the attitudes expressed in the interviews. By the waning years of the National Party's regime, the judges were surely aware that apartheid would not survive. The aggregate of their decision making reflects a concomitant decrease in support for the apartheid government.

For civil rights and liberties cases, most of which are criminal appeals, the results suggest that the Constitution Act of 1961 is positively associated with the government winning. The Constitution Act of 1961 represented a separation from British control and a consolidation of the apartheid philosophy within the National Party. Moreover, it clearly delineated the limitations of courts. However, decreasing support of the government follows the Soweto uprising and the passage of the Constitution Act of 1983, suggesting increasing reluctance on the part of the Court to support the apartheid regime. The percentage of Afrikaans-speaking judges serving on the Court is positively related to the likelihood of the government winning in civil rights and liberties cases, though only to a modest degree by conventional levels of statistical significance.

For public law challenges, the overall slope of the series declines significantly over time. However, the only intervention to significantly affect the series was the Constitution Act of 1983. It should be noted that the apartheid challenges have been removed from the public law category and were included in the civil rights and liberties section, narrowing the category of cases included here to less controversial decisions, such as tax cases and water regulation, for example. The results suggest that the overall decision making of the Court was driven in large part by its criminal, civil rights, liberties and apartheid decisions. The percentage of Afrikaans-speaking judges on the Court does significantly increase the likelihood of the government winning these cases.

Conclusion

These results indicate that courts do not function in isolation of either external or internal forces. Both the composition of the Court itself and external interventions affected regime support. These results of course cannot be interpreted to mean that chaos erupts in Soweto and the Appellate Division begins ruling against the government. Such a conclusion would be crude and simplistic, and, in this as in other areas of social science, crass inferences are seldom helpful. These results should rather be interpreted to mean that as the political and social climate began to deteriorate as evidenced in Steve Biko's death and the Soweto uprising, the Court's sensitivity to those challenging the regime was heightened. Where the government had been evaluated more generously in the past, the Court's decisions suggest that abruptly changed in the late 1970s. In other words, these interventions serve as surrogates of the political and social crisis facing the nation. The Court is an arbiter of the disputes with the regime but also a product of the same social, political and legal circumstances in which these interventions arise. The way in which judges use their discretion inevitably will be affected by such important events.

This empirical analysis suggests that the South African Appellate Division significantly increased and decreased its support of the government in response to key political events. Future research will need to assess the implications of these decision-making changes to the broader question of institutional legitimacy. The presumption of this research is that courts seek to maximize their institutional legitimacy by ruling in ways that lead to the optimal outcome without risking long-term damage to the court's institutional integrity. In developing countries, and particularly in authoritarian regimes, judges are required to walk a tightrope between their own formal law training with its respect for neutrality, impartiality, independence, equality and due process and the repressive laws imposed by the executive and legislative branches (Haynie 1994, 1995). Courts that reside in authoritarian or nondemocratic regimes are particularly vulnerable. Defying the regime is a matter of greater concern than whether or not their decisions will be ignored or overturned. Courts can be abolished, replaced, reconstituted or jurisdictionally limited in polities where there is no established rule of law or where the court has yet to emerge as a stable political institution with sufficient legitimacy to protect it from the opposition's onslaught. Moreover, in systems where Parliament is supreme, judicial decisions can easily be altered by statute to assure dominance of the preferences of the regime majority.

Judges certainly understand the political nature of their decisions (Tate and Haynie 1993, 1994). This analysis suggests that even in nondemocratic courts with no constitutional or statutory power to effectively challenge the regime, courts decrease and increase support systematically in response to significant shifts in the social and political context.

CHAPTER SIX

Judicial Decision Making in Repressive Legal Systems

The central theme of this book has been a simple one: judges are decision makers affected by both legal and extra-legal factors–choices are not simply black or white. I have argued that as interactions among individuals and groups increase, the potential for conflict and the potential for behaviors that violate social norms increases. Initially, the regime resorts to brute force and coercion to maintain control. However, governance by authoritarian or repressive means is problematic to commercial interests that seek security in their transactions. To increase stability and civility in society, statutes are passed by governing authorities that articulate rights and duties. As conflicts arise in the application of these formal laws, governments establish theoretically neutral court structures to perform at least two critical functions in social systems. They resolve conflicts and enforce behavioral norms and expectations. In authoritarian regimes, judges are left to resolve the disputes within the conflicting dictates of the formal and repressive law. Moreover, judges are limited both structurally and politically in the use of their discretion.

As this text demonstrates, authoritarian regimes that profess allegiance to the rule of law incorporate the formal law but do not abandon the repressive law. Superficially all government action is guided by statutory and constitutional edict. However, the statutes and the constitution are infused with repressive mandates. The formal law in these systems is simply the manner by which the repressive law is institutionalized. The government argues that if it is duly passed by a legislative body and enforced by authorized government officials, the law represents reasonable government action. Despite the rhetoric and the parliamentary charade, the "law" is merely repression by a different means.

Since the primary motivation for the passage of formal laws is to remove the tension and instability associated with the repressive law, these systems are untenable for the long term. The formal law serves as a mask for the repressive law embedded within it. Judges attempt to disentangle these tensions and inevitably become entangled themselves.

Judging in Black and White

Judges of the apartheid-era Appellate Division functioned within a system in which the oppressive, centralized, authoritarian nature of the repressive law was enmeshed with the rules-oriented, procedurally detailed formal law. The goal of this book has been to examine the decisions of judges embedded in a system where the formal law and repressive law overlap. Those who study the United States legal system will find nothing unique in the assertion that extra-legal factors can influence judges and judging since this has been a core component of judicial research on the United States legal system since the early 1900s.

For over a century, political and social science scholars have embraced the notion that judges have discretion, that they exercise their discretion differently and that those differences lead to differing policy outcomes–or decisions. However, such is not the case universally. Indeed, the mechanistic or formal law paradigm remains a dominant force among many scholars in South Africa as well as many other legal systems. The positivist approach remains the general approach to legal education throughout most law schools. Law students are not taught to determine the probabilities of winning given Judge A as opposed to Judge B but are taught principled legal reasoning that guides the decisions of both Judge A and Judge B. Of course, in practice, lawyers deduce intuitively what social scientists do empirically.

Normatively, there is great value in the formal law paradigm.[1] It is desirable to have judges who aspire to be the "living oracles" of the law (Blackstone 1765, 69) and who intentionally attempt to ignore their own personal attitudes in reaching principled legal decisions based upon an independent and impartial understanding of the facts and the law. But this is desirable only in systems in which the law is presumed to be based upon the voices of the governed. When the laws are used to coerce behaviors that will be consistent with the repressive will of the minority, the normative value of the positivist approach to judging no longer exists. The formal law becomes the defense for those who are coopted into legitimizing the repressive aspects of the law.

Dugard, among others argued that the formal law approach was a self-serving legal fiction. He noted that "[i]f one can seriously believe that the judge's sole function is to 'declare' the law he is absolved of all blame for interpreting evil laws evilly and wicked law wickedly" (Dugard 1989, 61).

The formal law protects judges in these systems in two ways. First, judges are protected from criticism or scrutiny because their decisions are not a function of personal bias but are theoretically determined only by the law and the facts. Second, assertions to the contrary are treated as contemptuous, creating a chilling effect on empirical inquiry. Studies of judicial behavior are considered pointless, even irreverent, because judges are merely articulating the legally correct outcome. To assert otherwise is to undermine the judicial function.

While there were a number of studies over the apartheid era focusing on racial discrepancies in sentencing, particularly for the death penalty, authors were careful not to directly attribute these discrepancies to the individual atitutdes of the judges.[2] Even indirectly, such assertions could be grounds for "scandalization contempt." Under the common law, alleging bias or partiality in judicial decision making denigrates both judges and the courts, which can undermine the legal system and thus the rule of law. Under this doctrine, those whose words or actions could undermine the faith of the general populace in the fairness of the courts could, indeed should, be punished accordingly.

The infamous Van Niekerk cases demonstrated the difficulty in pursuing critical analysis. Barend van Niekerk, a senior law lecturer at the University of Witwatersrand, conducted a survey of South African attorneys concerning the influence of race in death penalty sentences in South Africa. The first of two articles describing the results was published in the *South African Law Journal* in 1969. According to Van Niekerk:

> the fact which emerges undeniably is that a considerable number of replying advocates, almost 50 per cent in fact, believe that justice as regards capital punishment is meted out on a differential basis to the different races, and that 41 per cent who so believe are also of the opinion that such differentiation is 'conscious and deliberate'(Van Niekerk 1969, 467).

Van Niekerk suggested that the attorneys' perceptions of bias were correct and that such bias was "conscious and deliberate." For this assertion he was charged with scandalization contempt but was acquitted because it was determined that he lacked the requisite *mens rea*. The latter was attributed in no small part to what essentially was a retraction printed in the *South African Law Journal* which stated, "Whatever explanation there may be for these figures, it is unacceptable to assume that it lies in the conscious discrimination between the races in capital cases for purposes of sentencing" (Van Niekerk 1970, 72). He was less successful in the two subsequent contempt cases brought against him for other writings critical of judges and their recalcitrance in challenging the government.[3]

As Van Niekerk's history demonstrated, asserting any paradigm other than the positive or formal law approach in apartheid South Africa was not only considered inappropriate from a legal reasoning standpoint, it was considered contemptuous by the courts. Such decisions had a purposively chilling effect on the scholarship conducted on the decision making of the South African high courts (Marcus 1984).

Thus, the positive law provided a distinct defense for the judges of the South African courts. Judges appropriately could claim that independence and impartiality prevented them from affecting change via decisions in the apartheid state. They were responsible only for the interpretation and application of the laws–never for their construction or passage. Outcomes are dictated by the facts, the common law, legislative intent, plain meaning, precedent, etc., or so the theory goes, but the examples provided in this text certainly demonstrate that the "correct" resolution of a dispute, and thus the court's definition of the law, is never so black and white.

Concomitantly, to reject the formal law is to undermine the responsibility courts have to resolve conflicts and control behaviors. To suggest that within the formal law the rules should be interpreted to limit the effects of the repressive law requires that judges abandon "the law" and embrace ideologically driven jurisprudence. To advocate that judges engage in ideologically liberal decision making would be contemptuous of the mandated independence and impartiality required of their decision making. The positive law paradigm creates a win-win situation for judges in a repressive legal order. The paradigm absolves judges of any responsibility for participating in a repressive regime. Moreover, to reject it is contemptuous.

Fortunately, academics are a proudly contemptuous lot, and by the mid- to late 1980s scholars began to critically evaluate the judges.[4] Scholars argued forcefully that the legal context is but one aspect of judicial decision making. Certainty within the law, and thus within judging, is impossible. The inevitable ambiguity in the law *requires* that judges *make* law. Calling it explication or interpretation or application does not alter the fact that courts ultimately determine what is and what is not "legal." The Appellate Division created policies which allowed rather lengthy absences from employment like Mr. Mthiya's. The Court's decision determined what was and was not considered "voluntary" in evaluating race classification testimony, an important distinction for Mr. Felton. Mr. Pitje would appear as an attorney in certain South African courts at a separate table or not all–not because of statute but because of the Appellate Division's choice.

Every judge comes to his or her understanding of the law with a slightly different vision. These individual perceptions facilitate the legal resolutions. Moreover, individualized social, political and economic experiences facilitate these belief structures. Thus, despite the fact that each judge begins with the same statutory text, facts, precedents and legal traditions–the individual decision making process can result in very different outcomes.

While recognizing that judges within the South African legal system were faced routinely with difficult moral dilemmas, Dugard argued that the essence of judging provides choices. Discretion fuels the capacity of judges who favor the individual, as opposed to the status quo, to reach outcomes that frustrate the underlying objectives of the regime in repressive legal systems. Dugard did not argue that judges are able to do this in every situation, but they certainly have the means to the liberal ends often enough. While I agree that judges possess discretion, I disagree that judges can use this discretion in a consistent manner to oppose the regime. As a number of the high-profile cases examined in this text demonstrate, such antagonism will not be tolerated for long.

The early history of the Appellate Division suggests exactly this. The Court initially overturned the decisions of the National Party to remove the Cape coloured voters. Parliament, of course, refused to accept the Court's action and created the High Court of Parliament. Again, the Court declared the creation of the "High Court" *ultra vires*. However, without sufficient institutional legitimacy and without any real power of judicial review, the Court was powerless to prevent Parliament from pursuing alternative routes to achieve its goal of removing the voters. Ultimately, by enlarging the membership of Parliament, the National Party was able to achieve the requisite two-thirds vote. Moreover, the size of the Appellate Division was increased and staffed by Afrikaners. These frontal clashes significantly altered the institutional health of the Appellate Division. Parliament's manipulation of its size as well as the newly enlarged Court's ultimate reversal of its previous decisions made painfully clear Parliament's superiority. Never again did the two institutions battle on such a visibly political level.

I argue that is predictable. Courts that necessarily lack institutional resources will not challenge regimes persistently on the major issues brought before them. In addition, such courts frequently do not have the constitutional powers of judicial review or justiciable rights, necessary to challenge the regime directly. Courts that lack these resources will ultimately demure when faced with politically charged cases or will challenge the government infrequently in these major disputes. If the court persists, as the 1950s Appellate Division did, it will lose in repressive regimes. Those cases which are politically crucial to the regime, such as *Harris, Collins,* and *Omar,* are the black and white cases. Outcomes are, at least in large part, affected by external politics. The Court is neither ignorant of, nor immune from, the significance of the case and the potential consequences for the Court in challenging the regime, which it will do on occasion as demonstrated by *Hurley*. But these challenges will be limited as the Court attempts to preserve its institutional health. However, persistent support of the regime can be equally detrimental to the perceived independence and impartiality of the Court. I argue that the Court meets this challenge by balancing its decisions in the handful of major challenges in which the Court cannot substantively challenge the regime with the bulk of its docket. The bulk of the docket, and I would argue the grey of the docket, can provide opportunities for judges to use their discretion where the major clashes do not. Decisions like those in *Omar* come to define the Court without evaluating the entirety of the Court's decision making.

I certainly do not argue that cases were equivalent across the docket; some clearly have greater policy consequences than others, and this is particularly so given a court that lacks docket control. Clearly the Court's decisions in *Omar* and *Hurley* were far more significant than decisions focusing on whether a particular debt was owed or whether negligence existed in an automobile accident.

What I do argue is that focusing only on the major controversies decided by the Court can be equally misleading. I also do not argue that judicial decisions ignore facts and law; judges function within a legal context, and judicial decisions are the products of decision making processes that involve interpretation of facts alongside constitutional and statutory language. Nonetheless, judges have numerous alternatives available to them, and our understanding of court behavior suggests that outcomes represent a complex individualized judicial calculus enveloped by external political and social forces.

Winners, Losers and Discretion in South Africa

The critics of the South African Appellate Division focused on the alleged "pro-executive" bias of the Court's decision making. Chapter 2 explored a number of the decisions of the Court that led to that reputation. The early challenges to the National Party's removal of the Cape coloured voters and the consequent High Court of Parliament Act fueled a reputation for independence among the English-dominated Appellate Division. The subsequent capitulation by the Court and the packing of the Court with Afrikaners damaged the perceived impartiality of the Court, damage from which the Court never recovered. The appointment and then promotion of Judge Steyn to the Chief Justiceship in the 1950s, in blatant disregard for the norm of seniority, also weakened the Court's perceived independence from politics. The decisions of the Court in the 1980s state of emergency were also seen as supportive of the regime (Ellmann 1992), and these decisions were helmed by Chief Justice Rabie, who served as Acting Chief Justice during this period, despite his having reached the mandatory retirement age.

Chapter 2 suggests that the Court's reputation as supportive of the regime was due in part to the success of the government in several high-profile challenges. Based on these high-profile cases, the reputation for a conservative institution ensued. A few cases were used to infer bias in the general decision making of the court. I do not equate the high-profile cases with the less politically charged cases. In other words, I am not attempting the reverse—using the whole of the docket as exemplary of the Court's behavior. Cases are not equal in either import or impact, neither alone provides a complete picture. Only when the aggregate *and* the specific are explored can we more fully understand the true nature of judicial decision making in the South African Appellate Division.

The bulk of the court's decision making is not indicative of an ideologically driven, executive-minded institution, particularly in the waning years of apartheid. Chapter 3 suggests that the South African Appellate Division was not overwhelmingly supportive of the South African government, even in areas where one would have anticipated high success rates. The government did have the highest averaged success rate when petitioning the Appellate Division as well as the highest averaged success rate as both appellant and respondent but only barely. The government enjoyed a few percentage points advantage that neither individuals nor businesses had. Two or three percentage points would not be the result anticipated among a pro-executive institution. Certainly the success of the government varied by issue. The government was most successful in civil rights and liberties cases but even then lost on average 40% of the time. In apartheid cases, an issue area on which one would anticipate the highest pro-government bias, the averaged success rate of the government as both petitioner and respondent demonstrates that the government won only slightly more than it lost. The results suggest that the Appellate Division partially behaved as Dugard urged.

Chapter 4 explores the individual decision making of the judges. The general view presumed that macro-level judging was the result of aggregated micro-level biases; that is, the conservative individual voting patterns of the judges led to decisions that supported the upperdog—the government, in particular—over the underdog—the individual, and vice versa. Afrikaans-speaking judges were assumed to be more conservatively biased than English-speaking judges. But again, these assertions have not been tested empirically. This is not surprising given the Van Niekerk case. It was his assertion of bias among judges in death penalty cases that led to the contempt charge, and it was his yielding on this assertion that led to his acquittal. Demonstrating variance in voting patterns and attributing this to something other than proper legal reasoning was contemptuous in apartheid South Africa. Chapter 4 of course, does just this.

The results in Chapter 4 suggest that some justices were clearly more conservative than others. Some judges, such as Judges Brink, Reynolds and Klopper, supported the underdog on average in only one out of every three cases. In some issue areas support for the underdog was particularly sparse for judges such as Judges Centlivres, H. H. W. De Villiers and Reynolds. Others were much more supportive of those with presumed fewer resources. Judge Diemont supported the underdog in almost 60% of the cases in which he participated. Judge A. S. Botha supported the underdog 64% of the time, while Judge Eksteen did so in 70% of the cases in which he voted. There was some variation in the different voting patterns of Afrikaans-speaking and English-speaking judges. Afrikaans-speaking judges were more likely to support the government in civil rights and liberties cases as well as tort cases (almost 10 percentage points) but were slightly (41% to 38%) more likely to support the accused in criminal cases. Most interestingly, there were identical overall voting percentages for Afrikaans-speaking and English-speaking judges in apartheid cases, 39%. The mean of the support for the government in the application of the most repressive of the laws was the same.

Over time, the support for the underdog increases as the apartheid era draws to a close. The tables show less support for the individual in the early years of the Court and more support by the 1980s.

Chapter 5 presents a longitudinal analysis of the support for the government. Not surprisingly, the support for the government parallels the individual voting patterns over time. The support for the government was highest just after the rise of the National Party and its subsequent "packing" of the court. However, that support declines significantly as the apartheid regime comes to its close.

The Appellate Division Mr. Pitje faced was a different political institution than the Appellate Division presiding over the South African legal system in 1990. The results presented in the previous chapters indicate that the Court was not overwhelmingly deferential to the government at either the micro or the macro level when the whole of the docket is examined. Moreover, the Court became less supportive of the government as the era came to its close.

Certain events were significantly related to increases or decreases in the Court's aggregate support for the government. The passage of the Constitution Act of 1961 increased the likelihood of the government's winning. The death of Steve Biko and the Soweto riots decreased the likelihood of the government's winning. The subsequent passage of the Constitution Act of 1983 also led to a significant decrease in the likelihood of the government's winning before the Appellate Division. These events were delineated in the analysis as watershed events that represent larger social and political movements. The Soweto riots symbolized increasing domestic opposition among black South Africans and externally among international investors. The Court was cognizant of the political and social context of their decisions. The Court did not function in isolation of the society within which it resided, regardless of the positivists' rhetoric. Courts inevitably respond to the social trends that surround them. They are products of that environment, and as it shifts, so will the behavior of the Court.

Alternative Explanations

Those who adhere to the formal law explanation for court outcomes would argue that in every case represented in these data, outcomes can be explained by proper interpretation of the law and the facts. Indeed, every case analyzed in this text was accompanied by the requisite legal explanation of the Court's decision. Precedents are cited. Statutes are explained. The constitution is examined. The appropriate application of the common law is deliberated. Nowhere in the Court's decisions will you find rhetoric which says, "We think apartheid is a failing enterprise and think it in the Court's institutional best interest to rule against the powerful a little more often." Positivists would argue such a concept fairly absurd because every case can be, and was, explained in legal terms.

Of course judges will use legal reasoning in their decisions, and I do not argue that these decisions are simply rationalizations for desired outcomes as some scholars would suggest (Segal and Spaeth 1993, 2002). Judges' choices are the product of careful evaluation of the facts and the law, and a legal conclusion is reached. However, judges' personal attitudes inevitably affect how those facts are understood within the legal context brought before the court. Of course, the law matters. Of course, the law restrains the choices available to judges, but it is within that legal context that the discretion resides.

Every judge can argue, and in fact does argue, that his or her decision was based solely on the appropriate application of the law. The most convenient aspect of the formal law is its inability to be tested empirically. Each of the cases presented in this text proffered reasonable alternatives, either of which could be a proper disposition of the case. The Court selects one side and then explains why it is "the" proper choice. How can we operationalize "proper" legal reasoning? How do we measure "appropriate" interpretation? How does one empirically determine "legislative intent"?

The Court's decision in *R. v. Abdurahman* (1950) created a legal fiction in which the Court argued that it was "unlikely that the legislature intended that users of the railways should, according to their race, have partial or unequal treatment meted out to them."[5] The fact that the major intent of apartheid, in general, was to do just that would seem to defy the Court's assertion. The Court's similar assertions that the legislature could not have intended to create a catch-22 with the work permits of individuals like Mr. Mthiya seem dubious. Perhaps Parliament did not intend to do so, but it likely would have supported such an interpretation, which, of course, was Chief Justice Steyn's argument as to why Mr. Pitje would be forced to sit at a separate table from his white colleague.

Similarly, exactly how does one identify the precise "plain meaning" of words? The Court's interpretation of "voluntary" in Mr. Felton's classification case was certainly not an obvious choice. The Court's definition of the words "in terms of" in the ouster clause cases was similarly quixotic as was the Court's insistence that "necessity" was not an appropriate factor to consider in the transfer of Mr. Garda's license as a butcher.

Interpretation of the facts is rarely straightforward either. The Appellate Division argued that Parliament could not have "approved" the withdrawal of the Magopa tribe without knowing its final dwelling place. This seems to ignore Parliament's resolution approving the removal. Were the actions of the board in Ms. Kuhn's liquor license dispute "reasonable" as the Court asserted?

And how does one determine which precedent is applicable and which is not? Cases in the South African Law Reports begin with advocates for each side presenting often lengthy descriptions of applicable precedent supporting the position of their client. Both Roman-Dutch and British citations, as well as South African and even foreign precedents, provide ample numbers of sources from which attorneys can base their arguments and on which judges can base their decisions. The advocates for Mr. Omar relied on the precedent established in *Hurley;* the Court did not.

The inability to empirically measure these concepts makes it impossible to falsify the legal myth of the formal law.[6] Thus judges will argue that their decisions are based on the black and white criterion of the law, and there is no way to prove empirically they are not. One can argue normatively, as Dugard and others did, that the decision is morally wrong. One can argue that alternative legal reasoning would have been more appropriate. But the discretion generated by the ambiguity in legal conflicts makes it possible for judges to reach conclusions that can be based on "appropriate" legal reasoning, however they choose to define that.

Formal law theorists could argue that the winners and losers presented in Chapter 3 merely represent the correct interpretation of the law and proper application of precedent and legal tradition. The fact that one group wins 42% of the time and another 39% of the time is a silly exploration of outcomes appropriately based on the law. As Cameron noted, "Forty judgements favouring the executive (or some manifestation of it) may mean nothing more than that in forty cases no other ruling was judicially tenable" (1982, 52). The fact that more bias is not evidenced in Chapter 3 could be considered supportive of the formal law approach.

Moreover, the fact that a judge in the 1950s favored the underdog in 38% of cases while one in the 1980s favored the underdog in 58% of cases is an absurd comparison. They were interpreting different statutes, with different facts and precedents. Only if we could give each judge the same case could we genuinely make conclusions about individual differences. Of course, that is not feasible, and so it is again impossible to refute such an argument.

However, the formal law proponents must provide an alternative explanation for the longitudinal analysis presented in Chapter 5. If we attribute the declining support for the government, which is empirically measured, to proper legal interpretation, then we must assume that the law became more supportive of the underdog, and the decisions of the Court simply reflect this. The laws, of course, became even more conservative as the National Party struggled to maintain white minority rule and became particularly draconian by the years of the emergency rule in the 1980s. Of course the support for the government includes all types of legal disputes where the government was involved, not just security legislation. It could be argued that the repressive years of the emergency rule would have had no effect on the Court's decisions in government tort liability, criminal disputes generally or labor and transportation disputes. However, the government's policies changed only incrementally if at all in these areas and seldom in a direction supportive of the underdog. It is not possible to explain the systematic and statistically significant decrease in the likelihood of the government winning following the interventions explored in the analysis. Something in addition to the facts and the law was driving the decisions of the Court.

Those who adhere to the formal law theory will not be convinced by this analysis, and the inability to appropriately test the formal law model makes it impossible to combat it as an alternative hypothesis. However, those who adhere to the mechanical thesis must provide some alternative explanation for the variation in the empirical data presented here.

Discretion, Outcomes and Politics

These results suggest that contrary to the general view, the apartheid-era Appellate Division was not a mere appendage of the National Party. While there is little doubt that a government with parliamentary superiority and no justiciable bill of rights will prevail, the Court was not the deferential Division it is typically portrayed as having been.

The question remains, of course, why was the Court not overwhelmingly supportive of the regime? I argue several points. Surely the professionalism of the Court played a part. As Motala noted, "many South African ideologues consistently assert the South African judiciary is independent and consists of the finest judges to be found anywhere in the world" (1991, 375). Cameron echoed this sentiment: "The South African judiciary can still look to an overall record of professionalism and relative autonomy which few would seek to pass off as discreditable" (1987b, 339).

Even the most severe of the Court's critics would agree that the Appellate Division remained incorruptible and above the possibility of bribery. While other developing countries battle graft at every level, there has never been to my knowledge any charge of explicit corruption directed at the Appellate Division. Its judges were considered professionally ethical and essentially above reproach. Indeed, the contempt charges leveled against Van Niekerk and others were driven in part by the Court's desire to protect its cherished reputation as being above the machinations of other governmental bodies.

Moreover, training in the Western legal tradition grounded the judges in a respect for equality and procedural fairness that would have created individual sympathies for the underdog in such a repressive legal system. Even though apartheid ignored it, the courts remained closely tied to these legal traditions and precedents within their decision making. The widely respected Dutch legal scholar Johannes Voet (1647–1713) noted that "A law has various requisites. In the first place indeed it ought to be just and reasonable—both in its matter, for it prescribes what is honorable and forbids what is base; and in its form, for it preserves equality and binds the citizens equally."[7] Dugard noted the irony of a court that "prides itself on its independence and professes allegiance to the legal traditions of the Western world" while constituting a part of a political order that denies basic rights to the majority of its population (1987, 487).

Under the leadership of Chief Justice Steyn, an effort did emerge to expunge, or at least severely curtail, the British common law influence in South African jurisprudence. The efforts of Chief Justice Steyn and others in the 1950s and 1960s to "purify" South African law from external influences were seen as an attempt to provide more conservative legal traditions in judicial decisions (Cameron 1982). Chief Justice Steyn's voting patterns certainly support a more conservative approach to judging as Mr. Pitje learned too well. However, as Cameron noted, these efforts were largely unsuccessful, and the English law and the Roman-Dutch traditions of equality and substantive fairness continued to affect judicial ideologies.[8]

Thus, judges who respected these concepts and who opposed apartheid abuses would have found sufficient precedent in either previous South African, British or Roman-Dutch precedents to reach conclusions that favored the underdog. The results suggest that as often as not, the Court did just that. While some individual judges did so more than others, the aggregate of the outcomes suggests that the Court was not as obsequious as its critics asserted.

In addition to the legal training emphasizing respect for equality and fairness, legal training imbues judges generally with the ideal of courts as bulwarks against the powerful interests in society. The rules are intended to structure the power game, limiting the powers of some and enhancing the powers of others. Courts are seen as the arbiters to ensure adherence to the rules. The Roman-Dutch law required that individual freedom be protected and only in those instances where Parliament specifically dictated inequality or specifically limited rights would courts sanction such restrictions. Judge Kotzé in 1882 noted that "The court is bound to do equal justice to every individual within the jurisdiction, without regard to color or degree, except where in the particular instance the law expressly provides to the contrary."[9] Of course, this tradition provided little support when eventually the majority of statutes provided "to the contrary," but the courts were perceived as an avenue to pursue justice by other means, and Abel suggested that they were effective respites for some oppositionists (Abel 1995). The results appear to confirm this.

Thus, ultimately, the formal legal training of South African judges may have shaped individual sympathies and respect for equality and fairness. Ironically, it was this same formal legal training that asserted the necessity of adhering to the repressive laws of apartheid.

The Consequences and Possibilities for Courts in Repressive Systems

Hund and Van der Merwe (1986) critiqued the developmental approach to understanding courts and legal outcomes. Their work correctly noted that the ideal types of repressive, formal and responsive law are not progressive stages of legal development that shape legal disputes, but these types overlap. These authors specifically noted the overlapping nature of the repressive and formal law that I have explored in the cases and pages of this analysis. What made South Africa unique was its insistence that the repressive law be encapsulated in the formal law. Similar to the Jim Crow laws of the American segregated South, the divisive nature of the law was recognized and embraced as essential to "civil" society.

Hund and Van der Merwe argued that the tension between the repressive law and the formal law led to bifurcated factions in apartheid South Africa, with one arguing for "racial capitalism" and the other for "revolutionary socialism" (1986, ii). They were pessimistic about Dugard's legal realist approach to judging in which judges would use their discretion to frustrate the repressive law. Hund and Van der Merwe believed the positive law framework—one they embraced as essential to the rule of law—constrained that option. I have argued that judges are constrained by the law, so Hund and Van der Merwe are correct in their pessimism, but judges are politically constrained actors as well, frustrating the capacity of judges who ideologically embrace Dugard's missive.

The results of the analysis of the aggregate of the Appellate Division's behavior suggest that the Court was responding to these tensions. Ironically, the reputation of the Court declined dramatically at the exact same time that the decisions of the Court began to favor the individual more systematically. If public opinion polls on Court support were consistently available throughout the period analyzed, one could empirically evaluate the relationship between declining support for the Court and the Court's decreasing support for the government. Without such data we are left to qualitative analysis that suggests the Court was either responding to its critics or the writing on the wall—or both—as apartheid came to its inevitable end. But such action was too little, too late. The judges were not viewed as either independent or impartial by the majority of the South African population but as appendages of the apartheid regime despite their professionalism.

Hund and Van der Merwe also argued that the questions of substantive fairness and justice raised by the responsive law would remain moot "until South Africa moves away from its repressive-formal law system of governance toward a responsive law model of participatory democracy" (1986, 121). In other words, the repressive law and the formal law of apartheid South Africa could overlap, but the responsive law was an untenable ideal within that context. Indeed the authors asserted that, "The present state of the South African legal system . . . can only bring increasing polarisation and violence"; polarization that they argued would "continue unabated until some catastrophy strikes" (1986, 118, 121). No doubt the authors were surprised, as was much of the world, by the largely peaceful transition to a democratic order. However, consequences followed for the Appellate Division under the new constitutional dispensation.

South Africa transitioned to democracy with the adoption of the Constitution of the Republic of South Africa Act of 1993,[10] which was followed by the passage of the Constitution of the Republic of South Africa Act of 1996.[11] In the new constitutional order, parliamentary action is reviewable, and a new and rather broadly defined set of rights and liberties are justiciable as well. The justiciability of these rights necessarily expands the authority of the courts to resolve conflicts and control social behaviors. The ANC-led regime was reluctant to entrust these questions to a judiciary that remained largely unchanged in the new democratic order. It was not feasible to disband the entire judiciary and appoint new judges, especially when the professional integrity of the bench was well respected. Moreover, few blacks had been allowed the training or experience that would have prepared them for judgeships.

However, expanding the power of the established judiciary also created problems given the critical attitude toward the apartheid legal apparatus. Rather than ceding expanded jurisdiction to the regular courts with the Appellate Division at its apex, the new constitution created a separate court for this responsibility—the Constitutional Court.

The Constitutional Court represents a new structure separate from the old legal system. The new Court lacks the legal baggage that plagued the Appellate Division, which had been responsible for enforcing and applying the statutory edifice of apartheid. The creation of the new Constitutional Court also gave the new majority-led government the capacity to appoint the entire Constitutional Court with individuals perceived to be supportive of its ideals. This was certainly believed to be necessary to enhance the perceived legitimacy of the legal system with the majority black population (Haynie 1997).

In addition, the new constitution creates a Judicial Services Commission (JSC),[12] which submits a list of nominees from which the President will staff the bench. The Commission conducts public "interviews" of potential candidates, similar to the Senate hearings of judicial nominees in the United States. Some judges find the process unsettling. One Appeal Court judge suggested that the hearings provide opportunities for "inquisitions" of judges who served during apartheid for their past judgments. It was argued that some judges would not allow themselves to be nominated for the Constitutional Court to avoid the hearings. It was also suggested that those who "survive" the gauntlet of the JSC are "tagged" as having "passed through the ANC machinery," which destroys the credibility of the individual with the older, more established white legal fraternity (Haynie 1997).[13]

Even with the newly created JSC, the ANC simply could have expanded the jurisdiction of the Appellate Division and used the new appointment process to determine nominees ideologically aligned with the new regime. That, of course, would have taken time, and it would have required that the new majority rest critical decisions with an almost entirely white male bench with a presumed sympathy for the old regime.

The *perception* of the Appellate Division as an appendage of the apartheid state—and a supportive one at that—certainly affected its diminished position in the new constitutional order of the democratic Republic of South Africa. Those judges that espouse the formal law approach to decision making in a repressive legal system face a difficult dilemma if they ultimately prefer the responsive law. If they oppose the repressive regime consistently, they will be punished by it, enhancing the repressive component of the law; if they are perceived to support the repressive regime, they will be punished by the incoming responsive majority.

Conclusion

This analysis suggests that there is a role for courts even within particularly unjust legal systems. As Cameron noted, judges "in the capacity of the system within which they operate [can] play a meaningful constitutional role in curbing executive excesses where these occur" (Cameron 1987b, 340). Certainly this capacity is a restricted and limited one, but discretion inevitably creates within the legal forum the potential to respond politically in politically sensitive situations. While courts in systems with parliamentary sovereignty are not able to challenge the governments in cases that substantively threaten the majority's resolute will, they may elect to use other portions of their docket to respond in a way perceived to be politically beneficial. These results suggest that the South African Appellate Division did just that. Further analysis of courts similarly situated will be necessary to determine if South Africa is the exception to the rule or the case to support it.

Mr. Pitje's battle to gain equal status before judges in apartheid South Africa was affected by the law, the judges and the political and social context in which he brought his challenge. The results suggest that time was a major ally for Mr. Pitje. The repressive law and the formal law are systematically opposed in their objectives. The former exists to ensure domination of a small powerful faction or ideology; the latter emerges to garner confidence more broadly in the legal system. The tension between these two undermines the legitimacy of the regimes that attempt to merge them. In the midst of this tension, the maturing repressive regime can maintain power only by increasing the repressive component of the law. Either the system will collapse or an alternative must emerge. Two alternatives are likely. Either another repressive law regime will emerge that may or may not profess adherence to the formal law, or a responsive law regime will emerge to purge the repressive law from the formal law. Repressive laws and the potential for repressive action within the formal law exist in all systems; however, systems with justiciable rights and liberties increase the role of judges for these systems. Whether the court's decisions apply the law in a manner that supports the regime or limits it is dependent upon the composition of the court and the political and legal context within which the dispute originates. In every system, these decisions can play a significant role in the determination of winners and losers.

For South Africa, the responsive law emerged as the developmental approach predicts it ultimately should. The instability of apartheid became evident and the pressure for social justice and fairness increased, ensuring that Godfrey Pitje would be given equal status in a court of law. Mr. Pitje lost his struggle for equality in 1960, but he went on to distinguish himself in the South African legal profession as an outstanding lawyer. He served prominently as a leader of the ANC in its struggle against apartheid. Before his death in 1997, Godfrey Pitje was able to enter a South African courtroom and stand before a black judge appointed by a black president. These newly appointed judges now stand to evaluate the conflicts arising under the rules of the new democratic order. They will be called upon to effect justice within the parameters of the facts, the law and the discretion available to them in that uniquely individual process that constitutes judging.

APPENDIX A

Logistic Regression Analysis of Outcomes Before the Appellate Division, 1950–1990

The tabular results reported in Chapter 3 suggest that the government enjoyed only a modest advantage in litigation outcomes before the South African Appellate Division. To more rigorously assess this assertion, a multivariate analysis was conducted. The relationship of multiple variables can be explored in this type of statistical analysis. In this case, the model is designed to predict the success of the government in litigation outcomes. Cases in which the government either partially lost or won were excluded. Only those cases in which an appropriate interaction existed were included in the analysis (N = 1,622). These include cases where the government either sued or was sued by a corporation or an individual, and were coded 1 if the government won and 0 otherwise.

Several independent variables were included in the model to determine their relationship to the likelihood of the government's winning. The major issue areas were included as independent variables, coded 1 if the issue was present and 0 otherwise. This assessed the likelihood of the government's winning in certain types of cases, civil rights and liberties for example. Litigant interactions were also included and coded 1 if the interaction was present and 0 otherwise to determine, for example, if the government was more likely to win in cases when it challenged an individual or was challenged by an individual.

A common understanding of the Appellate Division assumed Afrikaans-speaking judges to be more supportive of the government than their English-speaking colleagues, but the results reported in Chapter 3 suggest minimal difference. To test the hypothesis that regime support varied among Afrikaans-speaking and English-speaking judges, a variable was included that measured whether or not the majority opinion writer was Afrikaans-speaking as opposed to English-speaking.

As reported in Table A.1, of the issue variables only one was significantly related;

torts were significantly and negatively related to the government winning. In other words, the presence of a tort case significantly reduced the likelihood of the government's winning. None of the other remaining issue variables was significantly related to the government winning. However, when the government was the respondent, it was significantly more likely to win. When an individual sued the government, the likelihood of government success increased significantly. When the government was sued by a corporation, it had a similar increase in the likelihood of success. Given the general advantage of respondents, this is not surprising. There was no support to the theory that, overall, the home language of the majority opinion writer was related to government support. Afrikaans-speaking majority opinion writers were no more likely than English-speaking majority opinion writers to favor the government. The model is highly significant and correctly predicts 61.4% of cases, a modest increase over the modal category at 57.5%. The results do not suggest a significant overall advantage for the government across issue categories or litigant interactions.

TABLE A.1
Regression Coefficients for Pro-Government Decisions

Variable	B	Std. Error	R
Intercept	−0.044	0.272	—
Criminal	−0.199	0.272	—
Civil Rights	−0.126	0.439	—
Public Law	−0.158	0.260	—
Torts	−0.722	0.345*	.03
Procedural	−0.052	0.504	—
Individual v. Government	0.780	0.215**	.07
Corporation v. Government	0.813	0.235**	.07
Government v. Individual	−0.094	0.227	—
Afrikaans Opinion Writer	−0.068	0.104	—

N = 1,615
−2 Log Likelihood = 2144.91
Model χ^2 = 56.65**
*$p < .05$, two-tailed; **$p < .01$, two-tailed

APPENDIX B

Codebook for the South African Data Set

CODER ID	Record your 2 digit code
COURT	50 = South Africa
CITATION	Year-volume-page (e.g., 9020441=1990 volume 2, page 441)
DATE	Decision Date–yymmdd (e.g., March 20, 1945 = 450320)
PROV INITIAL	The province in which the case was initially heard. Use the attached list.
PROV SOURCE	The province immediately below from which this case came. Use the attached list.
AFRIKAANS	Was the majority opinion written in Afrikaans? 1 = Yes 0 = No
APPELLANT	Code first appellant as listed in the title of the case using attached codes. All other codes are applicable to the first applicant only in cases with multiple appellants.
RESPONDENT	See appellant codes and directions.
TREATMENT	Treatment of the decision of the court (or agency) below: 0 = Review denied 1 = Affirmed, dismissed 2 = Affirmed in part & reversed in part (or modified or modified and affirmed) 3 = Reversed or vacated or remanded

	4 = Standing, venue or jurisdiction not addressed below
	5 = Advisory opinion issued
	6 = Granted motion/appeal/delay/without ruling and/or discussion on/of merits
	7 = Original jurisdiction; ruled on merits
	8 = Unable to determine
	9 = Certification to another court
WINNER	1 = Appellant
	2 = Appellant won in part and lost in part
	3 = Respondent
	4 = Other (e.g., intervener who was not originally a party to the suit)
	5 = Not ascertained
MAJORITY VOTES	(Include those who concur in result even if not with the majority opinion.)
DISSENT	Number of dissents (include partial dissents)
	0 = Unanimous
ISSUE	See attached list.

Note: In general, code the most important issue as the one about which the majority of the opinion is focused.

DIRECTIONALITY	See attached directionality specifications for details for each issue
	0 = Not ascertained
	1 = Supports the upperdog
	2 = Mixed (e.g., most decisions which affirm in part and reverse in part)
	3 = Supports the underdog
CRIMINAL ISSUE	0 = Not applicable (not a criminal case)
	1 = Murder (e.g., first or second degree murder)
	2 = Other unlawful killing (e.g., negligent homicide)
	3 = Rape
	4 = Other crimes of violence against persons (assault, child abuse, armed robbery, etc.)
	5 = Property crimes—felonies

      6 = Property crimes—minor

      7 = Crimes against public morality (liquor, narcotics, obscenity, disorderly conduct, gambling)

      8 = Business regulation & license violations

      9 = Government corruption or attempts to corrupt government officials

      10 = Political crimes (rebellion, subversion, sedition, illegal participation in political activities or demonstrations)

      11 = Perjury, contempt

      12 = Unknown

      13 = Income or business tax crimes

      15 = Criminal defamation/slander

      16 = Draft evasion

      17 = Violation of Group Areas Act or other race statute

      20 = Other

Note: If there are multiple crimes, code the offense that is the most severe.

JUDGE CODES   Record the five digit code for each judge who participated in the case. See separate list of judge codes. The first judge coded for the opinion (CODEJ1) should always be the code for the judge who wrote the majority opinion.

VOTES OF JUDGES

FIRST DIGIT: 1 = Wrote majority opinion (note: An "opinion" must have some minimal statement of a reason for the position taken, but it need not be more than a few sentences.)

      2 = Joined majority (Includes those who agree with the majority opinion and do not write a separate opinion.)

      3 = Wrote concurring opinion

      4 = Joined concurring opinion

      5 = Wrote dissenting opinion

      6 = Joined dissenting opinion

      7 = Dissented without opinion

8 = Joined *per curiam* opinion/judgement of the court

9 = Unable to determine

SECOND DIGIT: Directionality of vote (See codes for each issue below.)

Directionality of Decisions and Votes

Note: For all issues, use a "2" when the decision supports both sides in part. Use a "0" when the ideological direction of the decision cannot be ascertained.

Criminal issues:

3 = For position of the defendant

1 = For government

Civil rights :

3 = For position of person alleging a civil rights violation

1 = Opposite

Freedom of expression & religion:

3 = For position of person alleging a violation of rights of expression and religion

1 = Opposite

Private economic relationships:

3 = For the economic underdog if one of the parties is clearly an economic underdog compared to the other

1 = For upperdog

(Code as 0 if no clear underdog.)

Torts:

3 = For the injured party

1 = For party allegedly causing the injury

Copyrights, patents, trademarks:

3 = For the economic underdog

1 = Opposite

(Code as 0 if no clear underdog.)

Public law (except for public employment and government benefits):

    3 = For the government

    1 = Opposite

Apartheid related issues:

    3 = Against government regulation of the races

    1 = For government regulation of the races

Public employment & benefits:

    3 = For employee or the recipient of benefits

    1 = For government

Family:

    3 = For the economic underdog

    1 = Opposite

    (Code as 0 if no clear underdog.)

Appellant and Respondent Codes

Note: All codes are 4 digits. If there are multiple appellants or respondents, code the first appellant/respondent.

    7000 = Natural person

    1000 = Private business

    2000 = Business or trade association, professional association, political organizations, co-operatives, educational or religious schools or organizations, or civil, social, fraternal or charitable organizations

    2100 = Union

    3100 = All federal agencies and officials

    4100 = City/town government or agency

    4500 = Other unit of substate government

    5100 = All provincial agencies and officials; includes administrators of provinces

    5200 = All tribal authorities/tribes

    6100 = All independent territories

    9999 = Missing or ex parte/no respondent involved

Codes for Province of Immediate and Initial Origin

4000	Appellate Division Original Jurisdiction
2500	Northern Cape Division
2510	Cape Provincial Division
2520	Transvaal Provincial Division
2530	Eastern Cape Division
2540	Orange Free State Provincial Division
2550	Natal Provincial Division
2570	South West Africa Division
2580	Rhodesia High Court
9990	Other

Administrative/bureaucratic agencies/specialized courts

3591	Commissioner for Inland Revenue
3514	Minister of Justice
3501	Minister of Defense
3592	Minister of Labor
3594	Commissioner of Customs & Excise
6598	Court of the Commissioner of Patents
3599	Administrative agencies/councils/boards/officers
6590	Special Income Tax Court
6599	Other specialized courts
9999	Undetermined

Issue Codes

Criminal

100	Interpretation of criminal statute
101	Confession, incriminating statement
102	Admissibility of evidence (includes search & seizure)
104	Right to counsel or adequacy of counsel

105	Jury-related issue (e.g., instructions to jury, composition of jury)
106	Admissibility of testimony, prejudicial remark at trial; includes refusal to testify; swearing-in of interpreter; no cross-examination allowed; forcing to testify
107	Challenge to death penalty; what constitutes mitigating circumstances; if reduced to life sentence, code directionality 3
108	Other challenge to sentence; if overturned code directionality 3; if reduced code directionality 2
109	Sufficiency of evidence
110	Other criminal issue; includes challenges to indictments and charge sheets; double jeopardy
111	Crimes of military personnel
199	Unclear criminal issue

Note: For criminal prosecution of race statute violations, code criminal issue 17; do not code 617

Civil Rights

201	Civil rights claims by prisoners (does not include challenges to their sentences or to the legality of their confinement; includes claims of cruel and unusual punishment while in prison)
202	Voting rights
211	Race, ethnic discrimination alleged by white
212	Discrimination based on religion or nationality
220	Gender discrimination alleged by a woman
221	Gender discrimination alleged by a man
230	Age discrimination or rights of handicapped
240	Civil rights of juveniles
250	Suspension of right of *habeas corpus*
260	Privacy rights (including abortion, birth control)
290	Other civil rights; includes rights of squatters
296	Unlawful detention

Freedom of Expression and Association

310	Commercial speech or regulation of advertising (if opposed on freedom of expression grounds)
320	Libel or slander, defamation
330	Freedom of religion
340	Obscenity, expression offending standards of decency
350	Freedom of press (includes open meeting law questions)
360	Freedom of association
370	Expressive conduct (e.g., picketing, parades, demonstrations, sit-ins, canvassing–directed at achieving racial equality)
371	Expressive conduct–protesting war or military policy or the draft
372	Other expressive conduct
380	Other rights of expression or association

Private Economic Relations

401	Debt collection; insolvency cases; actions to collect on or repossess property involving mortgages, credit purchases, etc.; debt surety disputes
402	Insurance disputes
403	Other contract disputes; includes options to purchase real property disputes
410	Disputes over real property; includes questions over servitude and water rights
411	Landlord–tenant disputes
415	Patents, copyright and trademarks
420	Corporate law–disputes over control or mismanagement of corporations; stockholders' and creditors' rights
430	Labor relations (in private business); includes disputes between unions
435	Workers' compensation

440	Other; includes challenges between private parties to government granting of licenses, etc.; challenges for costs of lawsuits, awards

Torts–Various claims for "damages"

510	Motor vehicle accidents
520	Injured workers
530	Medical or legal malpractice
540	Government tort liability
550	Other personal injury (includes product liability)
560	Civil suits for police misconduct
590	Other torts

Public Law

610	Government health & safety regulation
611	Government environmental regulation
612	Government regulation of power and natural resources; includes water rights disputes
613	Other government regulation of business
614	Government regulation of land use (includes eminent domain and condemnation); and mineral rights; if Group Areas Act involved, code as 617
617	Government regulation of races
620	Taxation
630	Abuse of governmental authority (other than those in 610–620 or topics included in the civil rights or tort categories above)
631	Territorial boundary disputes
640	Public employment
650	Immigration, deportation, citizenship, passport disputes
660	Disputes over public office; challenges to elections, removals from office

670	Disputes between different units of government
671	Challenges between independent states and the national government
675	Challenge to judge action
680	Disputes over government benefit programs (e.g., welfare, unemployment compensation, government medical benefits; workers' compensation)
690	Other public law

Family and Estates

710	Divorce, child custody disputes
720	Inheritance, probate disputes
730	Other family law disputes

Procedural and Other

800	Only procedural or threshold issues decided by the court (e.g., if court has jurisdiction to hear the dispute)
900	Other issue or unable to classify
910	Attorney or judge discipline; includes those by law societies

Codes for Judges of South Africa

50001	Watermeyer, E. F.
50002	Centlivres, Albert van der Sandt
50003	Greenberg, Leopold
50004	Schreiner, Oliver Deneys
50005	Van den Heever, Francis Petrus
50006	Hoexter, Oscar
50007	Fagan, Henry Allen
50008	Murray, John Murray
50009	Ramsbottom, William Henry
50010	Steyn, L. C.
50011	De Beer, Edmund Maree

50012	Beyers, David Otto Kellnet
50013	Malan, Alfred Christo
50014	Van Blerk, P. J.
50015	Hall, Cyril Godfrey
50016	Price, Justice Norman
50017	Ogilvie Thompson, Newton
50018	Reynolds, Frederick George
50019	Smit, A. J.
50020	Rumpff, Frans Herman Lourens
50021	Botha, D. H.
50022	Holmes, George Neville
50023	Van Winsen, Louis de Villiers
50024	Van Wyk, Jacques Theodore
50025	Williamson, Arthur Faure
50026	Wessels, Petrus Johannes
50027	Potgieter, Hendrik Johannes
50028	Trollip, William Grey
50029	Miller, Solomon
50030	Rabie, Pieter Jacobus
50032	De Villiers, H. H. W.
50033	Muller, Gerhardus van Rhyn
50034	Jansen, E. L.
50035	Corbett, Michael McGregor
50036	Hofmeyr, Servass
50037	Van Zijl, Jacobus Wilhelmus
50038	Klopper, Hendrik Willem Olivier
50039	Joubert, C. P.
50040	Muller, W. G.
50041	Kotze, Gerhardus Petrus
50042	Trengove, John James
50043	Diemont, Marius Anne
50044	Smalberger, Johan Wilhelm
50046	Hoexter, G. G.

50047	Viljoen, Gerrit van Niekerk
50048	Galgut, Oscar
50049	Cillie, Petrus Malan
50050	Van Heerden, H. J. O.
50051	Smuts, Francis Sleigh
50052	Nicholas, Herbert Cecil
50053	Hefer, J. J. F.
50054	Jacobs, Hendrik Rudolf
50055	Grosskopf, Frans Heinrich
50056	Boshoff, Wessel Groenewald
50057	Nestadt, H. H.
50059	Eloff, Christoffel Frederik
50060	Nienaber, Petrus Millar
50061	Vivier, Werner
50062	Friedman, Gerald
50063	Milne, Alexander John
50064	Goldstone, Richard Joseph
50065	Kumleben, Mark Ernest
50066	Steyn, M. T.
50067	Eksteen, Johannes Paulus
50068	Grosskopf, E. M.
50069	Preiss, H. J.
50070	Botha, A. S.
50071	De Villiers, Jacob Nicolaas Carel
50072	Newton-Thompson, C.
50073	Jennett, A. G.
50074	Brink, C. P.
50075	Dowling, W.
50078	Howard, J. A.
50079	James, N.
50080	Marais, J. F.
50085	Beyers, A. B.
50086	Bekker, S.

APPENDIX C

Reliability Estimates for the South African Data Set*

Province of Initial Origin

    Pearson Correlation   .941
    Kendal's Tau b   .951
    Spearman's rho   .955

Province of Immediate Origin

    Pearson Correlation   .993
    Kendal's Tau b   .940
    Spearman's rho   .950

Majority Opinion in Afrikaans

    Pearson Correlation   .984
    Kendal's Tau b   .984
    Spearman's rho   .984

Appellant

    Pearson Correlation   .982
    Kendal's Tau b   .982
    Spearman's rho   .982

Respondent

    Pearson Correlation   .963
    Kendal's Tau b   .963
    Spearman's rho   .964

Treatment

    Pearson Correlation   .972
    Kendal's Tau b   .959
    Spearman's rho   .964

Outcome for Appellant

    Pearson Correlation   .993
    Kendal's Tau b   .986
    Spearman's rho   .991

Number of Votes in Majority

    Pearson Correlation   .964
    Kendal's Tau b   .958
    Spearman's rho   .963

Number of Votes in Dissent

    Pearson Correlation   .922
    Kendal's Tau b   .936
    Spearman's rho   .940

Issue

    Pearson Correlation   .971
    Kendal's Tau b   .972
    Spearman's rho   .972

Directionality

    Pearson Correlation   .973
    Kendal's Tau b   .964
    Spearman's rho   .967

Criminal Offense

    Pearson Correlation   .982
    Kendal's Tau b   .978
    Spearman's rho   .991

Code of First Judge

    Pearson Correlation   .999
    Kendal's Tau b   .997
    Spearman's rho   .999

Vote of First Judge

    Pearson Correlation   .971
    Kendal's Tau b   .968
    Spearman's rho   .979

Code of Second Judge

    Pearson Correlation   .999
    Kendal's Tau b   .994
    Spearman's rho   .998

Vote of Second Judge

    Pearson Correlation   .959
    Kendal's Tau b   .905
    Spearman's rho   .908

Code of Third Judge

    Pearson Correlation   1.00
    Kendal's Tau b   1.00
    Spearman's rho   1.00

Vote of Third Judge

    Pearson Correlation   .992
    Kendal's Tau b   .960
    Spearman's rho   .963

Code of Fourth Judge

    Pearson Correlation   .987
    Kendal's Tau b   .986
    Spearman's rho   .996

Vote of Fourth Judge

    Pearson Correlation   .943
    Kendal's Tau b   .952
    Spearman's rho   .961

Code of Fifth Judge

    Pearson Correlation   .997
    Kendal's Tau b   .991
    Spearman's rho   .998

Vote of Fifth Judge

    Pearson Correlation   .998
    Kendal's Tau b   .964
    Spearman's rho   .954

*All are significant at the .01 level.

APPENDIX D

Measurement of Judicial Ideology

In his seminal analysis of the United States Supreme Court, Pritchett (1948) evaluated the voting patterns of members of the United States Supreme Court. Pritchett established a schema that has been emulated by judicial behavioralists since. This schema was based on the premise that an underlying liberal to conservative continuum exists in the voting patterns of judges. Specifically, Pritchett statistically assessed the existence of certain blocs or groups within the Court that he argued fell into liberal and conservative categories. Subsequently, Schubert (1965, 1974, 1977, 1980) argued that certain issues stimulate responses that vary according to individual preferences. The more libertarian, egalitarian judge will favor the party in each case that is broadly understood to represent the "underdog" in legal disputes. The underdog typically is the less powerful while the upperdog tends to represent the powerful or the status quo. Subsequent analyses adapting this methodology have resulted in a standard approach to voting behavior studies (Spaeth 1961, 1963; Rohde and Spaeth 1976; Segal and Cover 1989; Segal and Spaeth 1993, 2002; Spaeth 1994, 1995, 1998; Segal, Epstein, Cameron and Spaeth 1995). For an extensive evaluation of the literature, see Baum (1997).

Evaluation of the support for upperdogs and underdogs is typically divided between civil rights and liberties disputes, including criminal cases, and economics disputes between the government and businesses or between individuals and businesses.

For civil rights and liberties disputes, the classic examples of underdogs are those who challenge governmental limitations of civil rights and liberties. If the judge supports the rights of the individual and the limitation of the governmental power to limit civil rights and liberties, that is considered to support the underdog. If the judge hears 10 disputes involving civil rights and liberties and favors the underdog in 6 of these disputes, he or she is said to be voting liberally in 60% of the cases involving civil rights and liberties.

For economics disputes, businesses are considered to be the upperdog in cases where the government attempts to regulate business in the interest of the public good. This can include regulation of wages, hours and workplace safety. This can also include regulation of the environment or other natural resources. The coding scheme was derived from the inability of the government to successfully regulate businesses during President Roosevelt's New Deal given the pervasive *laissez-faire* approach to the economy. The Court's subsequent capitulation and support of the government's over businesses' interests was considered a liberal reversal. Thus, if the judge supports businesses' capacity to operate without government intervention in 6 of 10 public law disputes, these are considered conservative votes, and the judge would be said to vote conservatively in 60% of cases.

There are some caveats to this coding. First, there are certain issues that do not fit neatly in the categories above but are presumed to have underlying upperdog/underdog dimensions. For example, if the government is attempting to limit employee benefits, this is an economic case where the individual employee would be considered the underdog. Similarly, if a party is alleging a harm or injury in a tort case, the party demanding compensation is considered the underdog and a vote for the party alleging injury is considered a liberal vote.

Second, there are some issues in which there is no underlying upperdog/underdog dimension. These would include disputes between different government agencies. These could include disputes between two large corporations over contract disputes. Probate and family law issues do not contain inherent upperdogs and underdogs. However, there may be cases, divorce, for example, where one party is clearly the upperdog in the dispute. Only when clearly defined upperdogs and underdogs exist in the case will a liberal or conservative vote be coded.

Third, South Africa represents a particularly unique coding dilemma. Any support for the apartheid government coded as pro-underdog is obviously problematic. In all cases involving government regulation of race, opposition to the government was coded as pro-underdog. The government regulated businesses to ensure white superiority. To code support for this as pro-underdog underlies the entire theoretical premise of categorizing votes on a liberal/conservative continuum. As a result in public law regulation, all but cases involving regulation of health and the environment were excluded in the calculation of overall voting records.

Fourth, this measure is limited in its utility. This measure allows only the crudest of comparisons across judges. It in no way evaluates the opinion or doctrine established. Thus the Appellate Division's decision in the Magopa case was coded as pro-underdog since the Magopa were the clear underdogs in the dispute, but the decision provided no relief to the tribe. The measure is also limited when there are very few disputes decided by the judge. Small numbers of votes allow for distortion. Only in those cases where judges participated in a sufficient number of cases can scholars make substantive inferences from the patterns. While I used 5 votes as the minimum number for inclusion in analyses, this number was clearly an arbitrary choice. See Appendix B for the specific coding instructions provided to the coders.

Despite its limitations, adapting this schema is useful because it allows systematic comparison across countries. Its use for over 50 years in judicial behavioral studies attests to its acceptance as a methodology. It is also replicable. This coding scheme can be adapted to a broad range of courts and dispute resolution processes. Moreover, the results are reliable according to the reliability measures reported in Appendix C.

Notes

Chapter One

1. Mr. Pitje served as an "articled clerk," a requirement for qualifying as an attorney.
2. *R. v. Pitje* 1960 (4) SA 709 (A) at 711.
3. Chief Justice Steyn was elevated over the more senior Judge Schreiner. Judge Schreiner alone had dissented in *Collins v. Minister of the Interior* 1957 (1) SA 552 (A), the "Senate-packing" case (see Chapter 2). Moreover, Judge Schreiner emphasized English precedent and tradition in his decisions. Chief Justice Steyn was to lead the charge of the Roman-Dutch purists who would ignore English law as an interpretive force and focus on South Africa's Roman-Dutch legal heritage (Dugard 1978, 287; Cameron 1982).
4. 1960 (4) SA 709 (A) at 710.
5. 1960 (4) SA 709 (A) at 710.
6. 1960 (4) SA 709 (A) at 711.
7. Had the contempt citation not followed so swiftly, Mr. Pitje, like Mr. Tambo before him, would have resigned from the case rather than move to the "non-European" table. Mr. Pitje's conceding this was considered evidence of his "deliberate and premeditated" contempt (*R. v. Pitje* 1960 (4) SA 709 (A) at 712).
8. A number of the courts did not separate. Judge President Beyers of the Cape High Court in the mid-1960s angrily rejected a government department's attempt to segregate the Cape High Court.
9. It is interesting to note that the Appellate Division examined the concept of a "court of law" in *Minister of the Interior v. Harris* 1952 (4) SA 769 (A), and found that the "High Court of Parliament" was in substance not a true court. The case is discussed more fully in Chapter 2.
10. Much of the discussion that follows is derived from Shapiro's approach to understanding the role and function of courts (Shapiro 1981).
11. Constitution of the Republic of South Africa Act 200 of 1993.
12. *President of the Republic of South Africa and Others v. South African Rugby Football Union and Others* 1999 (4) SA 146 (CC) at 185.
13. *President of the Republic of South Africa and Others v. South African Rugby Football Union and Others* 1999 (4) SA 146 (CC) at 186.
14. *President of the Republic of South Africa and Others v. South African Rugby Football Union and Others* 1999 (4) SA 146 (CC) at 187. See also Judge Cameron's opinion in *South African*

Commercial Catering and Allied Workers Union and others v. Irvin and Johnson Limited 2000 (3) SA 705 (CC).
15. See Dahl's classic thesis (1957) on the underlying power of majority preferences to influence the judiciary.
16. Nonet and Selznick (1978) referred to the second stage of the development of the law as "Autonomous Law" (see Chapter 3). I have adopted the verbiage of Hund and Van der Merwe, whose ideal types are more specifically formulated for the South African system. Much of the legal debate, as will be demonstrated below, has focused on the judiciary's, as well as the legal educational establishment's, emphasis on the formal law or the positivist approach to legal reasoning. Nonetheless, both sets of authors focused on similar criteria in their definitions of the autonomous or formal law stage.
17. See, of course, Weschler's classic assertion of neutral principles guiding the legal reasoning of judges (Weschler 1959).
18. The authors subsequently discussed the potential of responsive law to emerge in apartheid South Africa.
19. Of course, it should also be noted that economic pressures worked against South Africa's apartheid policy as many nations imposed economic sanctions such as trade and investment embargoes because of the apartheid policies.
20. This is not to suggest that racial discrimination did not exist in South Africa prior to the National Party's apartheid platform. Differential treatment on the basis of race was always a factor in South African politics since the establishment of the first white settlement in 1652.
21. *In re Dube* 1979 (3) 820 (N).
22. The Bantu Urban Areas Consolidation Act 25 of 1945 defined an "idle person" as one older than fifteen and younger than sixty-five who was capable of employment but had been unemployed for 122 days in the previous year. Exceptions were made for education and "other approved" activities. The commissioner in Dube's case had given him a 30-day reprieve to look for work.
23. *In re Dube* 1979 (3) 820 (N) at 821.
24. Dugard argued that the South African judiciary should abandon the "inarticulate premise" of positivism and embrace the "realism" of judicial policy making. He argued that after doing so, the apartheid-era courts should return to their Roman-Dutch heritage, stressing fundamental protection of individual rights and liberties through "realist-cum-natural-law" judicial reasoning. This approach to judicial decision making would create a "natural-law, value-oriented approach" to the legal process that would have expanded the capacity of the judiciary to protect human rights. He essentially argued for progression to progressive or responsive law.
25. The Group Areas Act 41 of 1950 (consolidated in Act 77 of 1957 and Act 36 of 1966) controlled the ownership and occupation of all of the land in South Africa.
26. As a cautionary note, Chief Justice Corbett specifically was addressing judging in private law issues, not the public law issues of this discussion. I am assuming he would offer similar instructions.
27. *In re Dube* 1979 (3) 820 (N) at 822.
28. As Etienne Mureinik argued "If we . . . argue that moral judges should resign, we can no longer pray, when we go into court as defence counsel, or even as the accused, that we find a moral judge on the Bench" (quoted in Dyzenhaus 1998, 57).
29. It must be noted that apartheid-related cases and other cases, for example, pass laws versus family law disputes, are not so easily delineated. After all, the "family" was a defined unit in South Africa in which the races legally could not be intertwined. The permeation of race within the legal structure was pervasive and complex, but overt apartheid statutes such as Mr. Dube's are clearly different from tort cases involving a motor vehicle accident. Nonetheless, the roads on which blacks

and whites could traverse leading to the accident were determined by statute. Even the damages awarded were differentiated on the basis of race (see *Radebe v. Hough* 1949 (1) SA (A) 380).
30. Beginning in 1950 Appellate Division decisions were no longer appealable to the British Judicial Committee of the Privy Council making it a logical starting date for analysis. Moreover, the two-year delay following the election of the National Party allows sufficient time for the appeals of the new regime to reach the Appellate Division. By 1990, the decline of apartheid and the National Party regime was evident. Many mark De Klerk's February 2, 1990, speech as the official beginning of the end of the apartheid order.

Chapter Two

1. See for example Saunders 1988, Smith 1988 and Worden 1993 for discussions of changing historical perspectives.
2. Du Plessis and Du Plessis refer to these collectively as South African "common law," but this should not be confused with the British common law, which was not similarly influenced by Roman law (1995:16–46).
3. Sachs (1973, 17) noted that the zebra was removed on Sundays for services held in the same illustrious venue.
4. Slaves were imported from all of the areas in which the Dutch East India Company traded as well as from West Africa (Sachs 1973, 20; Worden 1985, 8).
5. "Hottentots" refers to the Khoikhoi population.
6. The term "coloured" in South Africa refers to individuals of mixed race, and I replicate its use here. There is no intended derogation.
7. Eight members were nominated by the Governor-General, and eight were to be elected based on proportional representation from each of the four provinces (Barber 1999, 56).
8. Representation was as follows: 51 from the Cape, 36 from the Transvaal, 17 from Natal, and 17 from the Orange Free State (Barber 1999, 56).
9. Any man who earned 50 pounds annually or possessed property outside communal land in the African reserves worth 75 pounds technically could vote (Thompson 1990, 150).
10. Constitution Act 32 of 1961.
11. Forsyth (1985, 7) noted that the formal law technically required a quorum of four judges from the decision of two or more judges, but these cases were heard by panels of five. There are no examples of four-panel decisions in the data analyzed here. Forsyth noted some exceptions to the quorum rules adopted by the Court. Requests for the Court to sit outside of Bloemfontein were to be heard by the Chief Justice and two Appeal Court judges; appeals from special criminal courts were to be heard by five-judge benches; and petitions for leave to appeal were to be heard by the Chief Justice and/or other Appeal Court judges as he may appoint (sections 4; 12 (1) (1) (a) (5); 21 (3) of the Supreme Court Act 59 of 1959).
12. As a splinter from the South African Party, the National Party, formed in 1914 under the direction of J. B. M. Hertzog, represented the more nationalist Afrikaner sentiment (Barber 1999, 59–64).
13. Bantu Land Act 27 of 1913.
14. Immorality Act 5 of 1927.
15. Immorality Amendment Act 21 of 1950.
16. Prohibition of Mixed Marriages Act 55 of 1949.
17. White women were officially granted the franchise in 1930 (Women's Enfranchisement Act 18 of 1930).
18. *Kruse v. Johnson* (1898) 2 QB 91. Lord Russell establishes the rule of the "benevolent interpretation" of by-laws created by those in appropriate positions of the delegated parliamentary

authority. By-laws are deemed "unreasonable"when they are found "to be partial and unequal," "manifestly unjust," "disclosed bad faith," contain "oppressive or gratuitous interference" with the rights of the individuals involved, or had "no justification in the minds of reasonable men." If the by-law contained any of these flaws, the statute, and later for South African courts, the administrative action, was considered beyond the intentions of Parliament (at 99–100).

19. *R. v. Abdurahman* 1950 (3) SA 136 (A); *Tayob v. Ermelo Local Road Transportation Board* 1951 (4) SA 440 (A); *R. v. Lusu* 1953 (2) SA 484 (A). In the *Abdurahman* case the Court overturned a conviction of a non-European's use of the European first-class section of a rail car because the railways administration had failed to create a first-class section for non-Europeans. The Court, somewhat incredulously, ruled that Parliament could not have intended to mete out partial or unequal treatment. The Court similarly set aside a conviction in *Lusu* where a non-European waiting room had not been provided. In *Tayob* the Court overruled the refusal to grant a taxi-cab license to an Asian because of his race.
20. Act 49 of 1953.
21. Act 46 of 1951.
22. 1952 (2) SA 428 (A).
23. Act 35 of 1952.
24. 1952 (4) SA 769 (A).
25. 1952 (4) SA 769 (A) at 784.
26. Appellate Division Quorum Act 27 of 1955. In the 3,044 cases included in this analysis, the Court sat *en banc* in only three cases. The passage of the Supreme Court Act 59 of 1959 further altered the quorum requirements enabling quorums of three for some cases. Forsyth noted some exceptions to the quorum rules of the Court. See Forsyth (1985, 7 footnote 39).
27. Senate Act 53 of 1955.
28. The constitutional crisis of the 1950s had another significant impact on the legal system. The increasing numbers of Afrikaners on the bench began to pursue the National Party's prong of strengthening the Afrikaner roots of the South African Republic. Within the legal community and the bench, a "purge" of the British legal influence was pursued zealously by some.
29. 1957 (1) SA 552 (A).
30. The lone dissent of Schreiner is presumed by some to have contributed to his subsequently losing the Chief Justiceship to L. C. Steyn (Cameron 1982, 41–42).
31. Act 30 of 1950.
32. All individuals in South Africa were classified according to the Act into three broad categories: "white," "Bantu" or African, and "coloured" which included people of mixed race, Indians, Chinese and other Asians. However, Indians were considered by many South Africans as a separate group though not legally specified as such under the Act (Higginbotham 1990, 491).
33. Dugard (1978, 75) noted that pass laws in South Africa can be dated back to 1809. The 1952 act referred to here expanded the laws to include all blacks over the age of sixteen. It was ironically entitled the Native Abolition of Passes and Co-ordination of Documents Act 57 of 1952.
34. Act 27 of 1913.
35. Act 18 of 1936.
36. Act 41 of 1950. The statute was consolidated in Act 77 of 1957 and Act 36 of 1966.
37. Native (Urban Areas) Consolidation Act 25 of 1945 along with the Native Laws Amendment Act 54 of 1952 were passed to enforce segregation of the urban populations (Unterhalter 1987, 62).
38. Act 47 of 1953 amended by the Reservation of Separate Amenities Amendment Act 10 of 1960.
39. Act 45 of 1959.

40. According to the Surplus People Project, it is estimated that 3,548,900 blacks were removed from designated white areas between 1960 and 1983 (Thompson 1990, 194).
41. Act 25 of 1945 was substantially amended in 1952.
42. Act 49 of 1953; Section 1 of Act 10 of 1960.
43. Act 44 of 1950.
44. Prohibition of Political Interference Act 51 of 1968.
45. The African-centered Pan-Africanist Congress (PAC) was formed in 1959 as a splinter group of the ANC. The PAC envisioned an Africa for Africans–though "Africans" were defined by Robert Sobukwe, its initial chairman, as "everybody who owes his loyalty to Africa" (Davenport and Saunders 2000, 412).
46. The National Action Council was comprised of delegates drawn from the ANC, the South African Indian Congress, the South African Congress of Democrats, and the South African Coloured People's Organisation (later renamed Coloured People's Congress).
47. Mezerik (1964, 2) noted that "the Sharpeville killings marked a watershed for apartheid. The incident provoked an increase in the intensity of world condemnation of South Africa's racial policies."
48. Three statutes provided tremendous discretion to the executive to severely restrict an individual's movement and interaction with other people. These included the Bantu Administration Act 38 of 1927, the Internal Security Act 44 of 1950 and the Riotous Assemblies Act 17 of 1956.
49. Act 32 of 1961.
50. Section 59, Act 32 of 1961.
51. Created by the Bantu Self-Government Act 46 of 1959 with its amendments in 1970 (Bantu Homelands Citizenship Act 26) and 1971 (Bantu Homelands Constitution Act 21), the ten homelands were Gazankulu, KaNgwane, Kwa-Ndebele, KwaZulu, Lebowa, Qwaqwa, Ciskei, Bophuthatswana, Transkei and Venda. The latter four eventually were granted "independent homeland" status, though they were never fully independent of the South African Parliament (Dugard 1992, 10–13; Davenport and Saunders 2000, 478).
52. Constitution Act 110 of 1983.
53. Black Local Authorities Act 102 of 1982.
54. The Constitution Act of 1983 formally merged the previous symbolic State President with the true leader, the Prime Minister, to one premier referred to as the State President.
55. Immorality and Prohibition of Mixed Marriages Amendment Act 72 of 1985.
56. Abolition of Influx Control Act 68 of 1986.
57. Industrial Conciliation Amendment Act 94 of 1979 and Labor Relations Amendment Act 57 of 1981.
58. Discriminatory Legislation Regarding Public Amenities Act 100 of 1990.
59. Universities Amendment Act 83 of 1983.
60. Free Settlement Areas Act 102 of 1988.
61. De Klerk also lifted restrictions on the United Democratic Front, which had emerged in 1983 as a multi-racial opposition party to the National Party. Some 31 other organizations' bans were also lifted (Dugard, Haysom and Marcus 1992, 243).
62. Constitution of the Republic of South Africa Act 108 of 1996.
63. Judge Cameron noted before the Truth and Reconciliation Commission, "It is true that formal apartheid has been abolished. But we still live in a society characterised by extreme disparities of wealth and power. Our social system is democratic, and its political institutions now, fortunately, representative. But we live in a society still distinguished by extremes of dispossession. As a judge who proudly holds office under the Constitution of the Republic of

South Africa, I am nevertheless party to the injustices that still exist in our society; and my role in the enforcement of a system that contains injustices necessarily makes me complicit in them" (Cameron Submission to the Truth and Reconciliation Commission, page 3).
64. *Radebe v. Hough* 1949 (1) SA 380 (A).

Chapter Three

1. *Hurley and Another v. Minister of Law and Order* 1985 (4) SA 709 (D) at 710.
2. Act 74 of 1982.
3. Among these were the 90-day clause or Section 17 of the General Law Amendment Act 37 of 1963 and its extension, the 180-day detention clause (Section 7 of the Criminal Procedure Amendment Act of 96 of 1965). Under both statutes, no one could have access to the individual without the express consent of the Minister of Justice other than the magistrate who was required to visit the detainee weekly. The individual could be interrogated at will without access to counsel. The 180-day detention clause included an ouster phrase similar to Section 29: "No court shall have jurisdiction to order the release from custody of any person detained under [the statute]." Section 6 of the Terrorism Act 83 of 1967 allowed indefinite detention of suspected terrorists at the discretion of a senior police official. Dugard suggested that South Africa became a "police state" during the years of 1966–1978 with "uncontrolled powers vested in the police force" (1992, 22).
4. Internal Security Act 74 of 1982, Section 29 (6).
5. Internal Security Act 74 of 1982, Section 29 (1).
6. *Hurley and Another v. Minister of Law and Order* 1985 (4) SA 709 (D) at 711.
7. *Loza v. Police Station Commander* 1964 (2) SA 545 (A).
8. *Rossouw v. Sachs* 1964 (2) SA 551 (A).
9. *Schermbrucker v. Klindt NO* 1965 (4) SA 606 (A).
10. *Hurley and Another v. Minister of Law and Order* 1985 (4) SA 709 (D).
11. *Minister of Law and Order and Others v. Hurley and Another* 1986 (3) SA 568 (A).
12. 1987 (3) SA 859 (A). This case was decided along with *Fani and Others v. Minister of Law and Order and Others* and *State President and Others v. Bill*.
13. Act 3 of 1953.
14. Section 2(1)(a) Public Safety Act 3 of 1953.
15. Dullah Omar would go on to serve as the Minister of Justice under the democratic Republic of South Africa from 1994 to 1999. In 1999 he began service as Minister of Transport.
16. Public Safety Act 3 of 1953, as promulgated in Proclamation R121 of July 1985.
17. Regulation 9 (a) of the Public Safety Act gave the Minister of Justice the power to regulate detentions. Under this section, the Minister of Justice had issued several rules (5 (1) and (3) of Government Notice 2483 of October 26, 1985) that prevented legal advisors access to detainees without the express permission of the Minister of Law and Order or the Commissioner of the South African Police.
18. *Omar and Others v. Minister of Law and Order and Others* 1986 (3) 306 (C) at 330.
19. *Ultra vires* means "beyond the scope of the powers." Those actions of Parliament or the State President that are deemed to be passed in conflict with the requirements of the constitution or the statute can be declared void under this doctrine.
20. *Momoniat and Naidoo v. Minister of Law and Order* 1986 (2) SA 264 (W).
21. *Omar and Others v. Minister of Law and Order and Others* 1987 (3) SA 859 (A) at 892.
22. Judges could not be removed except on address from Parliament, which never occurred.

23. *R. v. Abdurahman* 1950 (3) SA 136 (A); *Tayob v. Ermelo Local Road Transportation Board* 1951 (4) SA 440 (A); *R. v. Lusu* 1953 (2) SA 484 (A).
24. *Collins v. Minister of the Interior* 1957 (1) SA 552 (A).
25. *Minister of the Interior v. Harris* 1952 (4) SA 769 (A).
26. For example, Cameron 1987a, 1987b; Davis 1987a, 1987b; Dugard 1978, 1984; Hahlo 1971; Haysom and Plasket 1988; Marcus 1984, 1985; Millner 1962; Mokgatle 1987; Wacks 1984, among others.
27. It should be noted that the South African Law Reports do not contain all of the decisions of the Court. A coding of a sample of years (1970 (45 cases), 1975 (45 cases), 1980 (50 cases), 1985 (78 cases), 1990 (81 cases) revealed that the majority of the unpublished opinions were criminal cases (1970 (53%) 1975 (69%) 1980 (78%), 1985 (79%), 1990 (70%), many revolving around appeals of sentence, particularly the death penalty. The remainder of the cases were divided equally among the remaining issue categories. While including all decisions would be preferable, cursory analysis of the data suggests that these cases do not differ systematically in outcome or substance from those in the analysis.
28. Criminal cases include challenges to various police and prosecutorial actions including interpretation of criminal statutes, sufficiency of evidence, challenge to appropriate sentence, as well as coerced testimony, inadmissable testimony, admissibility of evidence, and jury and counsel-related issues. These cases include challenges by individuals arrested for apartheid crimes.
29. These include debt collections, contract, property, landlord/tenant, corporate law, labor relations, copyright infringement, and workers' compensation disputes.
30. Public law cases include challenges to government regulations concerning health, safety, environment, natural resources, businesses, land use, taxation, public employment, immigration, government benefit programs and apartheid regulations.
31. While no constitutional rights or liberties existed for South Africans, the courts did recognize certain protections within the common law concerning procedural if not substantive fairness and equality. Thus individuals did challenge when speech, religion, press, association, equality, etc. were restricted. Moreover, protections for defamation also existed.
32. The respondent enjoyed a slight advantage in South Africa, with the appellant winning 37% of the time and the respondent winning 56% of the time. The Court favored the appellant in part and the respondent in part in 5% of cases. Approximately 2% of cases involved questions of law with no real issue in dispute.
33. Individuals are categories of natural persons. The government category includes all levels of government: national, provincial and local. The corporation category includes businesses, both small and large, as well as interest groups or other business associations such as unions. These categories are based on presumptions concerning resources. Clearly, a very wealthy individual would have greater resources than a very small business. But given the large N of the analysis, 3,044, on average, business groups should have greater resources than individuals.
34. Those cases in which the parties won in part and lost in part were excluded (178 or 6%). Approximately 47% of these are criminal cases. A separate analysis was conducted in which these partial victories were counted as the defendant winning. The results remain substantively the same.
35. These include cases challenging government race classifications of individuals as well as challenges to race-based statutes more generally. These cases are subsumed under public law challenges in Table 3.1.
36. The government was involved in some contract and ownership disputes with corporations and individuals that were coded as private economic disputes.

150 Judging in Black and White

37. These are cases where only a procedural issue, rather than a substantive issue, is decided by the Court.
38. Logistic regression analysis supports the tabular results presented above. These results are provided in Appendix A. It is evident that the government is particularly vulnerable in tort cases. This issue is significantly and negatively related to the government winning. However, the government does enjoy a significant advantage when challenged by an individual or a corporation. There was no significant relationship between Afrikaans-speaking judges and the government winning.

Chapter Four

1. Act 30 of 1950, Section 5 (1).
2. *Pitcher and Others v. Secretary for the Interior* 1968 (4) SA 238 (C) at 247.
3. *Felton v. Secretary for the Interior* 1972 (3) SA 886 (A) at 892-893.
4. *Felton v. Secretary for the Interior* 1972 (2) SA 497 (T).
5. *Felton v. Secretary for the Interior* 1972 (3) SA 886 (A) at 893.
6. *Felton v. Secretary for the Interior* 1972 (3) SA 886 (A) at 893.
7. *Felton v. Secretary for the Interior* 1972 (3) SA 886 (A) at 893.
8. 1985 (4) SA 754 (A).
9. The Transkei, located on the southeastern coast, was the initial territory set aside as a "homeland" to be "tutored" for eventual African "nationhood." The Transkei was declared "self-governing" in 1963 and "independent" in 1976 despite the fact that it was never allowed to be either. The Transkei is most famous as the birthplace of Nelson Mandela.
10. Act 25 of 1945.
11. In *East Rand Administration Board and Another v. Rikhoto* 1983 (3) SA 595 (A), the Appellate Division had ruled that the "call-in" requirement of returning to the individual's homeland to receive the annual employment certification during annual leave could not be considered a break in employment.
12. *Mthiya v. Black Affairs Administration Board, Western Cape, and Another* 1983 (3) SA 455 (C).
13. *Commission of Inquiry into Legislation Affecting the Utilization of Manpower (Excluding the Legislation Administered by the Departments of Labour and Mines),* Chair: Riekert, RP32–1979, Chapter 8.
14. *Black Affairs Administration Board, Western Cape, and Another v. Mthiya* 1985 (4) SA 754 (A) at 766.
15. 1986 (1) SA 102 (A).
16. Marcus noted that the Surplus People's Project estimated some 3.5 million people were forcibly removed under the statute between 1960 and 1982 (Marcus 1990, 13).
17. Allister Sparks in a November 27, 1983, front-page *Washington Post* article described the home of a sixty-one-year-old widow as a "modern ranch-style home with 10 rooms, tiled bathroom, carved front door and attached garage with an Alfa-Romeo inside."
18. Quoted in Abel (1995, 424).
19. Act 38 of 1927.
20. *More v. Minister of Co-operation and Development and Another* 1986 (1) SA 102 (A).
21. Judge Kriegler served on the Transvaal Provincial Division from 1984 to 1990 and subsequently on the Appellate Division. He was appointed to the Constitutional Court presumably in part for his opposition to apartheid.
22. See Chapter 6 for a discussion of Van Niekerk.
23. It should be noted that American scholars in exploring the voting patterns of its high court

judges compare voting records of judges who did not sit on the court at the same time. For example, scholars note that Warren was a more liberal judge than Rehnquist.
24. This description of the majority opinion assignment process was described by a number of Appeal Court judges during interviews conducted at the Supreme Court of Appeal, July 1996 and May 2001. The tradition of the senior judge on the panel assigning the opinion writer was continued by Mohammed and Acting Chief Justice (now President) Hefer.
25. The language measure was created with Forsyth's (1985) background data on judges from 1950–1985, supplemented by data in *Who's Who in Southern Africa, South African Legal Bibliography, South African Law Journal, De Jure, Judges of the Cape Provincial Division and Eastern Districts Local Division, Judges of the Appellate Division and Transvaal Bench from 1943 to 1970, Nuntius* and various biographies. Last, those who were not identified in these sources were identified as primarily Afrikaans-speaking or English-speaking through interviews with judges who served on the Appellate Division and South African academics.
26. Occasionally, these judges subsequently were appointed as Appeal Court judges.
27. The dates of tenure listed are derived from the data set and include those sessions in which the judge participated.
28. It should be noted that Judge Goldstone was appointed to the new Constitutional Court in part because of his presumed (and the evidence here suggests actual) support for the underdog.
29. Chi square is a measure of association that compares frequencies in a table to determine if the variance between observed and expected cells is statistically significant.
30. It should be noted that these include all cases involving apartheid issues before these judges, not merely those related to the state of emergency.
31. Only those judges who actually participated in an apartheid case are included in this mean.

Chapter Five

1. *Johannesburg Liquor Licensing Board v. Kuhn* 1963 SA (4) 666 (A) at 670.
2. *Johannesburg Liquor Licensing Board v. Kuhn* 1963 SA (4) 666 (A) at 671.
3. Act 30 of 1928.
4. *Johannesburg Liquor Licensing Board v. Kuhn* 1963 (4) SA 666 (A) at 671.
5. *Vanderbijl Park Health Committee and Others v. Wilson and Others* 1950 (1) SA 447 (A) at 458.
6. *Johannesburg Liquor Licensing Board v. Kuhn* 1963 (4) SA 666 (A) at 671.
7. *Johannesburg Liquor Licensing Board v. Kuhn* 1963 (4) SA 666 (A) at 672.
8. *Johannesburg Liquor Licensing Board v. Kuhn* 1963 (4) SA 666 (A) at 672.
9. *Johannesburg Liquor Licensing Board v. Kuhn* 1963 (4) SA 666 (A) at 672.
10. *Johannesburg Liquor Licensing Board v. Kuhn* 1963 (4) SA 672 (A) at 672.
11. *Johannesburg Liquor Licensing Board v. Kuhn* 1963 (4) SA 672 (A) at 672.
12. *Johannesburg Liquor Licensing Board v. Kuhn* 1963 (4) SA 673 (A) at 673.
13. *Johannesburg Liquor Licensing Board v. Kuhn* 1963 SA (4) 666 (A) at 667.
14. *Garda v. Livestock and Meat Industries Control Board* 1960 (3) SA 481 (T) at 484.
15. *Garda v. Livestock and Meat Industries Control Board* 1960 (3) SA 481 (T) at 485.
16. *Livestock and Meat Industries Control Board v. Garda* 1961 (1) SA 342 (A) at 346.
17. *Livestock and Meat Industries Control Board v. Garda* 1961 (1) SA 342 (A) at 347.
18. *Garda v. Livestock and Meat Industries Control Board* 1960 (3) SA 481 (T) at 486.
19. *Garda v. Livestock and Meat Industries Control Board* 1960 (3) SA 481 (T) at 482.
20. Marketing Act 26 of 1937, Sections 19 and 20, as amended by Proclamation 68 of 1952, Section 21 (3).
21. *Livestock and Meat Industries Control Board v. Garda* 1961 (1) SA 342 (A) at 342.

152   Judging in Black and White

22. See Chapter 4, note 25 for a description of the measurement of Afrikaans-speaking and English-speaking judges. Judges who served as Acting Appeal Court judges or who did not serve full terms at the beginning or ending of their tenure were included for the proportion of the year in which they served.
23. Republic of South Africa Act 110 of 1983.
24. Public law cases analyzed here include challenges to various kinds of government regulations, but do not include tort cases involving the government.
25. The $R2$, which represents the portion of the variance among the data "explained" or accounted for by the independent variables, is .67, suggesting that a significant portion of the variance is explained by the model. The Durbin-Watson estimate is 1.94. A score near 2 or lower suggests that the series does not exhibit a level of autocorrelation sufficient to contaminate the results. For time series analyses, it is important to disentangle the incremental effects of time from the effects of the intervention. The Durbin-Watson establishes that the correlation from year 1 to year 2, year 2 to year 3, etc. is not contaminating the parameter estimates for the independent variables.
26. The $R2$ is .69 and the Durbin-Watson 2.01.
27. The $R2$ is also less at .62, while the Durbin-Watson is acceptable at 2.13.

Chapter Six

1. See Justice Kriegler's discussion of moral authority in judging in *S v Mamabolo* 2001 (3) SA 409 (CC).
2. These studies include (though not exclusively) Simons (1949), Kahn (1970), Welsh (1969), Salmon (1980–81) and Knoebel (1980–81). For an excellent discussion of these studies, see Van Blerk (1988).
3. The initial prosecution for the law journal article is reported at 1970 (3) SA 655 (T). In a second case Van Niekerk was found guilty in the lower court on a charge of contempt and acquitted on a charge of attempting to obstruct the cause of justice. In a public protest meeting, Van Niekerk had argued that judges should ignore evidence obtained under the draconian security legislation rules as inherently coerced and corrupt. The lower court found this to be an attempt to undermine the judicial responsibility to remain independent and impartial and argued that it was specifically designed to undermine the prosecution of a detainee which was underway at the time of his speech. The lower court held this to constitute contempt of court (*S. v. Van Niekerk* 1972 (2) SA 279 (D)). The Appellate Division not only upheld the contempt conviction but ruled that the necessary intent to uphold the obstruction of justice cause had been established as well (1972 (3) SA 711 (A)). In a third case, the *Sunday Times* published an article quoting criticisms of Van Niekerk directed at the government. The publisher, the South Africa Associated Newspapers, Ltd., was sued for defamation (*Pelser v. South African Associated Newspapers Ltd. and Another* 1975 (1) SA 34 (N)). Van Niekerk had been critical of a case in which a black man and a white man were both convicted of the murder of a white shopkeeper. Both were sentenced to death, but the white man's sentence was commuted and the black man was hanged. Van Niekerk asserted that "The execution of Makinitha must fill all South Africans with shame. Two persons of different races commit the same crime and are sentenced to the same punishment by a court of law; yet they are treated differently by the Executive on a plea of mercy" (1975 (1) SA 34 (N) at 36). The lower court ruled that the reference to the executive was determined to be independent of criticisms of the government which would have been protected. Reference to the "Executive" (Executive Council) reasonably could be presumed to refer to particular individuals, such as Minister of Justice Pelser in this case, and could be de-

famatory toward their individual motives. The Appellate Division upheld the conviction (*South African Associated Newspapers Ltd. and Another v. Estate Pelser* 1975 (4) SA 797 (A)).
4. However, it should be noted that Mathews's *Law, Order and Liberty in South Africa* was published in 1971, and Dugard's watershed *Human Rights and the South African Legal Order* was published in 1978. In addition, Cameron's classic piece assessing the executive mindedness of L. C. Steyn, considered by some to be academic heresy, was published in 1982. But these few voices were fairly distinct from the essentially silent cadre of South African academics. Scholars became more vocal by the 1980s when criticism of the courts became more strident and appeared more frequently.
5. *R. v. Abdurahman* (1950) 3 SA 136 (A) at 149.
6. Segal and Spaeth present an excellent criticism of the legal model (1993, 32–73).
7. *Commentarius ad Pandectas* 1.3.5. Translation by Percival Gane, 1955, vol. 1, p. 34.
8. For an excellent description of the purists' efforts to return to the Roman-Dutch legal heritage, see Du Plessis and Du Plessis (1995, Chapter 2).
9. *In re Marechane* 1882 (1) SAR 27 at 31.
10. Act 200 of 1993.
11. Act 108 of 1996.
12. According to Chapter 8, Section 178 of the Constitution of the Republic of South Africa Act, Act 108 of 1996, the JSC is comprised of 23 members, including the Chief Justice of the Constitutional Court, the President of the Supreme Court of Appeal, one Judge President of the Supreme Court, the Cabinet member responsible for the administration of justice (or a designated alternate), two practicing advocates, two practicing attorneys, one professor of law, six members of the National Assembly, four permanent delegates to the National Council of Provinces, and four persons designated by the President of South Africa. Additionally, whenever a matter affects a specific province or local division of the courts, the Judge President of that division and the Premier of the province concerned (or their designates) will preside as well. The JSC was initially established under the interim constitution.
13. Judges who sat on the bench at the time of the adoption of the Constitution of the Republic of South Africa Act, Act 200 of 1993, the interim constitutional legislation, retained their appointments.

Bibliography

Abel, Richard L. 1995. *Politics by Other Means: Law in the Struggle Against Apartheid, 1980–1994*. New York: Routledge.
Atkins, Burton M. 1991. "Party Capability Theory as an Explanation of Intervention Behavior in the English Court of Appeal." *American Journal Political Science*. 35:881–903.
Barber, James. 1999. *South Africa in the Twentieth Century*. Massachusetts: Blackwell Publishers, Ltd.
Baum, Lawrence. 1997. *The Puzzle of Judicial Behavior*. Ann Arbor: University of Michigan Press.
Beinart, William. 1994. *Twentieth-Century South Africa*. New York: Oxford University Press.
Blackstone, William. [1765] 1979. *The Laws of England*. Vol. 1. Chicago: University Press of Chicago.
Brookes, Edgar H. 1968. *Apartheid: A Documentary Study of Modern South Africa*. New York: Barnes and Noble, Inc.
Cameron, Edwin. 1987a. "Judicial Endorsement of Apartheid Propaganda: An Enquiry into an Acute Case." *South African Journal on Human Rights*. 3:223–229.
———. 1987b. "Nude Monarchy: The Case of South Africa's Judges." *South African Journal of Human Rights*. 3:338–346.
———. 1982. "Legal Chauvinism, Executive-Mindedness and Justice—L. C. Steyn's Impact on South African Law." *South African Law Journal*. 99:38–75.
Cardozo, Benjamin N. 1921. *The Nature of the Judicial Process*. New Haven, CT: Yale University Press.
Corbett, Michael M. 1987. "Aspects of the Role of Policy in the Evolution of Our Common Law." *South African Law Journal*. 104:52–68.
Corder, Hugh. 1989. "The Record of the Judiciary (2)." *Democracy and the Judiciary*. Ed. Hugh Corder. Cape Town: Institute for a Democratic Alternative for South Africa.
———. 1987. "The Supreme Court: Arena of Struggle?" *The State of Apartheid*. Ed. Wilmot G. James. Colorado: Lynne Rienner.
———. 1984. *Judges at Work: The Role and Attitudes of the South African Appellate Judiciary, 1910–1950*. Cape Town: Juta and Co., Ltd.
Dahl, Robert A. 1957. "Decision-Making in a Democracy: The Supreme Court as a National Policy Maker." *Journal of Public Law*. 6:279–95.
Davenport, Christian. 1996. "Constitutional Promises and Repressive Reality: A Cross-National Time Series Investigation of Why Political and Civil Liberties are Suppressed." *Journal of Politics*. 58:627–654.
Davenport, Rodney, and Christopher Saunders. 2000. *South Africa: A Modern History*. New York: St. Martin's Press, Inc.

Davis, D. M. 1987a. "Competing Conceptions: Pro-Executive or Pro-Democratic–Judges Choose." *South African Journal on Human Rights*. 3:96–105.

———. 1987b. "The Chief Justice and the Total Onslaught." *South African Journal on Human Rights*. 3:229–233.

De Kock, W. J. 1975. "The Anglo-Boer War, 1899–1902." *Five Hundred Years: A History of South Africa*. Ed. C. F. J. Muller. Cape Town: Academica.

Dugard, John. 1992. "The Law of Apartheid." *The Last Years of Apartheid: Civil Liberties in South Africa*. Eds. John Dugard, Nicholas Hayson, and Gilbert Marcus. Ford Foundation and the Foreign Policy Association.

———. 1989. "Should Judges Resign? (And Lawyers Participate?)." *Democracy and the Judiciary*. Ed. Hugh Corder. Cape Town: Institute for a Democratic Alternative for South Africa.

———. 1987. "The Judiciary in a State of National Crisis—With Special Reference to the South African Experience." *Washington and Lee Law Review*. 44:477–501.

———. 1984. "Should Judges Resign?–A Reply to Professor Wacks." *South African Law Journal*. 101:286–294.

———. 1978. *Human Rights and the South African Legal Order*. Princeton, N.J.: Princeton University Press.

———. 1971. "The Judicial Process, Positivism and Civil Liberty." *South African Law Journal*. 88:181–200.

Dugard, John, Nicholas Haysom, and Gilbert Marcus. 1992. *The Last Years of Apartheid: Civil Liberties in South Africa*. Ford Foundation and the Foreign Policy Association.

Du Plessis, J. S. 1975. "The South African Republic." *Five Hundred Years: A History of South Africa*. Ed. C. F. J. Muller. Cape Town: Academica.

Du Plessis, J. R., and L. Kok. 1989. *An Elementary Introduction to the Study of South African Law*. Cape Town: Juta and Co., Ltd.

Du Plessis, Lourens M., and A. G. Du Plessis 1995. *An Introduction to Law*. Cape Town: Juta and Co., Ltd.

Dworkin, Ronald. 1978. *Taking Rights Seriously*. Cambridge, Mass.: Harvard University Press.

Dyzenhaus, David. 1998. *Truth, Reconciliation and the Apartheid Legal Order*. Cape Town: Juta and Co., Ltd.

———. 1991. *Hard Cases in Wicked Legal Systems*. Oxford: Clarendon Press.

Ellmann, Stephen. 1992. *In a Time of Trouble: Law and Liberty in South Africa's State of Emergency*. New York: Oxford University Press.

———. 1989. "Legal Text and Lawyers' Culture in South Africa." *Review of Law and Social Change*. 17:387–417.

Epp, Charles R. 1998. *The Rights Revolution: Lawyers, Activists, and Supreme Courts in Comparative Perspective*. Chicago, IL: University of Chicago Press.

Forsyth, Christopher F. 1985. *In Danger for Their Talents*. Cape Town: Juta and Co., Ltd.

Fredrickson, George M. 1981. *White Supremacy: A Comparative Study of American and South African History*. N.Y: Oxford University Press.

Galanter, Marc. 1974. "Why the 'Haves' Come Out Ahead: Speculations on the Limits of Legal Change." *Law and Society Review*. 9:95–160.

Gane, Percival. 1955. *The Selective Voet, Being the Commentary on the Pandects. Volume 1*. Durban: Butterworth and Co.

Greenberg, Stanley B. 1987. "Resistance and Hegemony in South Africa." *The State of Apartheid*. Ed. Wilmot G. James. Colorado: Lynne Rienner.

Hahlo, H. R. 1971. "Scandalizing Justice: The Van Niekerk Story." *University of Toronto Law Journal*. 21:378–392.

Hahlo, H. R., and Ellison Kahn. 1968. *The South African Legal System and Its Background*. Cape Town: Juta and Co., Ltd.

Haynie, Stacia L. 1997. "Courts and Revolution: Independence and Legitimacy in the New Republic of South Africa." *Justice System Journal*. 19:167–179.

———. 1995. "Resource Inequalities and Regional Variation in Litigation Outcomes in the Philippine Supreme Court, 1961–1986." *Political Research Quarterly*. 48:371–380.

———. 1994. "Resource Inequalities and Litigation Outcomes in the Philippine Supreme Court." *Journal of Politics*. 56:752–72.

Haysom, Nicholas. 1992. "The Total Strategy: The South African Security Forces and the Suppression of Civil Liberties." *The Last Years of Apartheid*. Eds. John Dugard, Nicholas Hayson, and Gilbert Marcus. Ford Foundation and the Foreign Policy Association.

Haysom, Nicholas and Clive Plasket. 1988. "The War Against Law: Judicial Activism and the Appellate Division." *South African Journal of Human Rights*. 4:303–333.

Helmke, Gretchen. 2002. "The Logic of Strategic Defection: Court-Executive Relations in Argentina Under Dictatorship and Democracy." *American Political Science Review*. 96:291–303.

Higginbotham, A. Leon, Jr. 1990. "Racism in American and South African Courts: Similarities and Differences." *New York University Law Review*. 65:479–588.

Hindson, Doug. 1987. *Pass Controls and the Urban African Proletariat*. Johannesburg: Ravan Press.

Hund, John, and Hendrik W. van der Merwe. 1986. *Legal Ideology and Politics in South Africa: A Social Science Approach*. Lanham, Md.: University Press of America.

Jackson, Donald W. 1997. *The United Kingdom Confronts the European Convention on Human Rights*. Gainesville, Fla.: University Press of Florida.

James, Wilmot G. 1987. "The State of Apartheid: An Introduction." *The State of Apartheid*. Ed. Wilmot G. James. Colorado: Lynne Rienner.

James, Wilmot G., and Andrew Du Pisanie. 1987. "End of a 'New Deal': Contradictions of Constitutional Reform." *The State of Apartheid*. Ed. Wilmot G. James. Colorado: Lynne Rienner.

Jenkins, Carolyn. 1990. "Sanctions, Economic Growth and Change." *The Political Economy of South Africa*. Eds. Nicoli Nattrass and Elisabeth Ardington. Cape Town: Oxford University Press.

Kahn, Ellison. 1970. "The Death Penalty in South Africa." *Tydskrif vir Hedendaagse Romeins-Hollandse Reg*. 33:108–141.

Keith, Linda Camp. 1999. "Writing Constitutions that Protect Against Human Rights Abuse–How Important are Provisions for Judicial Independence and Judicial Review?" Presented at the Scientific Study of Judicial Politics Conference, Texas A&M University.

Knoebel, Lizette. 1980–81. "Judicial Discretion in Sentencing in the Supreme Court: A Computerized Survey and Analysis of Assault Cases in the Durban and Coast Local Division 1970–1979." *Natal University Law Review*. 3:553–579.

Kritzer, Herbert M. 1979. "Federal Judges and Their Political Environments: The Influence of Public Opinion." *American Journal of Political Science*. 23:194–207.

Lapping, Brian. 1986. *Apartheid: A History*. London: Grafton Books.

Laswell, Harold. 1936. *Politics: Who Gets What, When and How*. New York: McGraw-Hill.

Leach, Graham. 1986. *South Africa: No Easy Path to Peace*. London: Routledge and Kegan Paul.

Lijphardt, Arend. 1999. *Patterns of Democracy*. New Haven, Conn.: Yale University Press.

Lobban, Michael. 1996. *White Man's Justice: South African Political Trials in the Black Consciousness Era*. Oxford: Clarendon Press.

Lodge, Tom. 1983. *Black Politics in South Africa Since 1945*. New York: Longman.

Mallaby, Sebastian. 1992. *After Apartheid: The Future of South Africa*. New York: Times Books.

Marcus, Gilbert. 1990. "Section 5 of the Black Administration Act: The Case of the Bakwena ba

Magopa." *No Place to Rest: Forced Removals and the Law in South Africa.* Eds. Christina Murray, and Catherine O'Regan. Cape Town: Oxford University Press.
———. 1985. "Respect for the Courts: Myth and Reality." *South African Law Journal.* 1:236–244.
———. 1984. "Judging the Judges." *South African Law Journal.* 101:160–171.
Mathews, Anthony S. 1986. *Freedom, State Security and the Rule of Law.* Cape Town: Juta and Co., Ltd.
———. 1971. *Law, Order and Liberty in South Africa.* Cape Town: Juta and Co., Ltd.
Mathews, Anthony S., and R. C. Albino. 1966. "The Permanence of the Temporary: An Examination of the 90- and 180-Day Detention Laws." *South African Law Journal.* 83:16–43.
McCormick, Peter. 1993. "Party Capability Theory and Appellate Success in the Supreme Court of Canada, 1949–1992." *Canadian Journal of Political Science.* 26:523–540.
Mezerik, A. G. 1964. *Apartheid in the Republic of South Africa.* New York: International Review Service.
Millner, M. A. 1962. "Eclipse of a Judiciary: The South African Position." *International and Comparative Law Quarterly.* 11:886–891.
———. 1961. "Apartheid and the South African Courts." *Current Legal Problems.* 14:280–360.
Mishler, William, and Reginald S. Sheehan. 1993. "The Supreme Court as a Countermajoritarian Institution? The Impact of Public Opinion on Supreme Court Decisions." *American Political Science Review.* 87:87–101.
Mokgatle, D. D. 1987. "The Exclusion of Blacks from the South African Legal System." *South African Journal of Human Rights.* 3:44–51.
Motala, Ziyad. 1991. "Independence of the Judiciary, Prospects and Limitations of Judicial Review in Terms of the United States Model in a New South African Order: Towards an Alternative Judicial Structure." *Albany Law Review.* 55:367–405.
Myburgh, A. C. 1985. *Papers on Indigenous Law in Southern Africa.* Pretoria: J. L. van Schaik, Ltd.
Nonet, Phillippe, and Philip Selznick. 1978. *Law and Society in Transition: Toward Responsive Law.* New York: Octagon Books.
Ogilvie Thompson, Newton. 1972. "Address on the Occasion of the Centenary Celebrations of the Northern Cape Division of the Supreme Court of South Africa." *South African Law Journal.* 89:23–34.
Owen, Harold J. 1971. "The Role of Trial Courts in the Local Political System: A Comparison of Two Georgia Counties." Ph.D. Diss. University of Georgia.
Pitts, Joe W., III. 1986. "Judges in an Unjust Society: The Case of South Africa." *Denver Journal of International Law and Policy.* 15:49–94.
Pritchett, C. Herman. 1948. *The Roosevelt Court: A Study in Judicial Politics and Values 1937–1947.* New York: Macmillan.
Riley, Eileen. 1991. *Major Political Events in South Africa.* N.Y.: Facts on File.
Rhode, David W., and Harold J. Spaeth. 1976. *Supreme Court Decision Making.* San Francisco: W. H. Freeman.
Sachs, Albie. 1973. *Justice in South Africa.* Berkeley, Calif.: University of California.
Salmon, Owen. 1980–81. "Judicial Discretion in Sentencing in the Supreme Court: A Computerized Survey and Analysis of Rape Cases in the Durban and Coast Local Division 1970–1979." *Natal University Law Review.* 3:580–650.
Saunders, Christopher. 1988. *The Making of the South African Past: Major Historians on Race and Class.* Cape Town: David Philip.
Schubert, Glendon A. 1985. *Political Culture and Judicial Behavior, Volumes I and II.* Lanham, Md.: University Press of America.
———. 1980. "Subcultural Effects on Judicial Behavior: A Comparative Analysis." *Journal of Politics.* 42:951–92.

———. 1977. "Political Culture and Judicial Ideology: Some Cross-Cultural and Subcultural Comparisons." *Comparative Political Studies*. 9: 363–408.

———. 1974. *The Judicial Mind Revisited*. New York: Oxford University Press.

———. 1965. *The Judicial Mind: Attitudes and Ideologies of Supreme Court Justices, 1946–1963*. Evanston, Ill.: Northwestern University Press.

Segal, Jeffrey A., and Albert D. Cover. 1989. "Ideological Values and the Votes of U.S. Supreme Court Justices. *American Political Science Review*. 83:557–565.

Segal, Jeffrey A., Lee Epstein, Charles M.Cameron, and Harold J. Spaeth. 1995. "Ideological Values and the Votes of U.S. Supreme Court Justices Revisited." *Journal of Politics*. 57:812–823.

Segal, Jeffrey, and Harold D. Spaeth. 2002. *The Supreme Court and the Attitudinal Model Revisited*. New York: Cambridge University Press.

———. 1993. *The Supreme Court and the Attitudinal Model*. New York: Cambridge University Press.

Shapiro, Martin. 1981. *Courts: A Comparative and Political Analysis*. Chicago: University of Chicago Press.

Sheehan, Reginald S., William Mishler, and Donald R. Songer. 1992. "Ideology, Status, and the Differential Success of Direct Parties Before the Supreme Court." *American Political Science Review*. 86:464–71.

Simons, H. J. 1949. "The Law and Its Administration." In *Handbook on Race Relations in South Africa*. Ed. Ellen Hellmann. Cape Town: Oxford University Press.

Smith, Ken. 1988. *The Changing Past: Trends in South African Historical Writing*. Johannesburg: Southern Books.

Songer, Donald R. 1982. "Consensual and Nonconsensual Decisions in Unanimous Opinions of the United States Courts of Appeals." *American Journal of Political Science*. 26:225–239.

Songer, Donald R., and Reginald S. Sheehan. 1992. "Who Wins on Appeal? Upperdogs and Underdogs in the United States Courts of Appeals." *American Journal of Political Science*. 36:235–58.

Spaeth, Harold J. 1998. *United States Supreme Court Judicial Database, 1953–1998 Terms*. 8th ed. Ann Arbor, Mich.: Inter-University Consortium for Political and Social Research.

———. 1995. *Expanded United States Supreme Court Judicial Database, 1946–1968 Terms*. Ann Arbor, Mich · Inter-University Consortium for Political and Social Research.

———. 1994. *United States Supreme Court Judicial Database, 1953–1992 Terms*. 5th ed. Ann Arbor, Mich.: Inter-University Consortium for Political and Social Research.

———. 1963. "An Analysis of Judicial Attitudes in the Labor Relations Decisions of the Warren Court." *Journal of Politics*. 25:290–311.

———. 1961. "An Approach to the Study of Attitudinal Differences as an Aspect of Judicial Behavior." *Midwest Journal of Political Science*. 5:165–180.

Spies, S. B. 1975. "Reconstruction and Unification, 1902–1910." *Five Hundred Years: A History of South Africa*. Ed. C. F. J. Muller. Cape Town: Academica.

Stadler, Alf. 1987. *The Political Economy of Modern South Africa*. New York: St. Martin's Press.

Tate, C. Neal, and Stacia L. Haynie. 1994. "The Philippine Supreme Court Under Authoritarian and Democratic Rule: The Perceptions of the Justices." *Asian Profile*. 22:209–225.

———. 1993. "Authoritarianism and the Functions of Courts: A Time Series Analysis of the Philippine Supreme Court." *Law and Society Review*. 27:707–740.

Tate, C. Neal, and Torbjorn Vallinder. 1995. *The Global Expansion of Judicial Power*. New York: New York University Press.

Terreblanche, Sampie, and Nicoli Nattrass. 1990. "A Periodization of the Political Economy from 1910." *The Political Economy of South Africa*. Eds. Nicoli Nattrass and Elisabeth Ardington. Cape Town: Oxford University Press.

Thompson, Leonard. 1990. *A History of South Africa*. New Haven, Conn.: Yale University Press.

Trengove, John. 1988. "Perspectives on the Role of Judges in a Deeply Divided Society." *Democracy and the Judiciary*. Ed. Hugh Corder. Cape Town: Institute for a Democratic Alternative for South Africa.

Uunterhalter, Elaine. 1987. *Forced Removal: The Division, Segregation and Control of the People of South Africa*. London: International Defence and Aid Fund for Southern Africa.

Van Blerk, Adrienne E. 1988. *Judge and Be Judged*. Cape Town: Juta and Co., Ltd.

Van Niekerk, Berand. 1970. "Hanged by the Neck until You Are Dead: Some Thoughts on the Application of the Death Penalty in South Africa." *South African Law Journal*. 86:61–5.

———. 1969. "Hanged by the Neck until You Are Dead." *South African Law Journal*. 86:457–75.

Van Schoor, M. C. E. 1975. "The Orange Free State." *Five Hundred Years: A History of South Africa*. Ed. C. F. J. Muller. Cape Town: Academica.

Van Zyl, M. C. 1975. "States and Colonies in South Africa, 1854–1902." *Five Hundred Years: A History of South Africa*. Ed. C. F. J. Muller. Cape Town: Academica.

Verner, Joel. 1984. "Supreme Court Independence in Latin America: Review of the Literature." *Journal of Latin American Studies*. 16:463–506.

Wacks, Raymond. 1984. "Judges and Injustice." *South African Law Journal*. 101:266–285.

Wanner, Craig. 1975. "The Public Ordering of Private Relations: Part I Initiating Civil Cases in Urban Trial Courts." *Law and Society Review*. 8:421–440.

Welsh, David. 1969. "Capital Punishment in South Africa." *African Penal Systems*. Ed. Alan Miller. New York: Frederick A. Praeger.

Weschler, Herbert. 1959. "Toward Neutral Principles of Constitutional Law." *Harvard Law Review*. 73:1–35.

Wheeler, Stanton, Bliss Cartwright, Robert A. Kagan, and Lawrence M. Friedman. 1987. "Do the 'Haves' Come Out Ahead? Winning and Losing in State Supreme Courts, 1870–1970." *Law and Society Review*. 21:403–45.

Worden, Nigel. 1993. *The Making of Modern South Africa: Conquest, Segregation and Apartheid*. Oxford: Blackwell.

———. 1985. *Slavery in Dutch South Africa*. London: Cambridge University Press.

Index

Abel, Richard L., 58, 67, 68, 71, 115
Acting Judges of Appeal, 31
Advocates, 153 (n 12) (see also Bar and Lawyers)
African Community Councils, 40
African National Congress (ANC), 1, 30, 37–38, 41, 117, 118, 119, 147 (n 45)
African People's Organization, 30
African Political Organization, 30
Afrikaans-speaking judges, 2, 35, 75, 76, 77, 80–85, 94, 95, 97, 99–102, 110–111, 121–122, 151 (n 25), 152 (n 22)
Afrikaners, 27, 29, 33, 35, 50
Albino, R. C., 44
Anglo-Boer War, 28–29
Apartheid, Foundations, 32–33; Implementation of, 35–37; Judging and, 10–12, 16–23, 51–52, 70–71, 105–106; Opposition to, 37–38; National Party and, 32–37, 41, 62, 109–114; Violence and, 39–40
Appellate Division, 31; Chief Justice and, 2–3, 8, 10, 16, 19, 31, 80, 83–84, 143 (n 3), 145 (n 11) 146 (n 30), 151 (n 24); Constitutional Court and, 117–118; Constitutional crisis and, 33–35; Criticism of, 17–21, 105–109; Docket and, 54–55; Docket control and, 31, 72–73; Success of litigants and, 56–60, 109; Longitudinal analysis and, 95–102; Professionalism of 115–116 (see also Judges)
Appointment of judges (see Judges, appointment and)

Asian, 36, 40, 89, 91, 146 (n 32) (see also Indian, Malay)
Atkins, Burton M., 53
Attorneys, 28, 32, 106, 143 (n 1) (see also Bar and Lawyers)
Audi alteram partem, 45–47, 48, 61, 88, 91
Austin, John, 16, 19
Authoritarian regime, 2, 4, 5, 8, 9 10, 42–43, 103, 104, 105

Bakwena Ba Magopa (see Magopa)
Banning, 38, 41, 147 (n 48)
Bantustans, 38, 147 (n 51)
Bar, 26, 32 (see also Advocates, Lawyers)
Barber, James, 37, 145 (n 7, n 8, n 12)
Batavian Republic, 26
Baum, Lawrence, 139
Beinart, William, 30, 36, 37
Bekker, S., 78, 81
Bentham, Jermey, 16, 19
Beyers, A. B., 78, 81
Beyers, D. O. K., 77, 78, 81
Beyers, Judge President of the Cape, 143 (n 8)
Biko, Steve, 39, 92, 96, 101, 102, 111
Black Consciousness movement, 39
Black Sash, 70–71
Blackstone, William, 105
Bloemfontein, 30
Boer republics, 27–29
Bophuthatswana, 147 (n 51)
Boshoff, W. G., 77, 79, 82, 84

Botha, A. S., 76, 77, 79, 80, 82, 84, 110
Botha, D. H., 78, 81
Botha, Louis, 30
Botha, P. W., 39, 41
Brink C. B., 77, 78, 81
British Charter of Justice, 26
British common law, 2, 14, 67, 112, 113, 115, 145 (n 2) (see also English law)
British Judicial Committee of the Privy Council, 31, 145 (n 30)
British rule, 26–29, 31, 34, 102
Brookes, Edgar H., 62

Cabinet, 30, 31, 49, 153 (n 12)
Cameron, Charles M., 139
Cameron, Edwin, 2, 42, 83, 113, 114, 115, 118, 143 (n 3, n 14), 146 (n 30), 147 (n 63), 149 (n 26), 153 (n 4)
Cape, 27, 28, 64, 65, 66, 67, 145 (n 8); Voting rights in, 30
Cape Colony, 25–27, 32
Cape of Good Hope, 1
Cape High Court 143 (n 8)
Cape Provincial Division, 47, 63
Capital punishment, 106 (see also death penalty)
Cardozo, Benjamin N., 15
Centlivres A., 78, 81, 110
Chief Justice (see Appellate Division, Chief Justice)
Chinese, 36, 146 (n 32)
Cillie, P. M., 79, 80, 82
Ciskei, 147 (n 51)
Civil rights and liberties, 9; Court and, 54, 58, 59, 110, 121, 122; Votes and, 76, 77, 80, 81–82, 83, 84, 110; Trends and 98, 100, 102
Codebook, 123
Colonial judges, 26
Coloured People's Congress (see South African Coloured People's Congress)
Command theory of law, 16
Common law, 2, 14, 112, 145 (n 2), 149 (n 31) (see also British common law)
Communist Party (see South African Communist Party)
Community Councils (see South African Community Councils)
Conflict resolution, courts and, 4–8, 11–12, 15, 42, 70, 94

Consensus norm, 72–74
Constitution, of 1909, 29–30, 34, 35; of 1961, 31, 38–39; of 1983, 40–41; of 1993, 143 (n 11), 153 (n 13); of 1996, 41, 117, 153 (n 12)
Constitutional Court, 8, 117–118, 150 (n 21), 151 (n 28)
Constitutional crisis of 1950, 33–35
Corbett, M. M, 19, 77, 79, 82, 83, 84
Corder, Hugh, 17, 31, 49–50
Court packing, 35, 50, 109, 111
Cover, Albert D., 139

Da Gama, Vasco, 25
Dahl, Robert A, 9, 94, 144 (n 15)
Davenport, Christian, 54
Davenport, Rodney, 37, 38, 147 (n 45, n 51)
Davis, D. M., 18–19, 149 (n 26)
De Beer, E. M., 77, 78, 81
De Klerk, F. W., 41, 145 (n 30), 147 (n 61)
De Kock, W. J., 29
De Villiers, H. H W., 76, 77, 78, 81
De Villiers, J. N. C., 78, 81
Death penalty, 106 (see also capital punishment)
Defiance campaign, 37
Department of Plural Relations, 16, 69
Detention 20, 41, 44–48, 148 (n 3, 17)
Developmental theory, courts and, 5, 12, 39, 85–86, 116–117, 119
Diakonia, 44
Diamonds, discovery of, 11, 28, 33
Diaz, Bartholomew, 24
Didcott, J. M., 16, 20
Diemont, M. A., 79, 82, 110
Digest of Emperor Justinian, 25
Dowling, W., 78, 81
Du Pisanie, Andrew, 40
Du Plessis, A. G., 25, 145 (n 2), 153 (n 8)
Du Plessis, J. R., 31
Du Plessis, J. S., 27
Du Plessis, Lourens M., 25, 145 (n 2), 153 (n 8)
Dugard, John, 9, 16, 17, 19–22, 31, 32, 33, 35, 36, 37, 38, 40, 41, 51, 60, 62, 64, 67, 71, 105, 107, 110, 113, 115, 116, 143 (n 3), 144 (24), 146 (n 33), 147 (n 51, 61), 148 (n 3), 153 (n 4)
Durban and Coast Local Division, 44
Dutch East India Company, 25–26, 145 (n 4)

Dworkin, Ronald, 19
Dyzenhaus, David, 17–18, 42, 60, 144 (n 28)

Education, blacks and, 27, 36, 39
Eksteen, J. P. G., 79, 82, 84, 110
Ellmann, Stephen, 37, 52, 58, 60, 83–85, 109
Eloff, C. F., 79, 82
Emergency team, 83–85
En banc, 74, 146 (n 26)
Engcobo, 65
English-speaking judges, 71–72, 75, 77, 80–85, 95, 97, 110, 151 (n 25), 152 (n 22)
English law, 11, 21, 26, 43, 67, 106, 115, 143 (n 3), 149 (n 31) (see also British common law)
Entrenched clauses, 30, 34–35, 38
Epp, Charles R, 42
Epstein, Lee, 139
Executive mindedness of judges, 110, 153 (n 4)
Executive Council, 152 (n 3)

Fagan, H. A., 77, 78, 81
Forced removals, 36, 68–69
Formal law, 4–5, 12–23, 48, 56, 60, 67, 70, 85, 86, 92–93, 104, 105–107, 111, 112–114, 116–117, 118, 119, 144 (n 16)
Forsyth, Christopher F., 18, 34, 35, 49, 52, 71, 95, 145 (n 11), 146 (n 26), 151 (n 25)
Franchise, 29–30, 32, 34, 145 (n 17) (see also Voting rights)
Fredrickson, George M., 33
Freedom Charter, 37
Friedman, G., 47, 48, 76, 79, 82

Galanter, Marc, 53
Galgut, O., 79, 82, 84
Gane, Percival, 153 (n 7)
Gazankulu, 147 (n 51)
Goldstone, R. J., 76, 79, 82, 151 (n 28)
Gold, discovery of, 11, 28, 33
Governor-General, 30, 31, 69, 145 (n 7)
Great Trek, 27
Greenberg, L., 77, 78, 81
Greenberg, Stanley B., 40
Grosskopf, E. M., 77, 79, 82, 84
Grosskopf, F. H., 76, 79, 82

Hahlo, H. R., 24, 149 (n 26)
Hall, C. G., 77, 78, 81

Haynie, Stacia L., 7, 53, 56, 103, 117, 118
Haysom, Nicholas, 41, 147 (n 61), 149 (n 26)
Hefer, J. J. F., 79, 82, 83, 84, 151 (n 24)
Helmke, Gretchen, 94
Hertzog, J. B. M., 145 (n 12)
Higginbotham, A. Leon, 146 (n 32)
High Court of Parliament, 35, 50, 108, 143 (n 9)
Hindson, Doug, 33
Hoexter, G. G., 79, 82, 84
Hoexter, O., 78, 81
Hofmeyer, S., 77, 79, 82
Holmes, G. N., 77, 78, 80, 81
Homelands, 32, 36, 38, 39, 147 (n 51)
Hottentots, 26–27, 145 (n 5)
House of Assembly, 30, 40
House of Delegates, 40
House of Representatives, 40
Howard, J. A., 79, 81
Hund, John, 5, 12–14, 39, 116–117, 144 (n 16)
Hurley, Dennis, 44

Idle person, 16, 144 (n 22)
Inarticulate premise, 16–17, 144 (n 24)
Impartiality, Courts and, 4–10, 11, 13, 22–23, 42, 43, 49, 54, 86, 103, 105, 107, 108, 109, 116, 152 (n 3)
Independence, Courts and, 4–10, 11, 22–23, 33–35, 42, 43, 48, 49, 51, 52, 53, 54, 86, 103, 105, 107, 108, 109, 115, 116, 152 (n 3)
Index of net advantage, Definition of, 56
Indian, 28, 29, 30, 33, 36, 40, 146 (n 32) (see also Asians)
Industrial and Commercial Workers' Union, 30

Jacobs, H. R., 79, 82, 84
Jackson, Donald W., 42
James, N., 79, 82
James, Wilmont G., 40
Jansen, E. L., 78, 81
Jenkins, Carolyn, 39, 40
Jennett, A. G., 78, 81
Joubert, C. P., 79, 82, 84, 85
Judges, Afrikaans-speaking (see Afrikaans-speaking judges); Appointment, 2, 4, 9, 10, 31, 49, 50, 93, 97, 109, 117–118, 153 (n 13); Background of, 49; Conference and, 74; Consensus and, 72–74; Criticism of, 17–22,

Judges *(continued)*
   42, 51–52, 54, 105–106, 153 (n 4); Discretion of, 2, 7, 20–22, 50–52, 85–86, 102–103, 104–105, 107–109, 110–111, 114–116; Docket and, 31, 54–55; Home language of, 71–72, 151 (n 25); Opinion assignment and, 74, 151 (n 24); Impartiality and (see Impartiality); Independence and (see Independence); Oral argument and, 74; Positivism and, 15–20, 144 (n 24) (see also Positivism); Policy making and, 4, 5, 10, 16, 94, 105–107, 144 (n 24); Voting patterns and, 76–85
Judicial Services Commission, 117–118

Kahn, Ellison, 24, 152 (n 2)
KaNgwane, 147 (n 51)
Kearney, Gerald Patrick, 44–46
Keith, Linda Camp, 54
Khoikhoi, 26
Klopper, H., 76, 79, 82, 110
Knoebel, Lizette, 152 (n 2)
Kok, L., 31
Kotze, G. P. C., 79, 82
Kotze, T., 115
Kriegler, J. C., 72, 150 (n 21)
Kritzer, Herbert M., 9
Kumleben, M. E. 76, 77, 79, 82, 84
Kwa-Ndebele, 147 (n 51)
KwaZulu, 147 (n 51)

Labor, 26, 27, 32–33, 36, 65–68, 97; Trade unions and, 30, 41
Lapping, Brian, 36, 38, 39, 40
Laswell, Harold, 42
Lawyers, 20, 28, 105 (see also Advocates, Attorneys, Bar)
Leach, Graham, 33, 37
Lebowa, 147 (n 51)
Legal system, 31–32
Legitimacy of courts, 54, 60, 94, 101, 103, 108, 117–118
Liberal Party, 37
Lijphardt, Arend, 54
Lobban, Michael, 52
Local Divisions, Supreme Court and, 31
Lodge, Tom, 37
Logistic regression, 121–122, 150 (n 38)
Luthuli, Albert, 37

Magistrates, 10, 31
Magopa, 68–71, 74, 85, 112
Malan, A. C., 78, 81
Malan, Daniel, 33, 36
Malay, 36, 89 (see also Asian, Indian)
Mallaby, Sebastian, 36
Mandela, Nelson, 1, 37, 41, 150 (n 9)
Marais, J. F., 78, 81
Marcus, Gilbert, 42, 106, 147 (n 61), 149 (n 26), 150 (n 16)
Mathews, Anthony S., 44, 50–51, 153 (n 4)
McCormick, Peter, 56
Mezerik, A. G., 147 (n 47)
Miller, S., 78, 81
Millner, M. A., 9, 16, 52, 149 (n 26)
Milner, Alfred, 29
Milne, A. J., 79, 82
Mishler, William, 9, 59–60
Mixed-race, 11, 38–39, 40, 50, 63–64, 145 (n 6), 146 (32)
Mokgatle, D., 149 (n 26)
Moore, Isaac, 68
Moore, Jacob, 68, 69
Motala, Ziyad, 114
Mureinik, Etienne, 144 (n 28)
Muldergate affair, 39
Muller, G. v R., 79, 82
Muller, W. G., 79, 82
Murray, C. J., 78, 81
Myburgh, A. C., 28

Natal, 27–28, 29, 30, 145 (n 8)
National Action Council, 37, 147 (46)
National Party, 3, 9, 11, 14, 17, 32, 33–34, 35–36, 39, 40, 145 (n 12), 147 (n 61)
Nattrass, Nicoli, 37, 39
Nestadt, H. H., 77, 79, 82, 84
Newton-Thompson, C, 76, 78, 81
Nicholas, H. C., 76, 79, 82
Nienaber, P. M., 79, 82
Nonet, Phillippe, 11–13, 24, 39, 144 (n 16)

Ogilvie Thompson, N., 8, 16–17, 78, 80, 81
Omar, Abdulah Mohamed, 46–47, 113, 148 (n 15)
Orange Free State, 27, 29
Ouster clause, 44–46, 48, 112, 148 (n 3)
Owen, Harold J., 53

Index

Pan-Africanist Congress (PAC), 37, 41, 147 (45)
Parliamentary sovereignty, 17, 21, 23, 30, 52, 54, 60, 70, 85, 95, 103, 108, 118
Pass laws, 32, 33, 36, 37, 65–67, 144 (n 29), 146 (n 33)
Peace of Vereeniging, 29
Pitje, Godfrey, 1–3, 6, 7, 9, 10, 23, 24, 118–119, 143 (n 1), 143 (n 7)
Pitts, Joe W. III., 31, 32, 36
Plaskett, Clive, 149 (n 26)
Positivism, 15–20, 144 (n 24)
Preiss, H. J., 76
Price, N., 78, 81
Pritchett, C. Herman, 139
Privy Council (see British Judicial Committee of the Privy Council)
Progressive Party, 37
Pro-Underdog measure, 76, 139
Pro-Upperdog measure, 76, 139
Provincial Divisions, 31

Qwaqwa, 147 (n 51)
Quorum, 32, 35, 145 (n 11), 146 (n 26)

Rabie, P. J., 74, 77, 79, 80, 82–85, 109
Racial classification, 36, 62–64, 70, 149 (n 35)
Ramsbottom, W. H., 79, 82
Regime control, courts and, 7–14, 21–23, 48, 60, 85–86
Repressive law, 4, 5, 12–13, 14, 15, 16, 17–18, 19–22, 25, 32, 38, 41, 42–43, 48, 52, 60, 61, 67, 70, 71, 85–86, 92, 103, 104–105, 107, 108, 111, 114, 116–117, 118, 119
Responsive law, 13–14, 19, 116–117, 119, 144 (n 18, 24)
Retirement age, 31
Reynolds, F. G., 78, 81
Riekert Report on Manpower Utilisation, 67
Riley, Eileen., 25
Rohde, David W., 139
Roman-Dutch law, 2, 11, 14, 18, 20, 21, 25, 26, 27–28, 29, 43, 67, 113, 115, 143 (n 3), 144 (n 24), 153 (n 8)
Rule of law, 2, 4, 9, 11, 13, 24, 47, 48, 52, 60, 103, 104, 106, 116, 144 (n 24)
Rumpff, F. L. H., 78, 81

Sachs, Albie, 25, 26, 27, 28, 94, 145 (n 3), 148 (n 8)

Salmon, Owen, 152 (n 2)
San, 26
Saunders, S., 30, 37, 38, 145 (n 1), 147 (n 45), n 51)
Schreiner, O. D., 77, 78, 79, 81, 143 (n 3), 146 (n 30)
Schubert, Glendon, 42, 139
Second team, 80
Segal, Jeffrey A., 112, 139, 153 (n 6)
Selznick, Philippe, 1–13, 24, 39, 144 (n 16)
Senate, 30; Packing and, 35, 145 (n 7)
Separate but equal doctrine, 34, 50
Shapiro, Martin, 5, 6, 7, 49, 143 (n 10)
Sharpeville, 37–38, 96, 147 (n 47)
Sheehan, Reginald S., 9, 53, 54, 56, 57, 59–60
Simons, H. J., 152 (n 2)
Slavery, 25, 26, 27
Smalberger, J. W., 76, 77, 79, 82, 84
Smith, K., 145 (n 1)
Smit, A. J. A., 78, 81
Smuts, F. S., 79, 82
Social control, courts and, 4, 6–9, 11–12, 15, 25, 48, 70, 85, 94, 107, 117
Songer, Donald R., 53, 54, 56, 57, 59–60, 73
Sophiatown, 36
South African Coloured People's Organisation, 147 (n 46)
South African Communist Party, 30, 41
South African Congress of Democrats, 147 (n 46)
South African Council of Churches, 70–71
South African Indian Congress, 147 (n 46)
South African Native National Congress, 30
South Africa Party, 145 (n 12)
South African police, 37, 38, 39, 40, 44, 45, 46, 51, 87, 89, 148 (n 3, n 17)
Soweto, 39–40, 94–95, 96, 98–102, 111
Spaeth, Harold J., 112, 139, 153 (n 6)
Spies, S. B., 29
Stadler, Alf, 39
State of emergency, 41, 46–47, 61, 113, 151 (n 30)
State President, 31, 41, 46, 47, 69, 147 (n 54)
Statute of Westminster of 1931, 34
Steyn, L. C., 2–3, 10, 78, 80, 81, 109, 112, 115, 144 (n 3), 146 (n 30), 153 (n 4)
Steyn, M. T., 77, 79, 82, 84
Strydom, J. G., 37
Supreme Court of Appeal, 151 (n 24), 153 (n 12)

Table Bay, 26
Tambo, Oliver, 1, 3, 143 (n 7)
Tate, C. Neal, 7, 42, 103
Terreblanche, Sampie, 37, 39
Thompson, Leonard, 26, 27, 28, 29, 30, 37, 39, 145 (n 9), 147 (n 40)
Transkei, 65, 66, 67, 70, 147 (n 51)
Transvaal, 24, 27, 28, 29, 30, 145 (n 8)
Transvaal Provincial Division, 68, 150 (n 21)
Treason Trial, 37
Trekboers, 26
Trengove, J. J., 79, 82
Trengove, John, 9
Tribal law, 14, 24, 27, 28
Trollip, W. G., 78, 81
Truth and Reconciliation Commission, 147 (63)

Ultra vires, 47, 50, 108; Definition of, 148 (n 19)
Underdog, Definition of, 73–74
United Democratic Front, 147 (n 61)
Unreasonableness, 3, 47, 87–88, 145 (n 18)
Upperdog, Definition of, 73–74
Uunterhalter, Elaine, 146 (n 37)

Vallinder, Torbjorn, 42
Van Blerk, Adrienne E., 17, 52, 92, 152 (n 2)
Van Blerk, P. J., 78, 81
Van den Heever, F. P., 77, 78, 80, 81
Van der Merwe, Hendrik W., 5, 12–14, 39, 116–117, 144 (n 16)
Van Dyk, J., 68
Van Heerden, H. J. O., 79, 80, 82, 84

Van Niekerk, Barend, 72, 106, 110, 150 (n 22), 152 (n 3)
Van Schoor, M. C. E., 27
Van Winsen, L. de V., 78, 81
Van Wyk, J. T., 78, 81
Van Zijl, J. W., 79, 82
Van Zyl, M. C., 28, 29
Venda, 147 (n 51)
Verner, Joel, 7
Verwoerd, Hendrik Frensch, 36, 37, 38
Viljoen, G., 79, 82, 83–84
Vivier, W., 79, 82, 83–84
Voet, Johannes, 115
Voortrekkers, 27
Vorster, Balthazar Johannes, 38, 39
Voting rights, 29–30, 32, 34, 145 (n 17) (see also Franchise)

Wacks, Raymond, 19, 20, 72, 92, 149 (n 26)
Wanner, Craig, 53
Watermeyer, E. F., 77, 78, 81
Welsh, David, 152 (n 2)
Weschler, Herbert, 144 (n 17)
Wessels, P. J., 76, 78, 80, 81
Wheeler, Stanton, 53
Williamson, A. F., 78, 80, 81
Witwatersrand, 28
Worden, Nigel, 25, 26, 27, 30, 32, 37, 145 (n 1, 4)

Xhosa, 26

Youth League, 37

Index of Statutes

Abolition of Influx Control Act 68 of 1986, 41, 147 (n 56)
Appellate Division Quorum Act 27 of 1955, 146 (n 26)

Bantu Administration Act 38 of 1927, 147 (n 48)
Bantu Education Act 47 of 1953, 36
Bantu Homelands Citizenship Act 26 of 1970, 38, 147 (n 51)
Bantu Homelands Constitution Act 21 of 1971, 38, 147 (n 51)
Bantu Land Act 27 of 1913, 32, 36
Bantu Self Government Act 46 of 1959, 38, 147 (n 51)
Bantu Trust and Land Act 18 of 1936, 36
Bantu Urban Areas Act 25 of 1945, 36, 70, 147 (n 41)
Black Administration Act 38 of 1927, 69
Black Local Authorities Act 102 of 1982, 147 (n 53)

Colonial Laws Validity Act of 1865, 34
Constitution Act 32 of 1961, 38–39, 96, 102, 111
Constitution Act 110 of 1983, 40–41, 96, 102, 111
Constitution of the Republic of South Africa Act 200 of 1993, 117, 143 (n 11), 153 (n 13)
Constitution of the Republic of South Africa Act 108 of 1996, 117, 147 (n 62)
Criminal Procedure Amendment Act of 96 of 1965, 148 (n 3)

Development Trust and Land Act 18 of 1936, 69
Discriminatory Legislation Regarding Public Amenities Act 100 of 1990, 41, 147 (n 58)

Extension of University Education Act 45 of 1959, 36

Free Settlement Areas Act 102 of 1988, 41, 147 (n 60)

General Law Amendment Act 37 of 1963, 148 (n 3)
Group Areas Act 41 of 1950, 18, 36, 90, 144 (n 25), 146 (n 36)
Group Areas Act 77 of 1957, 144 (n 25), 146 (n 36)
Group Areas Act 36 of 1966, 144 (n 25), 146 (n 36)

High Court of Parliament Act 35 of 1952, 35, 50

Immorality Act 5 of 1927, 32
Immorality Amendment Act 21 of 1950, 32, 145 (n 15)
Immorality and Prohibition of Mixed Marriages Amendment Act 72 of 1985, 41, 147 (n 55)
Industrial Conciliation Amendment Act 94 of 1979, 41, 147 (n 57)
Internal Security Act 44 of 1950, 147 (n 48, n 50)

Internal Security Act 74 of 1982, 44–45, 46, 48, 60

Labor Relations Amendment Act 57 of 1981, 41, 147 (n 57)

Liquor Act 30 of 1928, 87

Marketing Act 26 of 1937, 91, 151 (n 20)

Native Abolition of Passes and Co-ordination of Documents Act 57 of 1952, 146 (n 33)
Native (Urban Areas) Consolidation Act 25 of 1945, 65, 66, 70, 146 (n 37)
Native Laws Amendment Act 54 of 1952, 146 (n 37)

Population Registration Act 30 of 1950, 36, 62, 70
Population Registration Act 61 of 1962, 63
Prohibition of Mixed Marriages Act 55 of 1949, 32, 145 (n 16)
Prohibition of Political Interference Act 51 of 1968, 37, 147 (n 44)
Public Safety Act 3 of 1953, 46, 48, 60, 148 (n 17)

Reservation of Separate Amenities Act 49 of 1953, 36–37
Reservation of Separate Amenities Amendment Act 10 of 1960, 146 (n 38)
Riotous Assemblies Act 17 of 1956, 147 (n 48)

Senate Act 53 of 1955, 35, 146 (n 27)
Separate Amenities Act 49 of 1953, 34
Separate Representation of Voters Act 46 of 1951, 34, 146 (n 21)
South Africa Act of 1909, 29–30, 34, 35, 37
Statute of Westminster of 1931, 34
Suppression of Communism Act 44 of 1950, 37
Supreme Court Act 59 of 1959, 145 (n 11), 146 (n 26)

Terrorism Act 83 of 1967, 148 (n 3)

Universities Amendment Act 83 of 1983, 41, 147 (n 59)

Women's Enfranchisement Act 18 of 1930, 145 (n 17)

Index of Cases

Black Affairs Administration Board, Western Cape, and Another v. Mthiya 1985 (4) SA 754 (A), 64–68

Collins v. Minister of the Interior 1957 (1) SA 552 (A), 35, 50, 108, 143 (n 3), 149 (n 24)

East Rand Administration Board and Another v. Rikhoto (1983) 3 SA 595 (A), 66–68, 150 (n 11)

Fani and Others v. Minister of Law and Order and Others 1987 (3) SA 859 (A), 148 (n 12)
Felton v. Secretary for the Interior 1972 (2) SA 497 (T), 62–64
Felton v. Secretary for the Interior 1972 (3) SA 886 (A), 62–64

Garda v. Livestock and Meat Industries Control Board 1960 (3) SA 481 (T), 89–92

Harris v. Minister of the Interior 1952 (2) SA 428 (A), 34–35, 50, 108
Hurley and Another v. Minister of Law and Order 1985 (4) SA 709 (D), 44–48, 51, 52, 61, 108, 109, 113

In re Dube 1979 (3) 821 (N), 16
In re Marechane 1882 (1) SAR 27, 115, 153 (n 9)

Johannesburg Liquor Licensing Board v. Kuhn 1963 SA (4) 672 (A), 87–89

Kruse v. Johnson (1898) 2 QB 91, 145 (n 18)

Livestock and Meat Industries Control Board v. Garda 1961 (1) SA 342 (A), 89–92
Loza v. Police Station Commander 1964 (2) SA 545 (A), 46, 148 (n 7)

Minister of Law and Order and Others v. Hurley and Another 1986 (3) SA 568 (A), 44–48
Minister of the Interior v. Harris 1952 (4) SA 769 (A), 35, 50, 108, 143 (n 9)
Momoniat and Naidoo v. Minister of Law and Order 1986 (2) 264 (W), 148 (n 20)
More v. Minister of Co-operation and Development and Another 1986 (1) SA 102 (A), 68–69
Mthiya v. Black Affairs Administration Board, Western Cape, and Another 1983 (3) SA 455 (C), 64–68

Omar and Others v. Minister of Law and Order and Others 1986 (3) 306 (C), 46–48
Omar and Others v. Minister of Law and Order and Others 1987 (3) SA 859 (A), 46–48, 51, 52, 61, 108, 109

Pelser v. South African Associated Newspapers Ltd. and Another 1975 (1) SA 34 (N), 152 (n 3)
Pitcher and Others v. Secretary for the Interior (1968) 4 SA 247 (C), 150 (n 2)
President of the Republic of South Africa and Others v. South African Rugby Football Union

President v. Rugby Football Union (continued) and Others 1999 (4) SA 146 (CC), 8, 143 (n 12, 13, 14)

Radebe v. Hough 1949 (1) SA (A) 380, 144 (n 29), 148 (n 64)
R. v. Pitje 1960 (4) SA 709 (A) at 709, 1–3
R. v. Abdurahman 1950 (3) SA 136 (A), 50, 112, 146 (n 19), 149 (n 23)
R. v. Lusu 1953 (2) SA 484 (A), 50, 146 (n 19), 149 (n 23)
Rossouw v. Sachs 1964 (2) SA 551 (A), 46, 148 (n 8)

S. v. Mamabolo 2001 (3) SA 409 (CC), 152 (n 1)
S. v. Van Niekerk 1970 (3) SA 655 (T), 106, 152 (n 3)
S. v. Van Niekerk 1972 (2) SA 279 (D), 106, 152 (n 3)
S. v. Van Niekerk 1972 (3) SA 711 (A), 106, 152 (n 31)

Schermbrucker v. Klindt NO 1965 (4) SA 606 (A), 46, 148 (n 9)
South African Associated Newspapers Ltd. and Another v. Estate Pelser 1975 (4) SA 797 (A), 152 (n 3)
South African Commercial Catering and Allied Workers Union and others v. Irvin and Johnson Limited 2000 (3) SA 705 (CC), 143 (n 14)
State President and Others v. Bill 1987 (3) SA 859 (A), 148 (n 12)

Tayob v. Ermelo Local Road Transportation Board 1951 (4) SA 440 (A), 50, 146 (n 19), 149 (n 23)

Vanderbijl Park Health Committee and Others v. Wilson and Others 1950 (1) SA 447 (A), 151 (n 5)

TEACHING TEXTS IN LAW AND POLITICS

David Schultz, *General Editor*

The new series Teaching Texts in Law and Politics is devoted to textbooks that explore the multidimensional and multidisciplinary areas of law and politics. Special emphasis will be given to textbooks written for the undergraduate classroom. Subject matters to be addressed in this series include, but will not be limited to: constitutional law; civil rights and liberties issues; law, race, gender, and gender orientation studies; law and ethics; women and the law; judicial behavior and decision-making; legal theory; comparative legal systems; criminal justice; courts and the political process; and other topics on the law and the political process that would be of interest to undergraduate curriculum and education. Submission of single-author and collaborative studies, as well as collections of essays are invited.

Authors wishing to have works considered for this series should contact:
>Peter Lang Publishing
>Acquisitions Department
>275 Seventh Avenue, 28th floor
>New York, New York 10001

To order other books in this series, please contact our Customer Service Department at:
>800-770-LANG (within the U.S.)
>(212) 647-7706 (outside the U.S.)
>(212) 647-7707 FAX

or browse online by series at:
>WWW.PETERLANGUSA.COM